Law and Visual Jurisprudence

Volume 17

The Series Law and Visual Jurisprudence seeks to harness the diverse and innovative work within and across the boundaries of law, jurisprudence, and the visual in various contexts and manifestations. It seeks to bring together a range of diverse and at the same time cumulative research traditions related to these fields to identify fertile avenues for interdisciplinary research.

In our everyday lives, we experience law as a system of signs. Representations of legality are visually manifested in the materiality of things we see and spatially experience. Methodologically, aesthetic texts of legality semiotically emerge as examples of visual jurisprudence and illustrate the constitutive waltz between social governance, formal law, and materiality.

In its tangled relationship to regulation, the visual complexity of law is semiotically articulated as an ongoing process of meaning imbued with symbolism, memory, and cultural markers. Through a legal semiotics framework of symbolic articulation and analysis, the examination of law that happens in conjunction with the visual expands understandings of how law is crafted and takes root. Additionally, such an inquiry challenges the positivist view of law based within the courtroom as disciplinary spatial practices, the observation of everyday phenomenon, and the visible tethering of regulation to cultural understandings of legality generate a framework of visual jurisprudence. The Series seeks to enliven such frameworks as those in which law happens precisely without formal institutions of law and through which a visual-based methodology of law is crafted through everyday instances of ordinariness that contextualize the relationship between law, culture, and banality.

The Series welcomes proposals – be they edited collections or single-authored monographs – emphasizing the contingency and fluidity of legal concepts, stressing the existence of overlapping, competing and coexisting legal discourses, proposing critical approaches to law and the visual, identifying and discussing issues, proposing solutions to problems, offering analyses in areas such as legal semiotics, jurisprudence, and visual approaches to law.

Keywords: Legal Visual Studies, Popular Culture, Everyday Law, Spatiality, Legal Semiotics, Legal Geography, Legal Materiality, Legal Transplant, Bioethics, Cyber Law, Communication, Heritage and Territory, Design, Marketing, Packaging, Digitalization, Arts.

Mateusz Stępień • Mateusz Klinowski

Fighting Air Pollution

A Socio-Legal Case Study of Małopolska

Springer

Mateusz Stępień
Department of Sociology of Law
Jagiellonian University
Kraków, Poland

Mateusz Klinowski
Department of Law and Administration
Jagiellonian University
Kraków, Poland

ISSN 2662-4532 ISSN 2662-4540 (electronic)
Law and Visual Jurisprudence
ISBN 978-3-032-23908-2 ISBN 978-3-032-23909-9 (eBook)
https://doi.org/10.1007/978-3-032-23909-9

This Springer imprint is published by the registered company Springer Nature Switzerland AG
The registered company address is: Gewerbestrasse 11, 6330 Cham, Switzerland

Contents

Chapter 1
Introduction

Mateusz Stępień and Mateusz Klinowski

Abstract By providing both a historical overview and an analysis of key trends in pollution levels, the Introduction situates the study within the broader context of the problem of air pollution in Małopolska (Lesser Poland)—a wealthy region of Poland, located in the south, with Kraków as its capital. The Introduction discusses two regional antismog resolutions adopted by the regional legislature almost at the same time: one introducing a total ban on the use of solid-fuel heating installations in the municipal area of Kraków and the other establishing a more refined, less strict phased replacement of inefficient heating systems throughout the region. The chapter preliminarily examines how air pollution emerged as a salient public issue and how support for policy intervention gradually developed. It also introduces the book's three main themes: growing public awareness of air-quality problems, the role of eco-advisors in facilitating policy implementation, and the analytical usefulness of the concepts of symbolic law and wicked problems in understanding the persistent challenges of air pollution mitigation. Finally, the *Introduction* outlines the research design and methodology adopted in the study.

Keywords Air pollution · Air quality · Antismog resolutions · Case study · Symbolic law · Wicked problems

---

This publication is part of the research project 2019/34/E/HS5/00018 financed by the National Science Centre, Poland.

M. Stępień (✉)
Department of Sociology of Law, Jagiellonian University, Kraków, Poland
e-mail: mateusz.stepien@uj.edu.pl

M. Klinowski
Department of Law and Administration, Jagiellonian University, Kraków, Poland
e-mail: mateusz.klinowski@uj.edu.pl

M. Stępień, M. Klinowski, *Fighting Air Pollution*, Law and Visual Jurisprudence 17, https://doi.org/10.1007/978-3-032-23909-9_1

1.1 A Broad Context

We both grew up in similar circumstances—in a single-family house on the outskirts of a small or medium-sized city in Poland, heated by coal and wood. As teenagers in the 1990s, we both remember the scent of burning leaves as a defining feature of autumn—both sweet and acrid, an inseparable part of the season. Another common sight was the slow-burning remnants of dried potato stems left in the fields after harvest. Adding to this was the smoke rising from chimneys, most often from coal- and wood-fired stoves, though frequently fueled also by anything that could burn. In a way, this smoke and its distinct smell were an iconic element of every winter in Poland, along with snow and frost. A snow-covered landscape with chimney smoke drifting into the gray sky evoked a sense of warmth and security.

At the time, no one was objecting. There were no mainstream public or private discussions about the harmful effects of smoke. If environmental pollution—especially air pollution—was mentioned at all, it was associated primarily and exclusively with heavy industry. So-called low emissions from residential buildings were not linked in the public mind to air pollution at all. This general attitude toward air quality and the environment persisted for years, remaining largely unchanged into the early twenty-first century. When we occasionally returned to our family homes, from Kraków, where we had studied and then worked, we observed that nothing had really changed.

In the meantime, at the turn of the first and second decades of the twenty-first century, important social processes were unfolding in Małopolska (Lesser Poland), particularly in Kraków, leading to the emergence of a grassroots movement dedicated to combating air pollution. It was also here that, after years of public debates, political disputes, and legal battles—during which air pollution silently contributed to thousands of premature deaths and adversely affected the health and quality of life of countless residents—the so-called antismog resolutions were finally adopted (see Tang & Chiocchetti, 2026). These legal measures introduced new instruments for addressing air pollution (discussed briefly below and in greater detail in Chap. 2). In many respects, they were pioneering solutions, not only in Poland but also in a broader European context. This book is devoted precisely to the social, political, and legal processes surrounding the fight against air pollution in Małopolska in recent years.

Małopolska is one of the 16 regions of Poland, a Central European country and a member of the European Union since 2004. Located in the south of Poland, Małopolska encompasses mountainous terrain, foothills, uplands, and river valleys. Its capital, Kraków, is one of the historical centers of the Polish statehood, the site of royal coronations, and home to the Jagiellonian University, founded in 1364. Kraków is a renowned tourist destination, recognized as a United Nations Educational, Scientific and Cultural Organization (UNESCO) World Heritage Site.

The city underwent profound transformations after World War II, when the Polish People's Republic was established as a Soviet-dependent state. The postwar period was marked by rapid industrialization, which became one of the ideological pillars of the new socialist regime. The economy grew heavily reliant on coal-based, energy-intensive industries and was characterized by a lack of diversified energy sources (see Andersson, 2002; Cole, 1991, 1995). Smoking factory chimneys became iconic symbols of progress, modernization, and the promise of a better future. Against this backdrop, numerous industrial facilities were built or expanded in Kraków and its surrounding areas, including steelworks, energy plants, chemical and pharmaceutical factories, and other manufacturing enterprises. The rapid industrialization of Kraków was a deliberate undertaking by the current authorities of Poland, a socio-technical project designed to outweigh the influence of the city's intellectual elites with the working class and the new type of society promoted by the regime according to Soviet ideology. By the 1960s, these industries had already been identified as major sources of air pollution, particularly sulfur dioxide (SO_2) and nitrogen oxides (NO_n). Dłużniewska and Gorczyńska (1960, p. 57) warned: "The air quality of the city of Kraków in terms of dust, gas, and vapor pollution will continue to deteriorate, especially since the city and its surrounding terrain do not provide conditions for good ventilation." The authorities in Warsaw were reluctant to draw public attention to a problem that could undermine the official narrative of socialist modernization and industrial progress, and both local initiatives (e.g., Resolution No. 17/IV/65 of the National Council of the City of Kraków of 14 October 1965 on atmospheric air protection) and national legislation (Act of 21 April 1966 on the Protection of Atmospheric Air against Pollution) undertaken at that time remained largely ineffective.

The 1970s saw more systematic research on air pollution, notably at the Air Protection Department of the Faculty of Mining and Geodesy, AGH University of Science and Technology. Public awareness began to grow, with publications on the subject emerging—among them the 1977 book *SOS for Kraków*, which directly addressed not only industrial sources of pollution but also "local emitters—most often household stoves, where sulfurized coal is burned." A pivotal moment for environmental protection in Kraków came only in 1980.

Within the broader social movement represented by the so-called August Agreements—a result of negotiations between the government and representatives of striking factories, which secured limited civil liberties and freedoms—the Polish Ecological Club (PEC) was established in Kraków. PEC was the first organization of its kind in the Eastern Bloc to actively address air-quality issues.

Subsequently, PEC, together with other actors, worked to raise public awareness about a deplorable state of air quality in Kraków, which at that time contributed significantly to the degradation of cultural monuments in the city. In the second half of the 1980s, the organization coproduced radio broadcasts, initiated campaigns in local media, and organized expert debates, drawing residents' attention to the negative health and environmental impacts of polluted air. Meanwhile, at the central level, the Act on the Protection and Shaping of the Environment (Journal of Laws of 1980, No. 3, item 6) was passed. This legislation introduced a system for monitoring and planning air quality; however, it primarily focused on industrial sources and did not ensure effective enforcement of the obligations imposed. In the 1980s, Kraków also began installing the first automatic air-quality monitoring stations—an important step toward raising public attention to the problem and improving expert understanding of it. In the 1990s, actual levels of air pollutants measured in Kraków were displayed in the central part of the main square, also to indicate the city's commitment to improving air quality.

Meanwhile, the political transformation of the late 1980s and early 1990s fundamentally reshaped Poland's economic and environmental landscape. Following the collapse of the Polish People's Republic and the establishment of a new liberal democracy, deindustrialization began across the country as a result of economic crisis. In Kraków and its surrounding areas, many industrial plants were closed, production was reduced, and, in some cases, technological measures to limit industrial emissions were finally implemented during the rapid modernization to the new economic reality. As a result, air pollution levels—particularly concentrations of sulfur dioxide (SO_2) and nitrogen dioxide (NO_2)—gradually declined. This improvement was due largely to the contraction of highly polluting heavy industries rather than to proactive environmental policies. At the same time, Kraków introduced stricter air-quality standards, launched environmental protection programs, and began closing numerous local heating plants. These efforts were supported, in part, by the US Department of Energy in the early 1990s, which aimed to reduce low-stack emissions (Cole, 1995). As a result, several local heating plants were decommissioned, while the municipal district-heating network, based on the central heating unit (electric plant and heat generation facility "Łęg"), was expanded. By the end of the 1990s, however, air pollution levels—particularly concentrations of particulate matter (PM)—began to rise again, especially during winter seasons (see Millard, 1998). Individual household heating systems and the expansion of small commercial enterprises were the major culprits, gradually emerging as a serious environmental challenge not only for Kraków but also for the whole Małopolska region.

The beginning of the new millennium again brought significant changes—Poland joined the European Union in 2004, with all the accompanying obligations regarding air protection. As part of the preparations for accession, a new Act of Environmental Protection and other legal regulations outlining new methods for combating air pollution were introduced in 2001. At the same time, the air monitoring system was expanded. Meanwhile, in some places. the concentrations of harmful substances (especially PM10) in the air began reaching world-record levels. Kraków was one of the most polluted cities in Poland (see, e.g., Zgłobicki & Baran-Zgłobicka, 2024) and in the world generally. But this was the case not only in Kraków. According to a World Bank Group report published in 2019, 36 of the 50 most polluted cities in the European Union were located in Poland. This illustrates the scale of air pollution in the country at that time. Unfortunately, not much has changed to this day.

Thanks to new regulations, a shift in individual practices and air-quality perceptions began to emerge. Gradually, a significant part of society began to regard practices such as burning trash, burning biowaste (grass, leaves), and using uncertified stoves or low-quality solid fuels as harmful and ultimately unacceptable. Social awareness of the problem, however, did not automatically translate into specific actions, particularly when financial burdens were involved. Across different regions of Poland and among different age groups, recognition of air pollution progressed at different paces. Young and middle-aged people were the drivers of changing social perception of the problem, organizing themselves through social media channels. The visible turning point was the foundation of the Kraków Smog Alert (KSA—*Krakowski Alarm Smogowy* in Polish) in 2012. The mission of that grassroots organization—in their own words—was "to take matters into our own hands and start awareness-raising activities among the residents [of Kraków]." Their actions triggered a cascade, and mainstream media also began to highlight the issue, following growing public concern about air quality. A particularly symbolic moment occurred in 2013, when an antismog mask was placed on the statue of the poet Adam Mickiewicz in the heart of Kraków's Main Market Square.

We and our friends began wearing masks with high-efficiency particulate air (HEPA) filters outside our apartments during winters and using air purifiers inside (for similar patterns in China and the relationship between smog levels and demand for masks, see Zhang & Mu, 2018; see also Kim & Kim, 2021). Air pollution became a regular topic of discussion, influencing daily routines and even major life decisions—for some, as consequential as whether to have children or where to pursue a career. These personal and social changes unfolded in parallel with legal and political debates over how to tackle the air pollution problem.

The Environmental Protection Act (Journal of Laws 2001, No. 62, item 627), the principal statutory act establishing the legal and institutional framework for air pollution control in Poland, provides for so-called antismog resolutions. These are legal acts enacted by regional assemblies and are applicable within a specific territory (an entire region or part of a region) to prevent harm to the environment or public health. They establish limitations or prohibitions on the functioning of heating installations of particular types, as well as on the use of particular types of fuel for heating (Art. 96). Because of the exceptionally low air quality in Kraków and the city's international visibility as an important travel destination, Małopolska was the first region in Poland to consider using these legal instruments. Their opponents argued that antismog resolutions had originally been intended as instruments for addressing extraordinary and temporary circumstances rather than as long-term regulations. Concerns were also raised that they impose unconstitutional restrictions on fundamental rights and freedoms, as well as lead to economic disparities.

Divergent perspectives among experts, policymakers, and civic society representatives ultimately led to the establishment of two distinct legal regimes for combating smog in the Małopolska region, issued by the regional assembly. In Kraków, an effective ban on the burning of wood and coal—fuels that had been commonly used for household heating for decades—was introduced in 2016, with enforcement beginning on 1 September 2019. This measure was complemented by financial subsidies, regulated under separate local laws, to support households in replacing heating systems or connecting to the city's central heating network. In the area of Małopolska outside the Kraków municipality, a completely different regulatory approach was adopted finally in 2017: a gradual ban on inefficient stoves, requiring their phased replacement. This process mandated the elimination of the most polluting appliances first, followed by the sequential replacement of lower-emission class stoves, according to a schedule with three defined deadlines. Additionally, the resolution prohibited the use of certain types of fuel regardless of these deadlines, including cheap and popular coal dust (*miał*) and wood with high moisture content.

Both approaches differ in the underlying philosophies of regulation and thus in their restrictiveness. The regulation for Kraków imposed a blanket ban on coal and wood burning (reinforced by the generous financing scheme that covered up to 100% of the cost of replacing a banned device). In contrast, the regional resolution allowed the continued use of solid fuels of a certain quality and prolonged the use of highly emitting appliances, with the goal of their gradual removal supported by local, regional, and national financial subsidies. Coal bans were introduced to tackle air pollution in many historical periods and in various parts of the world. As early as 1257, the burning of "sea coal" (bituminous coal) was banned for the first time in an effort to combat air pollution in London (Cass, 2014, p. 389). Smokeless zones, where burning bituminous coal or wood in open fireplaces was prohibited, were established in England following the adoption of the Clean Air Act of 1956. The Irish government prohibited the marketing, sale, and distribution of coal in Dublin on 1 September 1990 (Regulations 1990, S.I. No. 123 of 1990). On 1 October 1995, a similar ban came into force in Cork, Ireland's second-largest city, and was subsequently extended to other urban areas (Regulations 1994, S.I. No. 403 of 1994). In Mongolia, after first introducing the measure in the capital city, the authorities also prohibited the use of so-called smoky coal (Ganbat et al., 2020). However, the measures implemented in Kraków were much more dramatic. Kraków prohibited the use of all types of coal, as well as wood, without exceptions and with a relatively short deadline.

From our perspective, the discrepancies between the legal measures introduced in Kraków and the rest of Małopolska immediately raise two important questions. Why did the same entity—Małopolska Regional Assembly—enact such drastically different regulations for Kraków and the rest of the region? And how effective have these two approaches been in reducing air pollution?

It is also important to note that those two regulations were the first so-called antismog resolutions passed in Poland. Their adoption set a precedent, later followed by other Polish regions. As mentioned earlier, the reasons were the reputation of Kraków and the ambitions of the city's authorities. Additionally, the region's unique geographical features (mountainous or foothill areas), its atmospheric conditions, and its capital's location in the Vistula River Valley, surrounded on almost all sides by higher terrain that reduces natural ventilation and encourages fog formation, were responsible for higher levels of pollution compared with other parts of the country. One must also remember that Małopolska is an area abundant in wood and bordering the Silesian coal basin. Its population is dominated by agricultural communities living across the majority of the region, which often declare attachment to conservative values.

Kraków is not only a city rich in history, culture, and monuments but also has socioeconomic conditions that favor progressive changes. For instance, Kraków houses academic institutions that have been conducting air-quality research for decades, dating back to the 1960s. It is difficult to assess the role of this social capital built over the years, but undoubtedly, the tradition of thinking about air protection and institutions has endured.

Supranational environmental policies and regulations regarding air quality were also an important factor in the implementation of both antismog resolutions in Małopolska. Poland, like other EU member states, was required to implement a range of measures, including the designation of air-quality zones, the establishment of air-quality standards at least as stringent as those defined by EU law, the adoption of air-quality plans and remedial programs, the monitoring of air pollution levels, and the provision of information to the public. The EU also financed a number of crucial projects aimed at strengthening the implementation of air-quality regulations. That way, EU membership obliged Poland to engage in a systematic effort to combat air pollution.

Therefore, our initial observation is that the adoption of antismog resolutions in the region was the result of the interplay between the increasing public awareness of air pollution and the spontaneous emergence of social activism, as well as the institutional mechanisms and obligations stemming from EU law. In a sense, the case of air-quality policies in Małopolska represents a new take on the ongoing debate about whether law shapes social awareness and drives social change or—the other way around—whether a change in public awareness leads to legal reforms. It may be the interaction between these two spheres, within the framework of the multilevel governance characteristic of the EU and its member states, that best explains the socio-legal dynamics.

In recent years, significant improvements in air quality have been observed in Kraków, where over 25,000 boilers were replaced between 2012 and 2020, including nearly 15,000 in the years 2017–2020, which coincided with the introduction of the antismog resolution for Kraków. The concentration of PM10 measured at the station with the worst annual results decreased by half. In 2010, it was 79 $\mu g/m^3$, whereas in 2020, the average fell below the permissible level, reaching 38 $\mu g/m^3$. In the rest of the voivodeship, improvements were not as dynamic as in Kraków, which corresponds to the number of boilers replaced outside the city. After the implementation of the antismog resolution for Małopolska (excluding Kraków), over 36,000 boilers were replaced. The average PM10 concentration in Małopolska decreased by 30% between the winter season of 2014–2015 and the season of 2019–2020, while in Kraków, it dropped by as much as 45%. However, this does not mean that the problem has been resolved. The Małopolska region still faces ongoing challenges with air pollution during certain periods and in specific locations. That is why we strongly believe that the analysis of the Małopolska case makes a significant contribution to the debate on the measures for combating air pollution at the subnational level, their operation, and the assessment of their effectiveness. In the literature, there is, of course, a discussion on command-and-control versus economic incentive methods (e.g., Beiser-McGrath et al., 2023), and there are case studies aimed at verifying which approach is more effective. However, we believe that our study could add something valuable to the problem.

1.2 Subject of the Study and Methodology Applied

The subject of this book is the study of the struggle against air pollution in the Małopolska region during the second decade and the early years of the third decade of the twenty-first century. The book focuses on how an important social problem—namely, severe air pollution—is addressed within a complex system of multilevel governance involving institutions operating at different levels, with particular attention paid to local actors. Improving air quality is certainly both a universal and a transboundary issue since air quality affects everyone and air pollutants cross administrative and national borders. While air pollution is often linked to broader socioeconomic processes, its consequences are primarily local, coshaped by regional and place-specific conditions. Therefore, we believe that our study, albeit limited to one particular region of Poland, could nonetheless be considered useful by all readers interested in the subject of air pollution. The book also examines and evaluates two popular conceptual frameworks frequently applied to environmental policy and environmental problems, namely, symbolic law and wicked problems. The case of Małopolska can be interpreted through these analytical lenses, providing an opportunity to assess their usefulness against empirical reality.

Our study does not address specific regional sources, types of pollutants, and their measurable health impacts in the region of Małopolska. Instead, we assume that a comprehensive approach to air pollution and its potential solutions requires insights from the social sciences. Moreover, we think that such insights should step beyond merely quantitative analyses of public opinion or attitudes toward air quality, i.e., the most popular applications of the social science perspective to the problem. Fortunately, we are not alone in this respect, and a shift in understanding the role of social sciences in the analysis of the problem has taken place already. For example, Giardullo et al. (2016) conducted in-depth interviews with residents in four European cities, highlighting how individuals experience and perceive air pollution in their everyday lives. Communication and media aspects have also been explored, including a review by Riley et al. (2021) on strategies to effectively communicate air pollution risks so as to influence public attitudes and behaviors. Questions of social justice have similarly been raised, particularly in relation to unequal exposure to harmful air (e.g., Maturo & Moretti 2018). Another significant strand of research has examined air pollution through the lens of policy design and implementation. For instance, Iza Yue Ding (2022) analyzed the work of municipal bureaucrats within China's Ministry of Environmental Protection, which operates across three hierarchical levels. Her ethnographic study, conducted in a city in the Yellow River Delta, traced the evolution of local environmental governance from inertia to performativity—at first constrained by scarce resources and strict oversight but later moving toward more substantive governance. Ding's research, one of the few extensive studies to rely on interviews and ethnographic methods, provides valuable insights into bureaucratic adaptation processes.

With these social-science-centered approaches in mind, this book seeks to demonstrate that interdisciplinary studies—conducted under the umbrella of the social sciences and focused on a concrete case of the fight against smog, here the example of Małopolska—can generate essential knowledge for understanding the social dimensions of organized efforts to mitigate air pollution. Stating that the subject of this work is the case of combating smog in Małopolska requires clarification: what exactly does this case concern, and what is it meant to illustrate and shed light on?

(1) The case under examination concerns a specific process unfolding in a particular place and time—the emergence of public awareness regarding air pollution and the perceived necessity of combating it. The example of Kraków illustrates how awareness of a pressing social problem develops—how apparent apathy gradually transforms into civic engagement. Central to this issue is the rise and activity of the grassroots social movement Kraków Smog Alarm (KAS), focused on air protection, as well as its influence on local authorities and, ultimately, on policy and regulation. Why did this movement emerge in Kraków at that specific moment? What strategies did Kraków Smog Alarm employ to mobilize society and influence decision-makers? And what role did Kraków Smog Alarm, together with the social mobilization it generated, play in the adoption of legal measures in the form of antismog regulations?

In the literature, there have already been attempts to answer the question of how environmental awareness emerges and how movements advocating for a better environment take shape. Particularly significant from a theoretical perspective is Veronica Herrera's book (2024; see also Fabricant 2022), which examines three case studies from cities in South America. The very title of her work highlights a focus on "slow harms," referring to pollution that exists alongside communities but often goes unnoticed until, for some reason, it becomes a matter of concern and a catalyst for social movements. Herrera investigates how issues "that long went unnoticed or were accepted as part of the everyday landscape" became recognized problems, prompting action and policy change. She explores "how citizen-driven efforts can push the state to implement environmental rights protections, and how ideas about pollution as a policy problem become institutionalized. Slow-moving harms are typically ignored or accepted parts of everyday life" (Herrera, 2024, p. 5). This is particularly relevant in the case of air pollution—without sufficient information, people may fail to perceive such pollution or may not consider it a critical threat to health. Notably, Herrera conducted ethnographic research based on interviews, observations, and document analysis. Her work can also be understood as a comparative case study, testing the significance of "bonding mobilization" (internal community integration) and "bridging activism" (finding external advocates) for the success of environmental movements. While her study does not specifically address air pollution, it provides insight into various contexts of social mobilization for environmental causes. Of course, there is also a broad range of smaller studies on the emergence of awareness regarding air pollution, including research on the role of the media in shaping public consciousness and the effects of environmental policies (see Bakaki et al., 2020; see Oltra et al., 2017; Szabo-Müller, 2019; Schmieder et al., 2021).

Fortunately, several studies have already examined the emergence of public awareness in Kraków. Sebastian Medoń (2021), for instance, conducted 12 interviews with members of Kraków Smog Alarm and the Polish Smog Alarm (a later umbrella organization bringing together local initiatives), applying the framework of actor-network theory. Also significant are the works of Tomas Maltby and colleagues (2024), who investigated activism around air quality in Poland and the ways in which society influences public policy. Their research highlighted how local initiatives—especially Kraków Smog Alarm—played a catalytic role in raising awareness and shaping policy, drawing on interviews with activists, including those directly involved in Kraków. Equally noteworthy are the studies of M. Burchard-Dziubińska (2019), who analyzed antismog movements across several Polish cities, and J. Frankowski (2020), who examined civic engagement in the struggle for clean air using web content mining, media discourse analysis, and interviews. While these works provide valuable insights into the rise of social awareness in Kraków, they do not yet offer a comprehensive account of the role this process played in the development of Poland's pioneering antismog resolutions of 2016 and 2017.

(2) The case also addresses the process and effect of implementing the European air protection law at the local level in Małopolska. It exemplifies how "policies are frequently re-shaped, re-defined, or even completely overturned" (Pülzl & Treib, 2007, p. 100). The implementation process follows the transposition of EU directives into national law. However, as Thomann and Sager (2017) point out, these actions are not automatic but are shaped by local contexts and influenced by political decisions and path dependency. In our study, we describe a key new element in this process that requires special attention—the role of eco-advisors (EDs), a form of street-level officials working partially as social workers and energy efficiency experts. In 2016, the position of eco-advisors was created in 16 municipalities as a trial, and eventually, all municipalities in Małopolska adopted the measure. Their role encompasses advising, assisting, and educating citizens on all issues related to energy efficiency and air protection, including enforcing antismog resolutions and coordinating local actions in this domain. As EDs in principle possess unique local knowledge about the adoption of antismog measures and play an essential part in the implementation process, they become an important part of our study.

Our case study also engages with the broader discussions about the EU's multilevel governance model. Several advantages of multilevel governance have been identified, such as decentralization, which takes local circumstances and knowledge into account, as well as spatial fit and increased participation from nonpublic actors. However, disadvantages, such as the risk of autonomization, superficial engagement, and additional costs, also exist. It is crucial to relate these discussions to the Małopolska case and assess, based on the specific context, the advantages and disadvantages of multilevel governance. By doing so, we can better understand how local dynamics shape the implementation of EU law and determine the effectiveness of decentralization in air-quality governance.

(3) The case of the fight against smog in Małopolska offers an opportunity to test the descriptive and explanatory potential of concepts that have been used to explain the difficulties associated with efforts to improve air quality. Among these, particular attention will be paid to the notion of symbolic law—or, more precisely, to a cluster of ideas grouped under this label—that has already been applied to examine the challenges of achieving environmental goals (including air protection) through

public policy and legal instruments. In this context, it is important to highlight John Dwyer's concept (1990), which emerged from his analysis of the US Clean Air Act, as well as Jens Newig's concept (2007), based on empirical material concerning environmental law in Germany.

Another widely used and influential concept in environmental studies is that of wicked problems, introduced by Horst W. J. Rittel and Melvin M. Webber in the 1970s. This concept has frequently been applied to the issue of air pollution. For example, leading policy scholars have argued that "nonpoint-source pollution is a challenging issue that can be considered a 'wicked' policy problem" (Head, Alford 2015, p. 712). The concept of symbolic law highlights the political factors that help explain the difficulty of solving environmental problems in an effective and timely manner, whereas the wicked problems approach draws attention to the intrinsic nature of certain problems that, in a sense, defy definitive solutions.

The case of Małopolska provides an opportunity to apply both frameworks in order to assess what insights—if any—they offer to explain and understand the region's ongoing struggle with smog (cf. the critique of the second concept by Pesch & Vermaas, 2020). The aim, therefore, is to test whether these two conceptual approaches help illuminate the processes by which actors attempt to cope with intractable challenges—here, air pollution in Małopolska. In doing so, the analysis contributes both to a better understanding of the Małopolska case and to a critical examination of the broader potential of these concepts.

In the literature on air pollution protection, there are case studies that focus on a single city, region, or country. Classic studies on smog episodes in London or Los Angeles are examples of this (but not only; see, regarding New Delhi, Véron, 2006). A notable example is the monograph on the fight against smog in New Delhi and Mexico City (2023), which represents a comprehensive study of how these metropolises are dealing with smog. Cities, in fact, become particularly important in this context—on the one hand, due to the concentration of problems and the scale of pollution and, on the other hand, because of the significant resources available and the possibility of implementing various local policies to protect air quality. Finally, we must mention monographs on entire countries—especially China, which has seen several monographs published over the course of a decade. However, it is important to note that rarely has the core of the research been the consideration of the effectiveness of antismog tools in an interdisciplinary way, combining various social sciences. What is important for the approach presented in this book is addressing the case of the fight against smog in Małopolska, not from the perspective of natural sciences but by combining threads closely related to legal science, public policy, sociology, the law and society approach, and conceptual analyses.

The considerations presented in this book have the following components: (1) legal (environmental protection law, EU influence, local legal institutions, legal problems, court cases, and rulings), (2) socio-legal (how awareness influences law and vice versa, how demands on the law are shaped, the effectiveness of two different regulations), (3) policy science (effectiveness of public polices, their limitations), (4) sociological (new social movements—ecological awareness of residents and its dynamics; social communication), and (5) conceptual (usefulness of certain conceptual categories).

The overarching methodological framework adopted in this book is the case study approach based on the conviction that attention to context, a focus on social actors, and an attempt to provide a "thick description" are essential for understanding social processes (Gerring, 2017). Against this backdrop—and taking into account such factors as legal and institutional path dependencies, political divisions, public awareness, and relations with the EU—the book examines key aspects of the struggle against smog in the Małopolska region. These include the emergence of public awareness of the smog problem, the functioning of the new profession of eco-advisors, and the usefulness of concepts such as wicked problems and symbolic law for understanding the complexities of air pollution policies. The book seeks to identify effective instruments for combating smog within this specific sociopolitical context. The case of Małopolska and its struggle against air pollution contributes to the wider discussion on strategies for air-quality protection and environmental governance. Accordingly, the book adopts an empirical-theoretical approach. Empirical data were collected during the research process, while theoretical concepts drawn from the social sciences provide the analytical framework for their interpretation.

While the case study approach provides the overall methodological framework—allowing the exploration of a relatively small area in depth to contribute to broader discussions—the research underlying this work employed a variety of research techniques. In-depth interviews were conducted with eco-advisors in Małopolska (17 interviews). Additionally, a quantitative research tool—an online survey—was used, targeting eco-advisors (160 completed surveys). The book also draws on numerous informal conversational interviews (as described by Patton 2015, pp. 426–431) conducted with the founders of Kraków Smog Alarm, as well as on interviews with high-ranking local government representatives responsible for air pollution policies (five interviews with persons responsible for decision-making processes at different levels of the Małopolska regional government). These interviews offered valuable insights into insider perspectives on the creation of antismog policies in Małopolska. In addition, this book draws on the analysis of existing data and official documents related to air pollution in both Poland and Małopolska. The literature review encompassed a broad thematic range.

Finally, it should be mentioned that one of the coauthors of the book was directly involved in the process of introduction and implementation of both antismog resolutions, first as an activist and civic journalist, then as a decision-maker. Such a personal and intimate perspective on the problem made it possible for us to include in the book information generally not accessible to typical researchers, as it formed part of insider knowledge and behind-doors discussions. Despite that personal perspective, though, our goal was to maintain high academic standards in the adoption of our research methodology and to avoid personal bias in the selection of data and facts for our analysis.

1.3 Synopsis

The *Introduction* presents the broader context of the air pollution problem in Małopolska. It provides a historical overview of the problem, with a focus on the twenty-first century. The *Introduction* outlines three key aspects of this study: the growing public perception of the problem, the implementation of solutions through the creation of eco-advisors, the potential usefulness of the concepts of symbolic law and wicked problems in explaining the challenges of combating air pollution at the local level. It also describes the methodology employed in the study.

The second chapter, *Context and Basic Information on the Fight Against Smog in Małopolska in the Twenty-First Century*, introduces the reader to the key issues addressed in this book. It begins with an overview of air pollution—its main types, sources, and health effects—before outlining the specific challenges that Małopolska, and Kraków in particular, faced. A crucial part of the chapter is an analysis of Poland's institutional and legal framework for air-quality protection. The focus is primarily on how Poland's legal and institutional system evolved through the transposition of EU air protection directives (e.g., Directive 2008/50/EC). The chapter then examines antismog resolutions, a legal instrument established under the Environmental Protection Act, which became the central—albeit belated—tool in Poland's fight against air pollution. Finally, it traces the legal history of two separate resolutions (for the Kraków municipality and for the Małopolska region), including the legal challenges they encountered. Particular attention is devoted to the outcomes of public consultations on the coal and wood-burning ban in Kraków.

The third chapter, *The Role of Public Awareness of the Air Pollution Problem for Its Solution: The Case of Kraków Smog Alarm*, explores how air quality concerns became a widespread public issue, leading to increased social and political pressure on policymakers. Drawing on previous research, as well as on conversations and interviews with the founders of Kraków Smog Alert, this chapter examines the movement's origins, objectives, strategies, and influence on state institutions and public policies. Particular attention is devoted to the role of social pressure and initiatives such as KAS in the development of antismog resolutions in Małopolska.

The fourth chapter, *Eco-Advisors: Their Roles and Views*, explores the emergence of eco-advisors as a pivotal new profession within Małopolska's public policies aimed at air-quality improvement. These professionals were introduced as part of the UE LIFE project and eventually placed in every municipality to coordinate and implement local environmental policies (mainly antismog regulations and energy-efficiency actions). The chapter draws upon both qualitative and quantitative research, including in-depth interviews and survey data, to thoroughly investigate the eco-advisors' roles, the challenges they face, and their perspectives on the legal measures that have been introduced. One of the key aspects explored is how eco-advisors view the effectiveness and limitations of the legal instruments in place, particularly the antismog resolutions, and their assessments of the impact these measures have had on air quality in the region. This analysis provides valuable insights into the practical realities of implementing environmental policies at the local level. The chapter contributes to broader discussions on the local implementation of European environmental law and the evolving role of such specialists in promoting sustainable practices.

The fifth chapter, *The Concept of Symbolic Law in Relation to Air Protection*, applies the framework of the theory of symbolic law to environmental legislation. Previous studies on the US Clean Air Act (J. Dwyer) and Germany's environmental laws (J. Newig) suggest that air protection laws often exist more for appearance than for effectiveness. This chapter compares these cases to Małopolska, identifying additional institutional and governance-related barriers that contribute to policy inertia.

The sixth chapter, *On the (In)Utility of the Wicked Problems Concept in the Context of Air Pollution*, critically assesses whether the framework of the wicked problems theory is useful for explaining Małopolska's air-quality challenges. It reconstructs the concept, evaluates its explanatory power, and ultimately argues that it does not adequately capture the region's specific obstacles. The chapter contributes to broader debates on the applicability of the wicked problems theory for environmental policies.

These two chapters shift from description to analysis, applying two well-known theoretical frameworks to the study of the difficulties in combating air pollution in Małopolska. The key idea was to deliberate whether these two concepts help explain the struggles observed in the region and also to evaluate the concepts' relevance for understanding the observed effectiveness of the anti-smog resolutions in the region. Symbolic law relates to the superficiality of some environmental regulations, while wicked problems emphasize the complexity of environmental challenges.

The book ends with the *Conclusion*, which highlights some broader issues that the case of combating air pollution in Małopolska brings to light.

References

Andersson, M. (2002). Environmental policy in Poland. In H. Weidner & M. Jänicke (Eds.), *Capacity building in national environmental policy*. Springer. https://doi.org/10.1007/978-3-662-04794-1_16

Bakaki, Z., Böhmelt, T., & Ward, H. (2020). The triangular relationship between public concern for environmental issues, policy output, and media attention. *Environmental Politics, 29*(7), 1157–1177. https://doi.org/10.1080/09644016.2019.1655188

Beiser-McGrath, L. F., Bernauer, T., & Prakash, A. (2023). Command and control or market-based instruments? Public support for policies to address vehicular pollution in Beijing and New Delhi. *Environmental Politics, 32*(4), 586–618. https://doi.org/10.1080/09644016.2022.2113608

Burchard-Dziubińska, M. (2019). Air pollution and health in Poland: Anti-smog movement in the most polluted Polish cities. *Economics and Environment, 69*(2), 76–90. https://doi.org/10.34659/2019/2/22

Cass, L. R. (2014). Acid pollution and acid rain. In P. G. Harris (Ed.), *Routledge handbook of global environmental politics* (pp. 395–406). Routledge.

Cole, D. H. (1991). Cleaning up Krakow: Poland's ecological crisis and the political economy of international environmental assistance. *Colorado Journal of International Environmental Law & Policy, 2*.

Cole, D. H. (1995). An outline history of environment law and administration in Poland. *Hastings international and comparative law review, 18*(2), 297–358.

Dłużniewska, K., & Gorczyńska, K. (1960). Zanieczyszczenie powietrza miasta Krakowa [Air Pollution in the City of Kraków]. *Roczniki Państwowego Zakładu Higieny, XI*(1)

Frankowski, J. (2020). Attention: Smog alert! Citizen engagement for clean air and its consequences for fuel poverty in Poland. Energy and Buildings, 207, Article 109525. https://doi.org/10.1016/j.enbuild.2019.109525

Ganbat, G., Soyol-Erdene, T.-O., & Jadamba, B. (2020). Recent improvement in particulate matter (PM) pollution in Ulaanbaatar, Mongolia. *Aerosol and Air Quality Research, 20*(10), 2280–2288. https://doi.org/10.4209/aaqr.2020.04.0170

Gerring, J. (2017). *Case study research: Principles and practices* (2nd ed.). Cambridge University Press. https://doi.org/10.1017/9781316848593

Giardullo, P., Sergi, V., Carton, W., Kenis, A., Kesteloot, C., Kazepov, Y., Kobus, D., Maione, M., Skotak, K., Fuzzi, S., & Pollini, F. (2016). Air quality from a social perspective in four European metropolitan areas: Research hypothesis and evidence from the SEFIRA project. *Environmental Science & Policy, 65*, 58–64.

Herrera, V. (2024). *Slow harms and citizen action: Environmental degradation and policy change in Latin American cities*. Oxford University Press. https://doi.org/10.1093/oso/9780197669020.001.0001

Kim, J., & Kim, Y. (2021). What predicts Korean citizens' mask-wearing behaviors? Health beliefs and protective behaviors against particulate matter. *International Journal of Environmental Research and Public Health, 18*(6), 2791. https://doi.org/10.3390/ijerph18062791

Medoń, S. (2021). The controversy about the smog phenomenon: The case study of Kraków Metropolitan Area. *Przegląd Socjologiczny, 70*(1), 41–64. https://doi.org/10.26485/PS/2021/70.1/3

Millard, F. (1998). Environmental Policy in Poland. *Environmental Politics, 7*(1), 145–161.

Oltra, C., Sala, R., Boso, À., et al. (2017). Public engagement on urban air pollution: An exploratory study of two interventions. *Environmental Monitoring and Assessment, 189*, 296. https://doi.org/10.1007/s10661-017-6011-6

Pesch, U., & Vermaas, P. E. (2020). The wickedness of Rittel and Webber's dilemmas. *Administration & Society, 52*(6), 960–979. https://doi.org/10.1177/0095399720934010

Pülzl, H., & Treib, O. (2007). Policy implementation. In F. Fischer, G. J. Miller, & M. S. Sidney (Eds.), Handbook of public policy analysis: Theory, politics, and methods (pp. 89–107). CRC Press/Taylor & Francis.

Riley, R., de Preux, L., Capella, P., et al. (2021). How do we effectively communicate air pollution to change public attitudes and behaviours? A review. *Sustainability Science, 16*, 2027–2047. https://doi.org/10.1007/s11625-021-01038-2

Schmieder, L., Scheer, D., & Iurato, C. (2021). Streams analysis for better air quality: The German lead city program assessed by the policy package approach and the multiple streams framework. *Energies, 14*(3), 596. https://doi.org/10.3390/en14030596

Szabo-Müller, P. (2019). Exploring the potential for "urban air quality transition management" in the EU – Lessons from the City of Aachen (Germany). *Urban Transformations, 1*, 3. https://doi.org/10.1186/s42854-019-0003-5

Tang, A.-M., & Chiocchetti, I. (2026). *Anti-smog resolution banning solid fuels for heating: Kraków case study*. Institute for European Environmental Policy. https://ieep.eu/publications/anti-smog-resolution-banning-solid-fuels-for-heating-krakow-case-study/

Thomann, E., & Sager, F. (2017). Toward a better understanding of implementation performance in the EU multilevel system. *Journal of European Public Policy*. https://doi.org/10.1080/13501763.2017.1314542

Véron, R. (2006). Remaking urban environments: The political ecology of air pollution in Delhi. *Environment and Planning A, 38*(11), 2093–2109.

Zgłobicki, W., & Baran-Zgłobicka, B. (2024). Air pollution in major Polish cities in the period 2005–2021: Intensity, effects and attempts to reduce it. *Environmental Research, 240*(Pt 2), 117497. https://doi.org/10.1016/j.envres.2023.117497

Zhang, J., & Mu, Q. (2018). Air pollution and defensive expenditures: Evidence from particulate-filtering facemasks. *Journal of Environmental Economics and Management*, 92, 517–536. https://doi.org/10.1016/j.jeem.2017.07.006

Chapter 2
Context and Basic Information on the Fight Against Smog in Małopolska (Lesser Poland) in the Twenty-First Century

Mateusz Klinowski and Mateusz Stępień

Abstract This chapter provides an overview of the context and key developments in the fight against air pollution in Małopolska (Lesser Poland), one of Poland's 16 regions, in the twenty-first century. It begins by outlining the phenomenon of air pollution, including its main types, sources, and health effects, before examining the specific challenges faced by the Małopolska region and, in particular, the city of Kraków. The chapter discusses the historical background of air pollution in the region, as well as the social and political factors that contributed to the adoption of antismog policies. Particular emphasis is placed on the legal and institutional framework, including Poland's transposition and implementation of EU air-quality directives (e.g., Directive 2008/50/EC), landmark court rulings, and the introduction of antismog resolutions under the Polish Environmental Protection Act. These resolutions became the central, albeit belated, instrument for regulating the use of solid fuels and the operation of residential heating installations—one of the principal sources of air pollution in the region. The chapter traces the legal development of two distinct antismog resolutions adopted during the same period: one applying to Kraków and the other to the remainder of the Małopolska region. It analyses their origins, content, implementation, and significance in the broader context of efforts to improve air quality.

Keywords Air pollution · Health effects of air pollution · Types of smog · Polish environmental law · Antismog resolutions

M. Klinowski
Department of Law and Administration, Jagiellonian University, Kraków, Poland
e-mail: mateusz.klinowski@uj.edu.pl

M. Stępień (✉)
Department of Sociology of Law, Jagiellonian University, Kraków, Poland
e-mail: mateusz.stepien@uj.edu.pl

M. Stępień, M. Klinowski, *Fighting Air Pollution*, Law and Visual Jurisprudence 17, https://doi.org/10.1007/978-3-032-23909-9_2

2.1 Initial Thoughts

As stated in the Introduction, this book does not focus narrowly on environmental law or environmental policy. Rather, it examines the sociopolitical and legal dynamics of the fight against smog in Małopolska (Lesser Poland), a region of Poland. The book addresses three central themes: (1) the factors that led to the adoption of legal measures aimed at reducing air pollution in Małopolska, (2) the ways in which the European Union's system of multilevel governance shapes air-quality protection efforts at the regional and local levels, and (3) conceptual frameworks that help explain the challenges and constraints associated with the struggle for cleaner air, particularly in the Małopolska context. The case of Małopolska is used here to illuminate the origins, development, and implementation of local antismog regulations as an example of multilevel governance in practice. By examining this case, the book seeks to contribute both to the understanding of air pollution governance and to broader discussions of environmental policymaking within complex institutional settings.

In this chapter, we clarify the concept of air pollution and outline its significance for public health. By providing essential background on the scope and nature of the problem in Małopolska, we establish the foundation for the subsequent analysis. Our second objective is to examine the institutional and legal contexts that have shaped the region's efforts to combat smog. Particular attention is devoted to the regional antismog resolutions, which have become crucial policy instruments in the absence of comprehensive nationwide measures.

2.2 Air Pollution and Its Health Effects

2.2.1 Unpacking the Concept of Air Pollution and Smog

Air pollution is—and has always been—a global phenomenon, transcending specific cultures, societies, or geographic regions. It is not exclusively associated with poverty, rurality, or cold climates. While the problem is often framed and communicated in varying ways, its structural causes remain largely universal. Air pollution is not primarily determined by weather, location, or geography—though these factors certainly influence its manifestations. Fundamentally, air pollution is a by-product of human civilization. Wherever people settle to live, the air, water, and soil are subject to degradation.

According to the World Health Organization (WHO), air pollution is any alteration of the natural characteristics of the atmosphere by chemical, physical, or biological agents. Climate change, environmental degradation, and human health problems are commonly discussed as consequences of air pollution. In Europe, the recently adopted EU Directive 2024/2881 on Ambient Air Quality and Cleaner Air for Europe continues the work of previous legislation (see Sect. 2.3.1), setting air-quality standards for member states in line with WHO recommendations (World Health Organization, 2021). The Directive regulates the following pollutants: particulate matter (PM10), fine particles (PM2.5), sulfur dioxide (SO_2), nitrogen dioxide (NO_2), lead (Pb), carbon monoxide (CO), benzene, ozone, arsenic (As), cadmium (Cd), nickel (Ni), and polycyclic aromatic hydrocarbons (PAHs) (mainly benzo(a) pyrene).

Among all those pollutants, it is currently PM that is typically considered to pose the highest risk to health, mainly due to its prevalence and its toxic and carcinogenic properties. PM is a complex phenomenon, as it consists of a heterogeneous mixture of solid and liquid particles of different origins, chemical composition, and reactivity, including acids, organic chemicals, metals, and dust particles. This mixture is responsible for the complex causal characteristics of PM. Although some fractions of PM present in the atmosphere are of natural origin (typically particles emitted by volcanoes, dust storms, and aerosolized sea salt), the most problematic are particles associated with human economic activities, such as industrial processes, energy and heat generation, and transportation.

In order to study PM, it is described either by the number of particles suspended in the air (total suspended particles (TSPs)) or, more often, by the size distribution of PM particles. The aerodynamic diameter (*aerodynamic equivalent diameter* (AED)) of particles characterizes their airborne ability as well as their ability to penetrate the human respiratory tract. Regulators distinguish primarily between two size categories of PM, in reference to which ambient air-quality standards are set: coarse particulate matter (PM10), with an aerodynamic diameter of 10 μm (or smaller), and fine particulate matter (PM2.5), with an aerodynamic diameter of 2.5 μm.

Recently, an additional size category has been defined: particles with an aerodynamic diameter smaller than 0.1 μm (UFP, PM0.1). The shift of researchers' attention to fine and ultrafine fractions of PM is a result of studies indicating that smaller fractions better explain PM's toxicity and possess a higher radical-generating capacity than coarser fractions (see, e.g., de Kok et al., 2006). Over the territory of Europe, PM2.5 amounts to 50–70% of PM10 (World Health Organization, 2013, p. 2).

PM10 is often associated with dust, fires, solid-fuel combustion, and emissions from smokestacks, while PM2.5 is typically associated with gasoline and diesel engine exhausts, industrial processes, and photocatalytic reactions in the atmosphere (Esworthy, 2013, p. 4).

In urban environments in Europe, traffic and residential heating together account for 77% of PM2.5 mass (with residential combustion responsible for 46% and traffic for 21%) (Juda-Rezler et al., 2020). While coal is the main culprit in Central Europe, on the global level, residential biomass burning is the major source of fine particulate matter in the atmosphere (Vicente & Alves, 2018).

Smog is a phenomenon often conflated with air pollution, especially in popular discourse, though the latter term is broader. Smog is usually defined as decreased air transparency due to the presence of particulate matter from anthropogenic sources. Typically, it takes the form of a thick fog with a characteristic smell and color, resulting from the presence of sulfur compounds. The phenomenon became prevalent in the industrialized West at the turn of the nineteenth and twentieth centuries, but it had already been observed in England and Scotland as early as the thirteenth century, when workshops in both countries started adopting coal for their production processes (Brimblecombe, 2011). The term is a combination of the English words "smoke" and "fog" and started to appear in the press toward the end of the nineteenth century. It is usually linked with Henry Antoine Des Voeux and his 1905 presentation, entitled *Fog and Smoke*, at the Congress of the Royal Institute of Public Health (although the term had appeared in the American and British press even decades before).

The formation of smog is facilitated by specific weather conditions, i.e., atmospheric temperature inversion, which often occurs over land in winter. Inversion shuts down the vertical circulation of heat in the atmosphere (convection) and prevents pollutants from being dispersed by wind and convection. The rising amount of particulate matter in turn acts as seeds for vapor condensation, eventually causing fog to appear. Yet smog is primarily caused by intensive solid-fuel combustion. This type of smog remains a frequent phenomenon in many poorer countries, including Poland and other Central European states, mostly due to their reliance on coal and wood for residential heating.

Apart from this type of smog, which is sometimes dubbed London-type smog, there is also a much newer phenomenon of a similar kind, called photochemical smog, characteristic of agglomerations with intense car traffic, for example, Los Angeles. Photochemical smog—or Los Angeles-type smog as it is often called due to its prominence in the L.A. basin—is composed of secondary pollutants formed from gases, primarily nitrogen oxides, and other pollutants emitted by vehicle exhausts, including PAHs (Dickerson et al., 1997; Finlayson & Pitts, 1976). The most well-known component of photochemical smog is ozone (O_3), but it also contains nitrogen dioxide (NO_2), peroxyacetyl nitrate (PAN), and various aldehydes. Ozone causes airway irritation, numerous health problems, and reduction in agricultural yields, since it interferes with plant photosynthesis. Nitrogen dioxide is a highly reactive gas causing airway irritation (Olszyk et al., 1989). PAN, in turn, is mutagenic and is suspected to contribute to the development of skin cancer (Aslam, 2021). Finally, aldehydes, due to their high reactivity, are also considered highly toxic (LoPachin & Gavin, 2014). The formation of photochemical smog also requires specific weather conditions, including light winds and air inversion, to severely limit the atmospheric dispersion of pollutants. Los Angeles-type smog requires sunny weather, as chemical reactions forming photochemical smog are driven by ultraviolet radiation (Brusseau, 2019, pp. 293–309).

Despite the fact that our book generally focuses on outdoor pollution, especially solid-fuel residential combustion for heat production, it is important for our readers to recognize that air pollution is a multifaceted phenomenon—with a complex genesis and a wide range of consequences. Among the most significant are effects on human health, which have already been studied for many years.

2.2.2 Health Consequences of Air Pollution

In the scholarly literature, it is the 5-day London smog of December 1952 that is usually mentioned as a turning point in understanding the significance of air quality for public health (Bell & Davis, 2001; Brimblecombe, 2011). Due to anticyclone weather conditions, the concentration of air pollutants rose to levels 19 times higher than current regulatory air-quality standards, effectively paralyzing the functioning of the city. Just after the episode, a government report estimated the death toll at over 4000—three times higher than expected in the normal course of events (U.K. Ministry of Health, 1954; Longan, 1953). The number of people seriously affected reached 100,000, mostly with cardiovascular or respiratory problems. Similar episodes, however, had occurred earlier and were subject to careful scientific examination. For example, a 3-day incident in the industrialized Meuse Valley in Belgium in 1930 caused acute pulmonary symptoms in several thousand people, allegedly leading to 60 deaths (Nemery et al., 2001). A similar "unusual smog episode" happened in the industrial town of Donora, Pennsylvania, in October 1948. Over the period of 1 week, 20 people died and several thousand, almost half of the population, became sick, which led to the first serious epidemiological investigation into atmospheric pollution by US authorities (Schrenk et al., 1949).

All of the mentioned episodes helped raise the attention of scholars and decision-makers, but translation into public policy was slow. Only in the 1970s and 1980s did the connection between airborne particulate matter and cardiopulmonary diseases become a consensus. Currently, it is beyond discussion that outdoor air pollution is associated with a number of health risks. Through observational studies, scientists were able to demonstrate, for example, that increased blood pressure, irregular heartbeat, elevated markers of inflammation and thrombosis, as well as cardiovascular hospital admissions and mortality are the expected effects of exposure to PM. Also, aggravated asthma, decreased lung function, increased respiratory symptoms (e.g., airway irritation, coughing), and premature deaths in patients with heart or lung disease are linked in the literature to air pollution. The short-term effects consist of, among others, premature mortality and hospital admissions, while the long-term cumulative ones include lung cancer, cardiovascular conditions, and cardiopulmonary diseases (Kim et al., 2015).

Solid evidence for the association between PM2.5 and life expectancy began to emerge, thanks to population studies in the second decade of the current millennium. An analysis of 2000–2007 data on yearly average PM2.5 and life expectancy in 545 US counties demonstrated that reductions in PM2.5 resulted in improvements in life expectancy (Correia et al., 2013). Another study, in turn, proved associations between global changes in PM2.5 and surface ozone with annual cardiopulmonary and lung cancer mortalities, and respiratory mortalities, respectively (Fang et al., 2012). Hospitalization or death from heart failure was proved to be associated with increases in air concentrations of carbon monoxide, sulfur dioxide, and nitrogen dioxide (Shah et al., 2013). PM is suspected to promote the production of reactive oxygen species in the human body, leading to cellular-level damage that initiates or exacerbates inflammation. It is inflammation that ultimately leads to tissue damage and airway irritation or injury (Hitzfeld et al., 1997). Studies also suggest that transition metals with redox potential contained in PM are responsible for many of these adverse effects, as they promote oxidative stress in lung cells (Aust et al., 2002).

Recently, science has also begun to understand the role of air pollution in brain functioning and cognitive impairment (e.g., Calderón-Garcidueñas et al., 2011; Kicinski et al., 2015; Lam et al., 2016; Costa et al., 2019). Evidence also indicates that air pollution is likely to contribute to central nervous system diseases, particularly Alzheimer's and Parkinson's, as air pollution exposure has been associated with increased expression of markers of neurodegenerative disease pathologies (Costa et al., 2020).

In the past, based on existing scientific evidence, the World Health Organization estimated that PM2.5 exposure was responsible for approximately 800,000 premature deaths per year. This made air pollution the 13th leading cause of mortality worldwide (Anderson et al., 2012). Nowadays, as new data have been collected, this estimate has changed significantly. Updated figures are much higher, as they encompass both indoor and outdoor air pollution from various sources. According to the newest data, air pollution contributed to 8.1 million deaths in 2021, advancing to the position of the second-leading risk factor for early death, surpassed only by high blood pressure (Health Effects Institute, 2024).

2.2.3 Glimpses on the Problem of Air Pollution in Małopolska

According to data published by WHO, out of 50 cities with the highest concentrations of fine particulate matter (PM2,5) in the EU, as many as 33 are located in Poland, mostly in Śląsk and Małopolska (see WHO Global Urban Ambient Air Pollution Database). Notably, the air in Poland is among the most polluted in Europe and—in certain periods of the year—in the world (Rolecki, 2022). The measured concentrations of various fractions of suspended dust often significantly exceed, on a daily basis, the air-quality levels set by the World Health Organization (WHO) and even the much looser national standards. A series of studies demonstrated that in the first decade of the twenty-first century, the major sources of pollution in most Polish cities were traffic emissions and domestic heating, with a shrinking role for industrial activities and long-range transport of pollutants (Juda-Rezler et al., 2020).

In 2022, the average number of "smog days" in Polish cities, i.e., those in which the permissible daily concentration of PM10 dust was exceeded, was 35. In Nowa Ruda, however, these exceeded 3 months (95 days) in total, and in several other cities in Śląsk and Małopolska, they surpassed 54 days (Polski Alarm Smogowy, 2023). Air pollution covers practically the entire area of the country, as it is not limited to large cities but also occurs in small towns and villages where coal and biomass are burned for domestic heating without any supervision from authorities.

It is also a mistake to attribute the poor quality of air in Poland merely to geographical conditions, since it is mainly political decisions that are responsible for the persisting pollution in the country. Many of those decisions have been made quite recently, despite existing knowledge on how air pollution influences human health. According to data from the Central Emission Register of Buildings (see Sect. 2.3.1), in mid-2022, there were 5.36 million individual heating systems for solid fuels in Poland, of which high-emission devices with the lowest energy efficiency accounted for as much as 2.24 million. For comparison, there were only 62,000 efficient and certified heating systems from the EcoDesign class. As stove owners constitute a large electorate, politicians have a reason not to act, perpetuating households' dependence on heat generated from hard coal or wood. In this way, necessary reforms were neglected, as was even rudimentary education about the impact of solid-fuel combustion on health and climate.

In recent years, air pollution has become an important topic of public debate in Poland. It was the effect not of scientific studies but mostly of rising civic activism and political pressure from the European Commission, disappointed by the slow adoption of air-quality standards by Poland. As mentioned previously, the capital of Małopolska—Kraków, the country's second-largest agglomeration and a popular tourist destination—was especially affected by air pollution due to its geographical as well as socioeconomic conditions. To address this problem, in 2015–2017, a number of local legislative attempts were undertaken.

2.3 Institutional and Legal Context of Fighting Smog in Małopolska

2.3.1 A System of Air Protection in Poland

The next step is to characterize the institutional and regulatory components of the system designed to combat air pollution in Poland, with particular attention to the Małopolska region. This overview does not aim to provide a comprehensive account of the relevant legal acts, institutional arrangements (whether European or domestic), or judicial decisions concerning air quality. Rather, its purpose is to identify and explain the key elements necessary for understanding the legal and institutional context that has shaped the challenges, opportunities, and dynamics of Małopolska's struggle against air pollution.

At the beginning of the twenty-first century, Poland's air protection system stood at the crossroads of two distinct eras. On the one hand, it retained the institutional and legal structures developed during the 1990s, rooted in domestic environmental legislation. On the other, it underwent rapid transformation in response to the requirements of the European Union accession process—concluded in 2004 (see, e.g., Radecka, 2021). This shift also reflected the growing influence of international environmental law, although the latter lies beyond the scope of this discussion. A key turning point came in 2001 with the adoption of a new framework law: the Environmental Protection Act (EPA) of 27 April 2001 (Journal of Laws 2001 No. 62, item 627). This foundational statute was later complemented by the Act of 3 October 2008 on providing information on the environment and environmental protection, public participation in environmental protection, and environmental impact assessments (Journal of Laws No. 199, item 1227) (for a general overview of air-quality management in Poland during this period, see Poskrobko & Poskrobko, 2012, pp. 211–246). At the same time, Poland undertook actions to implement the *acquis communautaire* in the field of air protection. However, for years, the system operated without providing considerable improvement in the levels of certain pollutants and with many problems. The air protection system shaped at that time—and still in operation with some changes—consists of several elements, which will be briefly characterized below.

EU Regulations and Policies

It is important to acknowledge the role of EU regulations and policies. The European Union's air protection system is among the most advanced and institutionalized worldwide (see, e.g., Jordan, 2012). Its foundation rests on the Treaty on the Functioning of the European Union, particularly Articles 191–193, which establish the general principles of EU environmental policy. Building on these provisions, a multilevel governance structure has emerged (see Chap. 3), encompassing EU-level secondary legislation, institutions responsible for implementation and oversight, and mechanisms for monitoring and reporting air quality.

The most important legal act regulating air quality during the period described in this book was Directive 2008/50/EC (the so-called CAFE Directive, revised in 2015), which consolidated previous regulations and introduced a comprehensive framework for air-quality monitoring and management in the EU. Although the new directive was issued in 2024, discussed below, the general framework and the philosophy underlying it remains the same. The CAFE Directive established, among others, the obligations to (1) designate zones and agglomerations in each member state (Section 3) where air quality is monitored; (2) conduct systematic monitoring at measurement points in accordance with location criteria (Annex III); (3) apply limit values, target values, alert thresholds, and long-term objectives for key air pollutants: PM10, PM2.5, NO_2, SO_2, CO, O_3, benzene, and lead (Pb) (Annexes XI and XII); (4) assess air quality based on measurement and modeling results; (5) develop and implement short-term action plans and air-quality programs in case of exceedances; and (6) inform the public about measurement results and air quality (Section 26).

The CAFE Directive was supplemented by Directive 2004/107/EC, which sets target values for arsenic, cadmium, nickel, and benzo(a)pyrene in suspended particulate matter, as well as the general requirements for air-quality assessment and management regarding these substances. In parallel, Directive (EU) 2016/2284 (the NEC Directive) established binding reduction commitments for member states with respect to five key pollutants: sulfur dioxide (SO_2), nitrogen oxides (NO_x), nonmethane volatile organic compounds (NMVOCs), ammonia (NH_3), and fine particulate matter (PM2.5) (see, in the Polish context, Radecka, 2020).

Among the above-listed features of the EU air-quality management system, its division into zones and agglomerations deserves special attention. This approach is intended to tailor remedial measures to local conditions and emission levels. In each zone, air quality is assessed based on data from monitoring stations, mathematical modeling, and statistical analyses. Measurements are conducted in accordance with the minimum requirements specified in the directive annexes (including the number and location of stations relative to the population and main sources of emissions). Moreover, reference values for individual pollutants have different legal status: (1) limit values are binding—their exceedance requires the preparation of remedial action plans; (2) target values and long-term objectives are indicative, aiming to improve environmental conditions over time; and (3) information and alert thresholds serve to protect public health during smog episodes.

The EU has developed a comprehensive system of institutions responsible for creating, implementing, and enforcing air protection policies and legislation. The European Commission—particularly the Directorate-General for Environment—plays a central role by initiating legislation, evaluating national reports, and referring cases against member states to the Court of Justice of the European Union (CJEU). The European Environment Agency collects and processes data from member states, analyzes trends, and publishes regular environmental reports. The CJEU, in turn, adjudicates treaty infringement cases related to air quality—for instance, judgments against several member states for exceeding PM10 and NO_2 limits. Poland has also faced such sanctions: in 2018, the CJEU ruled that Poland had violated the CAFE Directive due to persistent exceedances of air-quality standards (Case C-336/16; see Ward, 2018). The European Court of Auditors complements this framework by assessing the effectiveness of EU environmental policies and evaluating the use of financial resources. At the same time, national institutions remain responsible for air-quality monitoring systems, remediation programs, and enforcement measures at both national and local levels.

In recent years, EU air-quality policy has clearly shifted toward more ambitious goals and stronger integration with climate and health policies. In 2021, the European Commission announced the "Zero Pollution Action Plan" (https://environment.ec.europa.eu/strategy/zero-pollution-action-plan_en) as part of the European Green Deal. This plan includes aligning EU air-quality standards with the stricter WHO guidelines from 2021, significantly reducing emissions from transport and industry, and supporting cities in implementing integrated environmental management plans—thereby linking previously separate policy strands. Eventually, the revision of the CAFE Directive was adopted as Directive (EU) 2024/2881 of the European Parliament and of the Council of 23 October 2024 on ambient air quality and cleaner air for Europe. This directive lowers limit values for PM2.5 and NO_2, strengthens public information obligations, and introduces greater transparency in planning and oversight procedures. A 2-year period—until 11 December 2026—was set as the deadline by which member states must transpose Directive (EU) 2024/2881 into their national legislation. The new, more restrictive limit values for human health protection set out in this directive must be met by 1 January 2030 at the latest.

Polish Central Level Air Protection System

The air protection system in Poland is coshaped by national constitutional law. Environmental protection—including air protection—is a constitutional obligation of the Polish state. Article 5 of the Constitution of the Republic of Poland of 1997 states that the Republic of Poland "shall ensure the protection of the environment, guided by the principle of sustainable development." Article 74, paragraph 3, of the Constitution establishes that "Protection of the environment shall be the duty of public authorities." Furthermore, paragraph 3 states: "Public authorities shall pursue policies ensuring the ecological security of current and future generations." Meanwhile, paragraph 4 adds: "Public authorities shall support the activities of citizens to protect and improve the quality of the environment." Based on these constitutional provisions, the aforementioned framework law—the Environmental Protection Act—was enacted, replacing previous sectoral environmental regulations. This statute introduced many solutions aligned with EU directives, including the "polluter pays" principle, an integrated permitting system, environmental impact assessment, and—specifically in the field of air protection—a system of monitoring, zones, and remedial action plans in cases of exceedances of air-quality standards.

The Polish national system of air pollution management—originally established in its current form in 2001 and subsequently updated multiple times—operates across both central and local levels of government. Poland is a unitary state with a strong, three-tiered system of self-government, consisting of regions (*województwa*), counties (*powiaty*), and municipalities (*gminy*). At the central level, the Ministry of the Environment (operating under different names over more than three decades) has played—and continues to play—a key role. Its responsibilities include developing national strategies, drafting environmental legislation, ensuring the implementation of EU obligations, and engaging in international environmental cooperation. Alongside this system has operated—and continues to operate—the Chief Inspectorate of Environmental Protection, together with 16 Regional Inspectorates, responsible for monitoring air quality and overseeing compliance with emission standards (though only for industrial facilities). For many years, however, the monitoring infrastructure remained underdeveloped. In 2001, the Chief Inspectorate operated just around 100 monitoring stations, fewer than 20 of which were automatic (a strikingly low figure given Poland's size). Moreover, the network was concentrated in major urban areas, leaving significant "white spots" on the map of actual pollution levels across the country. Since then, the network has expanded considerably: today, it comprises more than 300 automatic monitoring stations. Around the same time, the National Centre for Emissions Management (KOBiZE in Polish), tasked with creating and maintaining a national emissions database, also began its activities. An important role is played by the Supreme Audit Office, which also oversees the effectiveness of the air protection system and has, on numerous occasions, highlighted its weaknesses and structural shortcomings.

In the case of national air-quality standards, these are specified by the minister responsible for climate matters (see Adamkiewicz et al., 2021). The legal basis is primarily provided by the EPA (Articles 85–92), which governs air-quality assessment and management. According to Article 91(1), the minister is authorized to determine, by regulation, the levels of certain substances in ambient air. The currently binding regulation is the Regulation of the Minister of Climate and Environment of 11 December 2020 on the levels of certain substances in the air (Journal of Laws 2021, item 92). It defines, among other things, limit values, target values, information and alert thresholds, and margins of tolerance for substances such as PM10, PM2.5, NO_2, SO_2, O_3, CO, benzene, and benzo[a]pyrene. Before that, these matters were governed by the Regulation of the Minister of the Environment of 24 August 2012 (Journal of Laws 2012, item 1031), which defined comparable categories and threshold values. Notably, an amending regulation issued in 2019 (Journal of Laws 2019, item 1931)—following sustained pressure from nongovernmental organizations and public health advocates—significantly lowered the information and alarm thresholds for daily PM10 concentrations: from 200 $\mu g/m^3$ to 100 $\mu g/m^3$ and from 300 $\mu g/m^3$ to 150 $\mu g/m^3$, respectively. This brought Poland's standards closer to those recommended by the World Health Organization and aligned them more closely with thresholds used in other EU member states. The 2020 regulation replaced the 2012 regulation to reflect administrative restructuring (e.g., the creation of the Ministry of Climate) and to clarify definitions, but it did not significantly alter pollutant limit values. For example, for now, the annual limit value for PM10 remains at 40 $\mu g/m^3$ and the daily limit value at 50 $\mu g/m^3$, which may be exceeded no more than 35 times per calendar year. The regulation also maintains the information and alarm thresholds for PM10 24-hour concentrations.

The second important legislation in the field of air protection is a regulation on the quality of fuels, first introduced in 2018 through the Regulation of the Minister of Energy of 27 September 2018 on Quality Requirements for Solid Fuels (Journal of Laws 2018, item 1890). This regulation came many years after serious air-quality problems had already been widely recognized in Poland—in this sense, it was introduced far too late (the Supreme Audit Office in 2000 pinpointed the problem and the need for regulation). The provisions were later amended in 2022 (Journal of Laws 2022, item 2856), but the standards remained relatively weak, setting low quality thresholds for solid fuels. As a result, households were still allowed to burn low-grade fuels, which continued to contribute significantly to air pollution.

These earlier regulations were replaced by the Regulation of the Minister of Industry and the Minister of Climate and Environment of 4 November 2024 on Quality Requirements for Solid Fuels (Journal of Laws 2024, item 1618), which introduced significant changes in the national regulatory framework for coal and other solid fuels. This legal act superseded the previous Regulation of 23 December 2022 (Journal of Laws 2022, item 2856) and offers a new approach to both the classification and quality parameters of fuels available on the market. The most notable novelty in the 2024 regulation is the introduction of a clear classification system for fuels, including new categories such as *węgiel kostka* (cube coal), *Orzech standard* (standard nut coal), *Groszek standard* ("standard pea coal"—replacing the previously used “premium pea” category), as well as *miał* (coal dust) and *antracyt* (anthracite). This classification is intended to facilitate the alignment of available fuels with the technical requirements of modern boilers, including those that meet EcoDesign standards. Each of these classes is associated with specific and detailed parameters regarding ash content, sulfur content, moisture level, calorific value, grain size distribution, and the Roga Index (RI). A second key innovation is the introduction of a timeline for the gradual tightening of fuel quality standards between 2025 and 2031. For example, for *węgiel kostka*, the permissible ash content is to be reduced from 12% to 10% by 2031, the maximum sulfur content is to be reduced from 1.7% to 1.2%, and the minimum calorific value is to be increased from 22 to 24 MJ/kg. This phased approach is intended to improve the quality of fuels used by households, albeit not in a substantial way, while simultaneously giving producers time to adapt to the new requirements.

In contrast to the 2018 and 2022 regulations, the 2024 regulation introduced a detailed implementation schedule and clearly defined procedures for quality control, to be carried out by accredited laboratories. The earlier acts lacked both a timeline for the introduction of stricter norms and a differentiated classification of fuels, which made them less precise and more difficult to enforce. Nevertheless, evaluations of the new regulation remain mixed. On the one hand, it has been welcomed for enhancing transparency in the fuel market and, in the long run, for promoting better air quality. On the other hand, critics have highlighted the practical challenges of implementation, including the need to train vendors and consumers in the new terminology and to expand the fuel-quality control infrastructure. From the perspective of antismog policy, however, the regulation represents an important step toward a more coherent and effective national regulatory framework.

Another initiative—not only significant for air pollution management but also introduced relatively late, in 2021—deserves mention: the Heating Sources Inventory Program, implemented as part of the Central Emission Register of Buildings (in Polish: *Centralna Ewidencja Emisyjności Budynków* (CEEB)). This nationwide system collects detailed data on heating installations and the technical parameters of buildings. Established under the amended Act on Supporting Thermomodernisation and Renovation (Journal of Laws of 2021, item 554), the program imposes a legal obligation on property owners to submit declarations specifying the type, age, and technical condition of their heat sources. This mandatory reporting is designed to create a reliable and up-to-date database of emission-intensive heating devices, which is essential for the development and enforcement of air protection policies. Data collected under CEEB supports targeted antismog measures, facilitates the monitoring of boiler replacement programs (such as Clean Air and Stop Smog), and enables more precise emission inventories at both national and regional levels. By linking individual heating choices with broader environmental strategies, the program strengthens the regulatory and planning framework for improving air quality in Poland.

These two regulatory measures—first, the standards for permissible pollutant concentrations and, second, the belated introduction of fuel quality regulations—together with the national subsidy program for heating system replacement and thermal modernization (discussed below), as well as the development of a database on household heating installations, represent the few substantial political decisions on air pollution adopted at the national level in Poland. However, all of these mechanisms were introduced far too late (see Citkowska-Kimla, 2019), and the first two, in particular, are considerably less ambitious and progressive than they could have been.

The devolution of responsibility for combating smog in Poland will be discussed below. As a counterbalance, the National Program for Air Protection (NPAP) was introduced as a complementary instrument in cases where local and regional efforts prove insufficient. According to Article 91c of the EPA, if permissible or target levels of air pollutants are exceeded across a significant area of the country and the measures undertaken by local authorities fail to achieve effective emission reductions, the minister responsible for climate policy may develop an NPAP. This program serves as a strategic framework that sets overarching objectives and directions for action, which should subsequently be reflected in regional and local air protection programs. The first NPAP, issued by the Minister of the Environment, entered into force on 1 October 2015 (and was updated in 2021). Its purpose was twofold: first, to ensure compliance with legally binding standards for pollutant concentrations (particularly particulate matter) in the shortest possible time and, second, to align, in the longer term (by 2030), with the more ambitious air-quality targets recommended by the World Health Organization.

With some serious delay and many challenges, national subsidy programs were developed to complement the obligations imposed by antismog resolutions. These included, among others, the KAWKA program, launched in 2013 by the Ministry of the Environment in cooperation with the National Fund for Environmental Protection and Water Management (NFEP&WM). It offered cofinancing of up to 90% of eligible costs and operated until 2016. KAWKA was later replaced by the Clean Air (*Czyste Powietrze*) program, as well as Stop Smog, both of which significantly expanded the availability of funds for replacing heat sources and improving building energy efficiency. Particularly noteworthy—though belated and imperfect—was the Clean Air program launched in 2018 (see, e.g., Sakson-Boulet, 2020; Rajchel & Rajchel, 2024). Its objectives were ambitious: reducing emissions from the residential sector, improving the energy efficiency of single-family homes, and supporting microlevel energy transformation, all with the aim of contributing to broader environmental goals. Beneficiaries could receive financial support for replacing heat sources (mainly stoves and boilers), insulating buildings, and installing renewable energy technologies. Managed by the NFEP&WM and implemented by regional funds in cooperation with municipalities, the program was allocated a budget exceeding PLN 100 billion for the period 2018–2029. By May 2025, when the program was suspended to be reopened in a new form later that year, over 1,037,465 applications had been submitted. According to official data, its reported environmental effect was an annual reduction of approximately 50,000 tons of PM10 (see https://czystepowietrze.gov.pl/efekty-programu/czyste-powietrze-w-liczbach; https://polskialarmsmogowy.pl/statystyki/).

Despite some successes, the Clean Air program—though undergoing successive changes and modifications—has been subject to sustained criticism. Although formally open to all, in practice, it has disproportionately benefited the middle class rather than those most affected by energy poverty and smog. Research by the Institute for Structural Research (2023) shows that the majority of beneficiaries are people with higher incomes, administrative skills, and the financial capacity to cover their own contribution. By contrast, those experiencing energy poverty—often living in old, energy-inefficient homes heated with coal—face substantial barriers: lack of creditworthiness, limited access to information, and insufficient advisory support (see Chap. 4). Territorial inequalities are also evident: program uptake is highest in voivodeships with strong local governments (e.g., Mazowieckie, Małopolskie), while participation remains weakest in peripheral regions (e.g., Podkarpackie, Podlaskie), even though air pollution there is often equally severe. It should be noted that the program initially had a very high entry threshold: application forms were complex, procedures time-consuming, and advisory networks largely absent in smaller municipalities (especially where eco-advisors were lacking—see Chap. 4). Reforms introduced since 2021—such as simplified application procedures, prefinancing options for the poorest households, and closer cooperation with municipalities—have improved accessibility, but significant disparities persist. The uneven quality of beneficiary service across voivodeships means that actual access to the program continues to depend heavily on the efficiency of local administrations, undermining the principle of equal treatment.

While the program has undoubtedly contributed to reducing PM (official data confirm significant declines in PM10 concentrations in cities such as Kraków, Rybnik, and Warsaw), its effectiveness as a tool for energy transformation is questionable. Most investments focus on boiler replacement, often with gas installations, which helps reduce smog but does not necessarily advance decarbonization of the residential sector. Furthermore, systematic monitoring of environmental outcomes remains lacking: as early as 2022, the Supreme Audit Office highlighted that data on emissions "before" and "after" investments were fragmentary or entirely absent. A further risk is the so-called rebound effect: new heating systems improve thermal comfort, which may increase energy consumption, especially when not combined with comprehensive thermal upgrades. These limitations illustrate the structural weaknesses of the program, which—despite its scale—cannot by itself guarantee a just and sustainable energy transition.

Regional-Level Air Protection System

At the self-government level, responsibilities for air-quality management have been highly fragmented. Since 2008, regional assemblies (*Sejmiki Wojewódzkie*)—legislative bodies at the regional level—have been required to adopt Air Improvement Plans in cases where air-quality standards are exceeded (see, e.g., Karpus, 2021). In accordance with Article 91 of the EPA, such a program must be developed for zones where exceedances of limit or target levels (together with any applicable margin of tolerance) have been recorded for at least one substance. These documents are both strategic and normative in character: they not only set out general goals and remedial measures but also constitute binding local law within the respective regions. At the same time, executive bodies of lower-tier local governments retain important competences. Under Article 379(1) EPA, the regional marshal, district governor (*starosta*), and commune administrator (*wójt*), mayor, or city president exercise control over compliance with and application of the EPA within the scope of their competences. These authorities may authorize employees of their subordinate offices—or, in the case of municipalities, also municipal guard officers—to perform inspection functions. According to Article 379(3)(1) EPA, inspectors are entitled, while performing such inspections, to enter the premises of a property, facility, or its parts where business activity is conducted (at any time, day or night) and to enter the remaining areas of a property between 6 a.m. and 10 p.m., accompanied by experts and with the necessary equipment.

Since 2015, local-level efforts to combat smog have intensified, particularly in heavily affected regions such as Małopolska. This shift was largely driven by the emergence of a new regulatory instrument: antismog resolutions adopted by voivodeship assemblies under the revised Article 96 of the EPA. These resolutions authorized regional authorities to restrict the use of specific fuels and impose technical standards on heating systems. The legal and political trajectory of this instrument—unused prior to 2013—is examined in more detail in the section that follows. Importantly, the implementation of these resolutions has resulted in a fragmented regulatory landscape across Poland. While some provinces adopted antismog measures imposing varying obligations on residents, others opted not to do so. A decentralized system thus emerged—characterized by coordination challenges and significant disparities in the level of protection afforded to residents across different regions. Paradoxically, it was not national policy or legislation but rather the resolutions enacted at the regional level that became the most significant instruments for addressing smog in Poland during the second decade of the twenty-first century and into the 2030s.

Even at this stage, it should be emphasized that the subnational air protection system continues to face persistent challenges: staff and financial shortages in municipalities, low detection rates of illegal practices, social resistance to bans and obligations, and the absence of large-scale effective instruments for controlling solid-fuel quality or assessing the actual effectiveness of Air Improvement Plans (see NIK, 2025). Despite gradual progress, the system remains reactive and fragmented, heavily dependent on the initiative of individual local authorities and the quality of cross-sectoral cooperation. In this context, local advisory and coordination networks have played—and continue to play—a crucial role. Among these, the institution of eco-advisors, discussed further in Chap. 4, has emerged as a central component of Małopolska's environmental policy, initially operating at the municipal level but quickly gaining broader importance.

To sum up, the air protection system in Poland—developed until 2001 largely in response to EU requirements—possessed all the necessary structural components: institutions, legal acts, and fundamental legal and environmental instruments. However, for many years, it remained underfunded and ineffective, with limited monitoring coverage and weak institutional capacity at the local government level. While numerous regulations were formally in place, they often had little practical impact on administrative or enforcement practices (NIK, 2025). The authorities' frequent use of postponed implementation dates for key pollutant standards further discouraged proactive and timely responses to smog. Although meaningful change only began after 2004—when Poland's accession to the European Union brought not only access to structural funds but also exposure to EU enforcement mechanisms, such as penalties for failure to comply with environmental directives and obligations to improve air quality—the immediate effects were far from transformative. Still, EU membership opened new avenues for negotiation, created new opportunities, and triggered important social processes. Over the two decades since accession, Poland's air protection system has undergone a profound transformation—from a fragmented and poorly functioning framework into an increasingly complex and structured public policy domain. Yet this evolution has been marked by a lack of coordination in the timing of reforms and by the delegation of responsibility to region-level initiatives, without a unified, command-and-control strategy to combat low emissions. The fight against smog has not followed a linear trajectory; rather, it has been shaped by a dynamic interplay of external legislative pressures from Brussels, national policy shifts, rising social awareness, and local-level activism (see Chap. 3).

2.3.2 The Case of Małopolska

The Political Context

As previously noted, the responsibility for combating smog in Poland was largely devolved to the regional level. Within this framework, Małopolska emerged as a pioneer, adopting two key regional legal acts during the second decade of the twenty-first century. These acts reflected distinct regulatory approaches and imposed differing obligations on residents in separate parts of the region. One introduced a significantly more restrictive regime for the city of Kraków, while the other established a comparatively more lenient framework for the rest of Małopolska. To understand the rationale behind the adoption of these divergent antismog regimes, it is essential to examine the interplay between environmental policy, the configuration of political power, and the structure of the electorate in the region.

This theme fits within broader theoretical frameworks present in the literature—that so-called postmaterialist values, such as environmental protection, correlate with the level of education and urbanization of society, which translates into greater support for proenvironmental policies in large cities than in rural areas (see Lubarda, 2024). In Małopolska, these differences produced a tension between Kraków—a more liberal city with a strong academic base, a large number of young people, and higher environmental awareness (although even here some groups held divergent views on the causes of and solutions to smog)—and, generally speaking, the more conservative municipalities in the rest of the region, where, as a rule, arguments emphasizing traditional coal heating and the high costs of restrictive regulations had much greater resonance (also expressed in municipal opinions submitted during the consultation of the drafts of the antismog resolutions). The conflicts surrounding the antismog resolutions, which surfaced in Małopolska's public sphere and during the legislative process in the regional assembly, to some extent mirrored broader political and ideological divisions.

It is worth briefly outlining the political landscape of Małopolska. Between 2009 and 2023, the Małopolska Regional Assembly (*Małopolski Sejmik Wojewódzki*) was governed by a coalition of the Civic Platform (PO), a centrist party, and the Polish People's Party (PSL), which represents conservative centrism. The main opposition force was the conservative Law and Justice (PiS) party, which simultaneously held power at the national level from 2015 to 2023. During this period, PiS often displayed skepticism toward ambitious environmental policies, promoting the coal industry and supporting controversial forestry initiatives. Notably, the PiS-led government, backed by Hungary and Romania, brought an action before the Court of Justice of the European Union seeking annulment of the NEC Directive under Article 263 TFEU (Case C-128/17 concluded by the CJEU judgment of 13 March 2019). The government argued that the Directive violated the principles of sincere cooperation, transparency, and proportionality by placing an excessive burden on Poland compared to other member states. The case was dismissed, but it highlighted the deep political resistance to EU climate and environmental policies. These divisions were also reflected at the regional level, where votes on antismog resolutions clearly exposed partisan lines. The final antismog resolution for Kraków, adopted on 15 January 2016, was supported by PO, PSL, and several independent councilors (22 votes in favor), while PiS councilors voted against it (11 votes), out of a total of 39 possible votes. In the case of the resolution covering the rest of the voivodeship (Resolution of January 23, 2017), which was much less stringent and allowed more time and flexibility for adjustment, a broader political compromise was reached: 29 votes in favor, one against, and two abstentions.

These divisions had both social and spatial dimensions. In Kraków, support for the ban on solid-fuel combustion was relatively widespread, with opposition remaining marginal. In rural municipalities, however, where coal heating was often perceived as an affordable and accessible option, the resolution was frequently framed as a top-down imposition—an initiative pushed by the urban center onto the periphery—thereby reinforcing local tensions. Political affiliation also appears to have played an important role: voters aligned with PiS largely mirrored the party's opposition to the ban on solid fuels, often justified by appeals to patriotism and the defense of the coal sector. In turn, PiS politicians tended to reflect the habits, interests, and environmental attitudes of a significant portion of Małopolska's rural population.

The First Ideas Behind Antismog Resolutions

The adoption of antismog resolutions in the Małopolska Voivodeship—particularly the groundbreaking (though ultimately repealed) resolution for Kraków in 2013 and the subsequent two attempts—was the outcome of a multiyear political, legal, and social process. Gradually, the idea of introducing restrictions on the types of substances burned in household stoves—or at least on the quality of those fuels or the stoves themselves—began to take shape and gain traction. Although the Małopolska antismog resolutions gained national attention as the first antismog resolutions in Poland, their substantive and analytical foundations had been developed much earlier. A key role was played by the *Expert Study on Introducing Restrictions on the Use of Solid Fuels in Kraków*, prepared by the consulting firm Atmoterm S.A. in 2010, commissioned by the authorities of Małopolska (Atmoterm, 2010). This was the first step—even the title of the report refers merely to "restrictions," not outright "bans."

This document represented the first relatively comprehensive attempt in Poland to create a technical as well as legal framework for a regional policy aimed at reducing low-stack emissions, clearly identified as the most significant source of air pollution. The Atmoterm report not only offered a diagnosis of air pollution in Kraków but also included a detailed legal analysis of Article 96 of the EPA, which at that time was under consideration as a legal basis for adopting local resolutions in the absence of national action. Notably, the provision—which had never before been applied—read as follows at the time:

> **Article 96 (prior to 2015 amendment):**
> *The regional assembly (sejmik) may, in order to prevent negative environmental impacts or to protect historical monuments, determine, by resolution:*
>
> 1. *the types or quality of fuels permitted for use within the entire voivodeship or part thereof;*
> 2. *the method of implementing and monitoring compliance with this obligation.*

Atmoterm experts observed that the typical narrow interpretation of this provision allows only for the introduction of quality standards for fuels but not a complete ban on their use. Importantly, Article 96 referred only to fuels, not installations, significantly limiting regulatory options in the latter area. It is also worth noting that the justifications for such restrictions were limited to the prevention of environmental harm or the protection of monuments—there was no mention of safeguarding human life or health, further underscoring the limited scope of the tool. The report also warned that the lack of clear provisions regarding enforcement and legal sanctions raised the likelihood that such a resolution might be annulled by administrative courts, which examine the legality of local regulations. Indeed, this is precisely what happened after the adoption of the 2013 Kraków resolution, which was invalidated by the Regional Administrative Court in Kraków (first-instance administrative court), a decision later upheld by the Supreme Administrative Court (second-instance administrative court). The courts ruled that the then-current version of Article 96 (quoted above) did not constitute a sufficient legal basis for enacting a general ban on certain fuels. We elaborate on this ruling further below.

The Atmoterm report proposed three regulatory scenarios aimed at tackling low-stack emissions: (1) the introduction of quality standards for solid fuels, (2) partial spatial or temporal restrictions on the use of certain solid fuels, and (3) a total ban on the use of solid fuels within Kraków. Each scenario was analyzed in terms of environmental impact, technical feasibility, and legal admissibility. Emphasis was placed on the argument that only a complete ban on the use of solid fuels (especially coal and wood) could meaningfully reduce emissions of PM10 and benzo[a]pyrene—the primary pollutants in Kraków. This conclusion played a crucial role in paving the way for future antismog resolutions in the region.

In response to the legal limitations identified in the current version of Article 96 of the EPA, the authors of the report proposed a revised version aimed at clarifying and expanding the legal powers available to regional assemblies. However, the proposed revision remained relatively limited, as it did not explicitly authorize a total ban on specific fuels. The suggested wording was as follows:

Article 96—Atmoterm Proposal (2010):

1. *The regional assembly may, in order to prevent negative environmental impacts or to protect historical monuments, adopt a resolution to establish:*
   (a) *permissible quality parameters for solid fuels (e.g., sulfur content, ash, moisture);*
   (b) *time periods and geographic zones for which restrictions apply;*
   (c) *fuel documentation and labeling requirements;*
   (d) *rules and powers for inspection bodies, along with administrative penalties.*
2. *The resolution may prohibit the use of fuels that do not meet the quality requirements.*
3. *Local authorities shall provide technical support and carry out educational campaigns.*

This proposal aimed to strengthen both the legislative mandate and the practical enforceability of the regulations while also addressing the need to support citizens during the energy transition. As such, the Atmoterm document served as an informal but significant cornerstone for future antismog policy in the region. It also served as a reference point during the drafting of the Air Improvement Plan for Małopolska in 2013. Moreover, as noted above, the validity of the legal predictions contained in the Atmoterm report was later confirmed by court rulings. To salvage the legal basis for adopting antismog resolutions, an amendment to the EPA was enacted on 10 July 2015 (Journal of Laws 2015, item 1223), coming into force on 12 November 2015. We discuss this development further below. In this context, it is important to emphasize that the Atmoterm expert report identified legislative gaps and proposed a coherent and realistic, albeit somewhat limited, regulatory model. With later modifications, this model was reflected in both the amended legislation and the subsequent resolution-making practices of the Małopolska Regional Assembly. Additionally, the technical-legal expertise provided by Atmoterm S.A. enriched public debate, as its conclusions and recommendations were frequently cited in consultations and stakeholder meetings. It helped shift the conversation from merely diagnosing the problem to exploring viable legal instruments for solving it.

Małopolska Air Improvement Plans of 2009, 2013, and 2017

As already noted, the adoption and implementation of antismog resolutions in the Małopolska region resulted from a complex interplay of social, institutional, and legal factors. From a legal perspective, a key element of this process was the development of the Małopolska Air Improvement Plans (MAIPs), which must be established whenever air-quality standards are persistently exceeded. MAIPs became the primary planning instrument for remedial actions aimed at improving air quality in the region. In particular, two documents—the MAIP of 2009 and its successor from 2013 (amended in 2017)—illustrate how the regional authorities' approach to low emissions evolved over a relatively short period.

The first MAIP was adopted by the Regional Assembly on 21 December 2009, several months after the statutory deadline set by Article 91 of the EPA. The document was a direct response to the chronic exceedances of permissible pollutant levels, particularly particulate matter (PM10) in Kraków and other parts of the region. The analysis identified individual solid-fuel heating installations as the main contributors to pollution—which, at the time, was a novel and important acknowledgment ("individual heating installations burning solid fuels"). The document also clearly distinguished between Kraków and the rest of the region, with more ambitious actions envisioned for the former.

While the program did not propose any legal instruments that would authorize a ban on the use of solid fuels, it did state—with regard to Kraków—the need to "introduce restrictions on the use of solid fuels" (2009: 56). Most of the proposed measures were technical and educational in nature (modernization of boilers, expansion of district heating, promotion of renewable energy sources, and establishing public information systems). The program did not contain a legal pathway for eliminating the most inefficient emission sources. Instead, it focused on goals such as "Reducing surface emissions through the intensification and continuation of the boiler replacement program in Kraków; reducing household waste burning through control and enforcement actions; introducing a Low Emission Zone for transport; limiting emissions from road transport; and conducting promotional and educational activities."

During the public consultations accompanying the preparation and adoption of the MAIP, it was reported that—again, specifically in relation to Kraków—a proposal was made to introduce a ban on solid fuels ("introducing a ban on the use of solid fuels … in Kraków"). Although this proposal was not incorporated into the final document, its appearance in the consultation process is worth noting. Legal doubts were also raised about introducing a coal ban *via* local land-use and zoning plans—a strategy that ultimately would not have been legally effective. In response to these concerns, the consultation summary mentioned a proposal to adopt a resolution by the Regional Assembly limiting the use of solid fuels in Kraków. Thus, the idea of restricting—though not fully banning—solid fuel use was formally raised, but only with respect to Kraków. At that stage, a comprehensive regional ban was not under discussion.

Outside Kraków, no comparable proposals were put forward. In Tarnów, a mid-sized city, a measure was adopted to eliminate coal heating in buildings owned by governmental and self-governmental institutions. In one of the air-quality zones, there was a call for "radical changes in legal provisions to grant greater authority to impose obligations on individuals to reduce their environmental impact (e.g., in terms of 'low emissions')." In general, however, the measures described focused on building new roads, which were presented as a way to reduce transport-related air pollution. In reality, this was largely a convenient gesture, allowing infrastructural investments to be framed as actions aimed at reducing low emissions. Altogether, this points to an early phase of policy exploration—marked by dilemmas, debates, and emerging objections—rather than a coherent or legally robust strategy for eliminating household emissions.

The second key document was the Air Protection Program for the Małopolska region adopted in 2013, titled *Małopolska 2023—In a Healthy Atmosphere*. Unlike the 2009 plan, the new program not only reaffirmed the dominant role of emissions from individual heating sources but explicitly listed the limitation of solid fuel use as a priority measure and a necessary starting point. It also introduced quantitative targets (compliance with PM10, PM2.5, and SO_2 standards by 2023) and a comprehensive plan, including expansion of district heating and gas networks, phasing out of low-efficiency boilers, promotion of renewables, thermal retrofitting of buildings, enforcement against waste burning, and support for public transport. Importantly, the program departed from previous reliance on soft instruments and called for the use of binding legal tools, such as local antismog resolutions from Article 96 EPA. Although the MAIP 2013 only referred to "introducing restrictions on the use of solid fuels," it acknowledged the legal limitations at the time, especially the ineffectiveness of the preamendment version of Article 96 of the EPA.

Following the 2015 legal amendment of—mentioned many times below—Article 96 of the EPA, a major revision of the MAIP was adopted in 2017, enabling more robust legal interventions. The revised program stated that previous actions had been insufficient and concluded that "only a complete ban on the burning of solid fuels in the municipal and residential sector in Kraków can deliver the necessary improvement in air quality" (MAIP, 2017, p. 204). The 2017 update also included a detailed comparative assessment of regulatory strategies based on their environmental effectiveness, technical feasibility, and social acceptability. Several policy scenarios were evaluated: Scenario 0—status quo (baseline), Scenario 1—ban on boilers below EcoDesign standards (or class 5 EN-303:5/2012), Scenario 2—ban on boilers below class 3, Scenario 3—total ban on solid fuels in the entire voivodeship, and Scenario 4—ban on boilers below class 4. Scenario 3 was projected to eliminate air-quality exceedances but was deemed too socially and economically burdensome to implement regionwide. Scenario 1 was ultimately selected as the most balanced option, combining reasonable environmental outcomes with public and economic viability. The program explicitly justified the differentiated approach between Kraków and the rest of the region. Kraków was prioritized for stricter measures, according to the plan, due to its higher population density, topography that worsens air stagnation, greater availability of clean heat sources, and more severe pollution levels. In contrast, rural and peri-urban areas of Małopolska—characterized by limited infrastructure access and a higher risk of fuel poverty—were seen by the drafters as requiring a more gradual, supportive strategy based on technical standards and incentives rather than outright bans. These distinctions reflected not only practical constraints but also a growing recognition of the need for socially—and, implicitly, also politically—sensitive environmental governance, in which policy instruments are tailored to local conditions as well as to the province's political divisions.

From Legislative Defeat to Legal Breakthrough

The landmark antismog resolution adopted by the Małopolska Regional Assembly on 25 November 2013 (No. XLIV/703/13), which *de facto* prohibited the use of solid fuels in the city of Kraków, became both a symbol of political determination and a case study of the tension between public health protection and the constraints of the existing legal framework. The resolution explicitly allowed only the following fuels for heating purposes: "natural gas and other gaseous hydrocarbons intended for heating purposes" and "heating oil and diesel oil intended for heating purposes, excluding heavy fuel oil." Consequently, by way of *a contrario* interpretation, the ban covered hard coal, brown coal, coal sludge, coal flotation concentrates, and wood, regardless of their emission class or combustion technology. The prohibition was universal in scope, applying to all installations within the administrative boundaries of the Municipality of Kraków used for heating buildings or producing domestic hot water. Although the resolution set clear deadlines for compliance (14 days after promulgation for new buildings and from 1 September 2018 for existing buildings), it did not include separate enforcement provisions, delegating these responsibilities to municipal authorities.

The resolution demonstrated that local governments could act as a regulatory initiator in the fight against smog, even in the absence of robust legal tools to ensure the effective implementation of the adopted measures. It is worth noting that the resolution was formally grounded in Article 97 of the EPA and, in a rather peculiar formulation, stated that its purpose was "to prevent negative impacts on the environment and on monuments," without explicitly mentioning human health. This omission stood in stark contrast to the justification for the draft resolution, which drew extensively on epidemiological data and scientific studies highlighting the harmful effects of air pollution on public health. Particularly influential were the initial findings of the long-term research project led by Wiesław Jędrychowski from Jagiellonian University Medical College (see Jędrychowski et al., 2016), which monitored the impact of air pollution on pregnant women and newborns for over a decade. The study revealed a clear correlation between maternal exposure to particulate matter and polycyclic aromatic hydrocarbons (PAHs) and adverse outcomes such as lower birth weights, smaller head circumferences, and reduced IQ levels in children. This discrepancy illustrates that the official axiological basis of the resolution did not fully reflect its real aims and highlights the inadequacy and fragility of

Article 97 EPA in its wording at the time. Moreover, the justification referenced international examples of cities that had introduced bans on solid fuels or outdated stoves in response to air-quality problems, including London (in 1956), Dublin (in 1990), Christchurch (in 2008), Sacramento (in 2007), and several Chinese urban centers or even provinces. However, not all of these cases can be directly attributed to identical policies.

Despite clear health justifications and strong public support, the resolution was annulled by the Voivodeship Administrative Court in Kraków and later also deemed unlawful by the Supreme Administrative Court. In its ruling on the antismog resolution of 2013 (Case No. II SA/Kr 490/14), the Voivodeship Administrative Court found that the resolution exceeded the legal authority delegated by the then-binding Article 96 of the EPA. The court held that the regional assembly had no legal right to impose a general and preventive ban on the use of specific fuels, such as coal and wood. According to the Voivodeship Administrative Court, Article 96 permitted territorial and qualitative differentiation but not a categorical prohibition of particular fuel types based on their purpose. The court emphasized that Article 96 should be interpreted narrowly and in line with the principle of legality (Article 7 of the Polish Constitution), which restricts public administration bodies to act strictly within legal limits. The resolution, in the court's view, created a new category of restrictions not envisaged in the statute and therefore violated the principles governing local legislation. This position was upheld by the Supreme Administrative Court in its judgment of 28 January 2015 (Case No. II OSK 255/15). The court found that the preamendment version of Article 96 did not provide a clear legal basis for a general ban on specific fuels for specific purposes (e.g., heating buildings). The court accepted differentiation in terms of quality standards but rejected the possibility of eliminating solid fuels as a category.

These rulings necessitated an amendment to Article 96 of the EPA, which was enacted in the second half of 2015. The amendment of 10 July 2015 (Journal of Laws 2015, item 1223), effective as of 12 November 2015, was a direct legislative response to the constraints imposed by administrative court jurisprudence. Its aim was to clarify the legal powers of regional assemblies regarding the adoption of antismog resolutions and to strengthen their position as a tool for combating air pollution. The amended Article 96 EPA states:

> ***Article 96. The voivodeship assembly may, by way of a resolution constituting a local law:***
>
> 1. *In order to prevent negative impacts on human health or the environment:*
>   a) *introduce restrictions or bans on the operation of installations in which fuels are burned;*
>   b) *define the types or quality of fuels permitted for use in the area covered by the resolution;*
> 2. *Define the area where the restrictions or bans referred to in point 1 apply;*
> 3. *Define the period during which the restrictions or bans referred to in point 1 apply;*
> 4. *Introduce exemptions from the restrictions or bans referred to in point 1;*

5. *Indicate the authorities responsible for enforcing the resolution and the measures for ensuring compliance.*

According to the explanatory memorandum to the government bill (Sejm Print No. 3437), the amendment was intended to "restore and consolidate the capacity of voivodeship self-governments to independently respond to serious problems related to exceedances of permissible air pollution levels, particularly PM10 and benzo[a]pyrene, in the context of the requirements of Directive 2008/50/EC of the European Parliament and of the Council." The memorandum further emphasized that (1) the amendment aimed to enable action "in advance," not only after damage had occurred (i.e., preventive rather than reactive action); (2) the amendment fulfilled the state's obligations under Article 23(1) of Directive 2008/50/EC to adopt "short-term and long-term actions" to improve air quality; and (3) the law allowed flexible legal responses to local emission problems.

The 2015 amendment was a fundamental milestone for antismog policy at the regional level. For the first time, the legislator explicitly authorized voivodeship assemblies to introduce direct bans on the operation of specific types of heating installations, define acceptable fuels and fuel quality, and establish the basis for enforcement and sanction mechanisms. This legal framework enabled the readoption of the antismog resolution for Kraków in 2016, which—this time—was issued based on the amended Article 96. However, as Szulecka and Szulecki (2017, p. 23) observed when commenting on the state of infrastructure for combating smog at the time, the 2015 amendment "gave local and regional governments concrete tools for fighting air pollution, but also visibly pushed the issue down the governance ladder. The bill does not force local authorities to act, only gives them space to do so and decide on municipal and regional emission limits, reduction targets and fuel bans. (…) However, the central government in Warsaw remained reluctant to act."

The Resolution Banning the Use of Coal and Wood in Kraków

The Małopolska Regional Assembly was the first in Poland to exercise the authority granted under the amended Article 96 of the EPA. On 15 January 2016, it adopted Resolution No. XVIII/243/16, introducing restrictions on the operation of fuel-burning installations within the Municipality of Kraków. This resolution, a direct response to earlier administrative court rulings and the subsequent legislative amendment to Article 96 of the EPA, effectively imposed a total ban on the use of coal, wood, and other solid fuels for heating within the city's administrative boundaries while also specifying the fuels permitted for use. According to § 4 of the resolution, only the combustion of high-methane or nitrogen-rich natural gas (including liquefied natural gas (LNG)), propane-butane, agricultural biogas, other combustible gases, and light fuel oil (as defined in the Act of 25 August 2006 on the System of Monitoring and Controlling Fuel Quality, Journal of Laws 2021, item 133) was allowed. This provision applied to all fuel-burning installations used for space heating or domestic hot water production, including boilers, stoves, and fireplaces. In practice, this meant a blanket ban on the use of other solid fuels—such as hard coal, wood, pellets, coal slurries, and flotocon centrates—in individual heating systems. Notably, the resolution also encompassed so-called ecological wood-burning devices that met EcoDesign standards, underscoring its stringent and systemic character. The resolution does not limit the possibilities of using district heat, electricity, heat pumps, photovoltaics, and solar collectors. A transition period was established, with compliance required by 1 September 2019, thus allowing over 3 years for adaptation.

From the public policy tool perspective, the 2016 resolution represents a textbook example of a command-and-control regulation—a hard legal instrument based on prohibitions, mandates, and clearly defined technical standards. In contrast to market mechanisms (e.g., environmental fees, subsidies, emissions trading, or tax incentives) or informational instruments (e.g., educational campaigns), command-and-control tools are characterized by a high degree of institutional coercion and, typically, a low level of flexibility for regulated entities (Howlett & Ramesh, 2003; Jordan et al., 2005). The mechanism applied was uniform—no exemptions were granted for low-emission stoves or renewable fuels; no permit systems, user-specific limits, or transitional periods for vulnerable groups (such as the energy poor) were introduced. The resolution thus functioned as an absolute ban, whose enforcement was entrusted to the Municipal Guard, the Regional Inspectorate for Environmental Protection, and local government units.

A crucial component in the adoption of the resolution was the process of public participation. In the autumn of 2015, local authorities employed a limited participatory framework that combined public consultations and town hall meetings. The draft resolution was made available at the municipal office and published online, allowing residents to submit comments via email without any formal requirements. Nongovernmental organizations, in turn, were asked to provide feedback using a simplified template, also submitted electronically. However, the consultation period was brief, as were the announcements and opportunities for public dialogue—reflecting the authorities' intent to bring the resolution to a vote during the January session. Overall, the mechanisms for public engagement were rudimentary and lacked sophistication, falling short of more robust models of public participation.

Particularly noteworthy are the critical comments submitted during the public consultation process. Of the 4799 comments submitted regarding the Kraków anti-smog resolution, only 25 expressed opposition to its core provision, namely, the ban on the use of solid fuels (see the consultation report: https://bip.malopolska.pl/pobierz/1343267.html). Although quantitatively marginal, these comments provide valuable insight into the arguments, concerns, frustrations, and alternative framings of the smog problem articulated by opponents of the proposed regulation during the consultation process.

The primary concern raised by critics related to the financial burden associated with the replacement of heating systems. Many respondents perceived the required transition as an overwhelming economic challenge. Some pointed out that, although public authorities promised subsidies, not all residents would be able to benefit from them. Others openly declared that financial constraints would make compliance with the regulation impossible. A recurring theme was the perception of unfairness, particularly among individuals who had previously invested substantial resources in modern heating installations only to learn that these would also have to be replaced. Critics frequently argued that the resolution would not solve the problem of air pollution but would instead expose residents to higher heating costs, especially in the context of rising gas and electricity prices.

Beyond economic concerns, some residents questioned the rationale behind the blanket ban on solid fuels. Several commentators argued that modern fifth-class boilers generate only limited emissions and therefore should remain permissible. Others maintained that wood should be treated differently from coal due to its renewable character and its status within broader European discussions on biomass. Another recurring argument involved the denial of household heating as the principal source of smog. Instead, opponents frequently pointed to road transport or transboundary pollution originating outside Kraków. According to this interpretation, public authorities were targeting the wrong sources of pollution while shifting the burden of adjustment onto ordinary residents.

The consultation process also revealed concerns regarding the legitimacy of state intervention. Some participants questioned the right of public authorities to decide how individuals heat their own homes. Others emphasized the possible consequences for businesses involved in the sale of fuels and heating equipment. Doubts were likewise expressed concerning the enforceability of the proposed measures and the practical capacity of public institutions to monitor compliance.

Particularly striking was the near absence of references to scientific research in the comments made by opponents of the antismog resolution for Kraków. In contrast to supporters of the resolution, who frequently cited studies on the health effects of air pollution and the sources of particulate emissions, opponents relied primarily on personal experience, intuition, and individual opinions. References to international examples, most notably Germany and Austria, appeared only occasionally and were generally formulated in a vague manner without supporting evidence. The limited use of scientific evidence significantly weakened the position of opponents and made their demands easier to dismiss during the decision-making process.

Most of these objections were not reflected in the final policy. In response to economic concerns (that the ban would not be viable due to financial constraints), drafters pointed to available financial support schemes. Arguments in favor of modern boilers were rejected on the ground that even the most advanced solid-fuel installations continue to emit harmful pollutants. Likewise, concerns relating to transport or transboundary pollution were regarded as extending beyond the direct scope of the resolution. Ultimately, opposition to the proposed measures remained limited in scale and relatively weakly substantiated, particularly when compared to the supportive comments that dominated the consultation process.

Nevertheless, these comments reflected genuine concerns present among parts of the population, relating not only to the ban itself but also to its anticipated social and economic consequences. For many critics, the resolution appeared to be another bureaucratic measure that imposed additional obligations on ordinary citizens while failing to address what they perceived as the underlying causes of the smog problem.

Next, as Baranyai et al. (2020) note, command-and-control instruments have limited effectiveness under weak enforcement conditions but can be effective when combined with financial support schemes and informational efforts. The city undertook initiatives in both areas. The resolution was supplemented by local social assistance programs and an extensive educational campaign (see Chap. 4) linked with enhanced air-quality monitoring.

Referring to the latter, in Kraków, the key financial mechanism supporting the replacement of solid-fuel heating systems was the Low Emission Reduction Program for the City of Kraków. The program offered subsidies to cover a substantial share of the costs of permanent heating system replacement: up to 80% of eligible investment costs in 2017 and up to 60% in both 2018 and 2019, as stipulated in Resolution No. CXXI/1918/14 of the Kraków City Council of 5 November 2014. While generous, these subsidies did not fully cover the justified costs of such investments, which could pose a financial barrier for lower-income households. To address this gap, the city introduced supplementary protective measures through the social support program adopted by Resolution No. XCVIII/2555/18 of 28 March 2018. This additional scheme allowed for the possibility of covering up to 100% of the costs for eligible residents, with the level of support determined based on income, family situation, and the amount of subsidy already received under the Low Emission Reduction Program. Together, these instruments formed a comprehensive support system designed to accelerate the transition to proecological heating solutions in Kraków.

The 2017 Małopolska Antismog Resolution

Following the experience of implementing the antismog resolution for Kraków, on 23 January 2017, the Małopolska Regional Assembly adopted Resolution No. XXXII/452/17, introducing antismog regulations for the entire region, excluding the Municipality of Kraków. This was the first regional-level antismog resolution in Poland, covering both urban and rural municipalities. Unlike the Kraków resolution of 2016, the 2017 regulation did not impose a complete ban on solid-fuel combustion. Instead, it introduced a system of gradually tightening emission standards for heating installations. The resolution was based on a clear implementation schedule, allowing residents time to adapt to the new requirements (Table 2.1). Transparency in timelines and regulatory phases helped reduce social resistance (Baranyai et al., 2020). In turn, the second resolution regarding the remaining area of Małopolska focused on the voluntary, incentive-based gradual replacement of furnaces, with a long adjustment period (in the case of some types of installations even until 2026) and with relatively little financial support from the state or local governments (30–50% of the investment value). The regulations also aimed to prohibit the use of the following fuels: "(1) fuels in which the mass share of hard coal or lignite with a grain size of 0-3 mm exceeds 15%; (2) fuels containing biomass with a moisture content in the working state exceeding 20%." The regulations thus targeted two key elements: fuel quality and appliance standards.

The resolution also included enforcement mechanisms, the effectiveness of which depended on cooperation between different levels of government and local

Table 2.1 Implementation schedule for the 2017 Małopolska antismog resolution

Effective date	Regulation	Remarks
1 July 2017	Ban on the use of coal slurries, flotoconcentrates, and lignite	Applies to all households
1 July 2017	Obligation to install only EcoDesign-compliant boilers/stoves (EU Regs. 2015/1189 and 2015/1185)	For new installations
by 31 December 2022	Obligation to replace boilers not meeting minimum emission standards	Applies to noncertified and class 1–3 boilers
by 31 December 2026	Obligation to modernize or replace fireplaces that exceed PM emissions > 40 mg/m^3	Option to retrofit with certified filters

institutions. Although market-based instruments (such as emissions trading or tax credits) were not adopted, the resolution was complemented by a range of support programs. At both the regional and local levels, grants were made available for replacing heating sources, investing in renewables, and implementing education and outreach initiatives—often cofinanced with EU funds.

The academic literature emphasizes that the strategy adopted in the 2017 Małopolska resolution aligns with the model of incremental environmental transformation, in which environmental standards are gradually tightened while social resistance is minimized by extending transitional periods and offering compensatory programs (Baranyai et al., 2020; Howlett & Ramesh, 2003; Jordan et al., 2005). This incrementalism is reflected in the resolution's design: rather than immediately banning the use of solid fuels, it introduced a phased system of obligations spread over several years but related to the quality of heating installations. The timeline—such as requiring boiler replacement by 2022 (later postponed once during Covid-19) and fireplace upgrades by 2026—helped distribute the regulatory burden over time, thereby increasing political consent and reducing the risk of citizen backlash. At the same time, the regulation was supported by informational and financial mechanisms, including the eco-advisor network (see Chap. 4) and grant programs for heating system replacement, which served as "soft" implementation tools. In this way, instead of pushing politically costly radical solutions, the authorities pursued a path of gradual change aligned with the logic of adaptive learning and cumulative reform, seen here as a kind of compromise (Jordan et al., 2005). This case thus illustrates how incremental logic can be employed in local climate and environmental policy to build public consent for energy transformation—particularly in regions where solid fuels are prevalent and traditional heating methods are deeply rooted (Baranyai et al., 2020). Although the final goal was not particularly ambitious—boiler replacement rather than full system transformation—the policy marked a significant shift against the previous lack of any substantial actions.

The 2017 resolution became a reference point for regulations in other voivodeships, which, in the following years, adopted their own antismog measures, drawing inspiration from both its structure and implementation mechanisms. For instance, the Silesian Voivodeship adopted its antismog resolution in 2017, initially based on a similar phased elimination of the worst emission sources and fuels. Subsequent amendments introduced final deadlines for boiler replacement (until 2027). In turn, Mazovia's 2017 resolution, covering the entire region, was also modeled on the Małopolska framework. It implemented identical bans on low-quality fuels and introduced EcoDesign requirements. Referring to the last example, the Lower Silesian Voivodeship introduced its resolution in 2018, applying territorial differentiation (between urban agglomerations and rural areas), which reflected the Małopolska approach of tailoring measures to local conditions. Although the scope and pace of implementation varied between regions (NIK, 2025), a shared feature of these regulations was their reliance on solutions pioneered in Małopolska—in terms of both legal instruments and educational implementation strategies. In this sense, the 2017 Małopolska resolution triggered a wave of regional antismog regulations in Poland and marked a breakthrough in shaping local air protection policies.

The Emergence of New Infosphere

The fight against smog in Małopolska has advanced not only through legal, infrastructural, and technological measures but also through a growing system of public information practices, shaped by both European and domestic legal obligations. In line with the CAFE Directive (2008/50), later the EU Ambient Air Quality Directive (2024/2881), and Polish national legislation, authorities are required to provide citizens with access to real-time air-quality information (see examples from Spain: Oltra & Sala, 2015). This obligation has produced a highly visible—but uneven and fragmented—landscape of information on air pollution that now characterizes the region's public spaces and media environments.

Local governments, particularly in urban centers such as Kraków, have introduced a range of visual communication tools designed to alert, inform, and mobilize public response (see Rosen et al., 2021). These include LED information boards at public transport stops, city websites showing hourly PM10 and PM2.5 levels, mobile applications (e.g., "Powietrze Kraków" or "AIRLY"), and the integration of pollution indicators into school closures and health advisories. In rural and suburban municipalities, similar practices have been adopted, often funded through regional or EU mechanisms, but implementation remains inconsistent. One of the most striking examples of awareness campaigns is the "See What You Breathe" initiative, established by Kraków Smog Alarm with the cooperation of some municipalities in Poland, featuring transparent lung-shaped installations filled with filters that visibly darken with accumulated particulate matter over time (see Chap. 5). These installations, often placed in town squares or near schools, provide a visceral and immediate visual representation of the invisible threat posed by polluted air. Alongside this, campaigns such as "Don't Burn Trash" and "Clean Air—Common Cause" have used billboards, local media, and social media platforms to target behavioral change at the household level, particularly in areas reliant on coal and wood for heating.

Despite these efforts, serious limitations persist. The infosphere of antismog action remains fragmented and aesthetically incoherent. There is no standardized visual language or communication protocol across municipalities, leading to varying levels of visibility, accessibility, and credibility. Digital inequality further compounds the problem: residents of poorer or rural areas may lack access to smartphones or reliable Internet, while elderly populations are often excluded from app-based warning systems. Moreover, some municipalities have failed to update online data regularly or provide any real-time displays in public space, in potential breach of legal obligations. What emerges is a hybrid information ecology: partially public, partially civic, partially commercial (e.g., private providers like Airly), and deeply uneven in coverage. Rather than a coordinated communication policy, what exists is a patchwork of symbolic signals—sometimes effective, often symbolic in the pejorative sense. While public communication has played a role in raising awareness and supporting legal changes (such as the antismog resolutions), its full potential as a tool for behavioral transformation remains underutilized.

2.4 Conclusion

Air pollution is one of the most pressing social problems worldwide, affecting nearly every region of the globe. It causes severe health risks, contributes to the degradation of ecosystems, and accelerates the deterioration of buildings and infrastructure. What is urgently needed, therefore, is a systematic accumulation of experiences and knowledge regarding the development, application, and implementation of specific measures to combat air pollution. Only by engaging closely with concrete contexts and particular instruments can we, in the long run, achieve the much-needed synthesis and formulate delicate, nuanced recommendations on how to address air pollution effectively. The case of Małopolska should be interpreted through this lens. Equally important is the context of multilevel governance. As a member of the European Union, Poland manages air quality through a complex policy process in which competences and obligations are distributed across multiple levels of authority—spanning supranational, national, regional, and local institutions. In this sense, the Małopolska case illustrates both the benefits and the challenges of multilevel governance in the domain of air pollution policy.

References

Adamkiewicz, Ł., Maciejewska, K., Skotak, K., Krzyżanowski, M., Badyda, A., Juda-Rezler, K., & Dąbrowiecki, P. (2021). Health-based approach to determine alert and information thresholds for particulate matter air pollution. *Sustainability, 13*(3), 1345. https://doi.org/10.3390/su13031345

Anderson, J. O., Thundiyil, J. G., & Stolbach, A. (2012). Clearing the air: A review of the effects of particulate matter air pollution on human health. *Journal of Medical Toxicology, 8*(2), 166–175. https://doi.org/10.1007/s13181-011-0203-1

Aslam, F. (2021). Toxicity of peroxyacetyl nitrate on human. *Global Journal of Research and Review, 8*(2), 60.

Atmoterm, S. A. (2010). *Ekspertyza w sprawie wprowadzenia ograniczeń w stosowaniu paliw stałych w Krakowie [Expert study on introducing restrictions on the use of solid fuels in Kraków]*. Raport na zlecenie władz Małopolski.
Aust, A. E., Ball, J. C., Hu, A. A., Lighty, J. S., Smith, K. R., Straccia, A. M., Veranth, J. M., & Young, W. C. (2002). Particle characteristics responsible for effects on human lung epithelial cells. *Research Report Health Effects Institute, 110*, 1–65; discussion 67–76. PMID: 12578113
Baranyai, N. H., Csutora, M., & Smajgl, A. (2020). Pro-environmental behavior and lifestyle change in climate change mitigation: Policy instruments and individual decision-making. *Climate Policy, 20*(1), 1–16. https://doi.org/10.1080/14693062.2019.1694490
Bell, M. L., & Davis, D. L. (2001). Reassessment of the lethal London fog of 1952: Novel indicators of acute and chronic consequences of acute exposure to air pollution. *Environmental Health Perspectives, 109*(Suppl 3), 389–394. https://doi.org/10.1289/ehp.01109s3389
Brimblecombe, P. (2011). *The big smoke: The history of air pollution in London since medieval times* (1st ed.). Routledge.
Brusseau, M. L., Pepper, I. L., & Gerba, C. P. (2019). *Environmental and pollution science* (3rd ed.). Academic Press.
Calderón-Garcidueñas, L., Engle, R., Mora-Tiscareño, A., Styner, M., Gómez-Garza, G., Zhu, H., Jewells, V., Torres-Jardón, R., Romero, L., Monroy-Acosta, M. E., Bryant, C., González-González, L. O., Medina-Cortina, H., & D'Angiulli, A. (2011). Exposure to severe urban air pollution influences cognitive outcomes, brain volume and systemic inflammation in clinically healthy children. *Brain and Cognition, 77*(3), 345–355. https://doi.org/10.1016/j.bandc.2011.09.006
Citkowska-Kimla, A. (2019). Poland and the problem of smog -Political action versus social expectations. *Krytyka Prawa. Niezależne studia nad prawem, 26*(2), 127–137. https://doi.org/10.17951/k.2019.26.2.127-137
Correia, A. W., Pope, C. A., III, Dockery, D. W., Wang, Y., Ezzati, M., & Dominici, F. (2013). Effect of air pollution control on life expectancy in the United States: An analysis of 545 U.S. counties for the period from 2000 to 2007. *Epidemiology, 24*(1), 23–31. https://doi.org/10.1097/EDE.0b013e3182770237
Costa, L., Cole, T., Dao, K., Chang, Y., & Garrick, J. (2019). Developmental impact of air pollution on brain function. *Neurochemistry International, 131*, 104580. https://doi.org/10.1016/j.neuint.2019.104580
de Kok, T., Driece, H., Hogervorst, J., & Briedé, J. (2006). Toxicological assessment of ambient and traffic-related particulate matter: A review of recent studies. *Mutation Research, 613*, 103–122. https://doi.org/10.1016/j.mrrev.2006.07.001
Dickerson, R., Kondragunta, S., Stenchikov, G., Civerolo, K., Doddridge, B., & Holben, B. (1997). The impact of aerosols on solar ultraviolet radiation and photochemical smog. *Science, 278*(5339), 827–830. https://doi.org/10.1126/science.278.5339.827
Esworthy, R. (2013). *Air quality: EPA's 2013 changes to the particulate matter (PM) standard*. Congressional Research Service Report No. R42934.
Fang, Y., Naik, V., Horowitz, L., & Mauzerall, D. (2012). Air pollution and associated human mortality: The role of air pollutant emissions, climate change and methane concentration increases during the industrial period. *Atmospheric Chemistry and Physics Discussions, 12*, 22713–22741. https://doi.org/10.5194/acpd-12-22713-2012
Finlayson, B., & Pitts, J. (1976). Photochemistry of the polluted troposphere. *Science, 192*(4235), 111–119. https://doi.org/10.1126/science.192.4235.111
Health Effects Institute. (2024). State of global air 2024: A special report on global exposure to air pollution and its health impacts, with a focus on children's health. Health Effects Institute. https://www.stateofglobalair.org/resources/report/state-global-air-report-2024
Hitzfeld, B., Friedrichs, K. H., Ring, J., & Behrendt, H. (1997). Airborne particulate matter modulates the production of reactive oxygen species in human polymorphonuclear granulocytes. *Toxicology, 120*(3), 185–195. https://doi.org/10.1016/s0300-483x(97)03664-0

Howlett, M., & Ramesh, M. (2003). *Studying public policy: Policy cycles and policy subsystems* (2nd ed.). Oxford University Press.

Jędrychowski, W., Perera, F. P., Mroczek, B., Flak, E., & Spengler, J. D. (2016). Prenatal exposure to fine particles and polycyclic aromatic hydrocarbons and birth outcomes: A two-pollutant approach. *International Archives of Occupational and Environmental Health, 89*(3), 341–351. https://doi.org/10.1007/s00420-016-1192-9

Jordan, A. (2012). *Environmental policy in the European Union: Actors, institutions, and processes*. Earthscan.

Jordan, A., Wurzel, R. K. W., & Zito, A. R. (2005). The rise of 'new' policy instruments in comparative perspective: Has governance eclipsed government? *Political Studies, 53*(3), 477–496.

Juda-Rezler, K., Reizer, M., Maciejewska, K., Błaszczak, B., & Klejnowski, K. (2020). Characterization of atmospheric PM2.5 sources at a Central European urban background site. *Science of the Total Environment, 713*, 136729. https://doi.org/10.1016/j.scitotenv.2020.136729.

Karpus, K. (2021). "Effective" air quality plan and constitutional guarantees of ecological security. *Przegląd Prawa Konstytucyjnego, 6*(61), 467–477. https://doi.org/10.15804/ppk.2021.06.37

Kim, K.-H., Kabir, E., & Kabir, S. (2015). A review on the human health impact of airborne particulate matter. *Environment International, 74*, 136–143. https://doi.org/10.1016/j.envint.2014.10.005

Kicinski, M., Vermeir, G., Van Larebeke, N., Den Hond, E., Schoeters, G., Bruckers, L., Sioen, I., Bijnens, E., Roels, H. A., Baeyens, W., Viaene, M. K., & Nawrot, T. S. (2015). Neurobehavioral performance in adolescents is inversely associated with traffic exposure. *Environment International, 75*, 136–143. https://doi.org/10.1016/j.envint.2014.10.028

Lam, J., Sutton, P., Kalkbrenner, A., Windham, G., Halladay, A., Koustas, E., Lawler, C., Davidson, L., Daniels, N., Newschaffer, C., & Woodruff, T. (2016). A systematic review and meta-analysis of multiple airborne pollutants and autism spectrum disorder. *PLoS ONE, 11*, e0161851. https://doi.org/10.1371/journal.pone.0161851

Logan, W. P. D. (1953). Mortality in the London fog incident, 1952. *The Lancet, 261*(6755), 336–338. https://doi.org/10.1016/S0140-6736(53)91012-5

LoPachin, R. M., & Gavin, T. (2014). Molecular mechanisms of aldehyde toxicity: A chemical perspective. *Chemical Research in Toxicology, 27*(7), 1081–1091. https://doi.org/10.1021/tx500079y

Lubarda, B. (2024). *Far-right ecologism: Environmental politics and the far right in Hungary and Poland*. Routledge.

MAIP (2017). *Małopolska Air Protection Programme*. Kraków, Poland.

Nemery, B., Hoet, P. H., & Nemmar, A. (2001). The Meuse Valley fog of 1930: An air pollution disaster. *Lancet, 357*(9257), 704–708. https://doi.org/10.1016/S0140-6736(00)04135-0

NIK. (2025). *Realizacja uchwał antysmogowych* (20/2025/P/24/069/LKR). https://www.nik.gov.pl/plik/id,31538,vp,34684.pdf

Olszyk, D., Bytnerowicz, A., & Takemoto, B. (1989). Photochemical oxidant pollution and vegetation: Effects of mixtures of gases, fog and particles. *Environmental Pollution, 61*(1), 11–29. https://doi.org/10.1016/0269-7491(89)90259-5

Oltra, C., & Sala, R. (2015). Communicating the risks of urban air pollution to the public: A study of urban air pollution information services. *Revista Internacional de Contaminación Ambiental, 31*(4), 361–375.

Peter Brimblecombe. (2011). *The big smoke: The history of air pollution in London since medieval times* (1st ed.). Routledge.

Polski Alarm Smogowy. (2023, November 2). Smogowy ranking PAS—Walka ze smogiem zaczyna przynosić efekty. https://polskialarmsmogowy.pl/2023/11/smogowy-ranking-pas-walka-ze-smogiem-zaczyna-przynosic-efekty

Poskrobko, B., & Poskrobko, T. (2012). *Environment management in Poland*. Białystok University Press.

Radecka, E. (2020). The national air pollution control programme in Poland -Selected legal issues. *Review of European and Comparative Law, 40*, 123–140.

Radecka, E. (2021). A legal model of air protection in Poland -selected issues. *Bratislava Law Review, 5*(1), 159–166. https://doi.org/10.46282/blr.2021.5.1.231
Rajchel, D., & Rajchel, A. (2024). The implementation of the "Clean air" programme in Poland including voivodeships. *Economics and Environment, 88*(1), 614. https://doi.org/10.34659/eis.2024.88.1.614
Rolecki, M. (2022, November 26). Do utraty tchu. Powietrze w Polsce jedno z najgorszych na świecie? *OKO.press*. https://oko.press/do-utraty-tchu-powietrze-w-polsce-jedno-z-najgorszych-na-swiecie-cala-prawda-o-rodzimym-smogu
Rosen, Z., Bice, C., & Scott, S. (2021). Visualizing the invisible: Visual-based design and efficacy in air quality messaging. *International Journal of Environmental Research and Public Health, 18*(20), 10882. https://doi.org/10.3390/ijerph182010882
Sakson-Boulet, A. (2020). The clean air priority programme -evaluation and perspectives. *Środkowoeuropejskie Studia Polityczne, 1*, 171–192. https://doi.org/10.14746/ssp.2020.1.9
Schrenk, H. H., Heimann, H., Clayton, G. D., Gafafer, W. M., & Wexler, H. (1949). *Air pollution in Donora, Pa.: Epidemiology of the unusual smog episode of October 1948*. Public Health Service.
Shah, A. S., Langrish, J. P., Nair, H., McAllister, D. A., Hunter, A. L., Donaldson, K., Newby, D. E., & Mills, N. L. (2013). Global association of air pollution and heart failure: A systematic review and meta-analysis. *Lancet, 382*(9897), 1039–1048. https://doi.org/10.1016/S0140-6736(13)60898-3
Szulecka, J., & Szulecki, K. (2017). *Polish environmental movement 1980–2017: (De)legitimization, politics & ecological crises* (ESPRi Working Paper No. 6). European Studies Centre, University of Oslo.
U.K. Ministry of Health. (1954). *Mortality and morbidity during the London fog of December 1952* (Reports on Public Health and Medical Subjects No. 95). Ministry of Health.
Vicente, E., & Alves, C. (2018). An overview of particulate emissions from residential biomass combustion. *Atmospheric Research, 199*, 159–185. https://doi.org/10.1016/j.atmosres.2017.08.027
Ward, K. (2018). ECJ rules that Poland failed to fulfil obligations under Ambient Air Directive. *European Journal of Risk Regulation, 9*(2), 372–379. https://doi.org/10.1017/err.2018.26
World Health Organization. (2013). *Health effects of particulate matter: Policy implications for countries in eastern Europe, Caucasus and central Asia* (p. 3). WHO Regional Office for Europe.
World Health Organization. (2021). *WHO global air quality guidelines: Particulate matter (PM2.5 and PM10), ozone, nitrogen dioxide, sulfur dioxide and carbon monoxide: Executive summary*. World Health Organization.

Cited Legal Acts

Acts and Statutory Instruments

Act of 25 August 2006 on the System of Monitoring and Controlling Fuel Quality. Journal of Laws 2021, item 133.
Act of 3 October 2008 on Providing Information on the Environment and Environmental Protection, Public Participation in Environmental Protection, and Environmental Impact Assessments. Journal of Laws No. 199, item 1227.
Act on Supporting Thermomodernisation and Renovation. Journal of Laws 2021, item 554.
Constitution of the Republic of Poland of 1997. Warsaw, Poland: Sejm of the Republic of Poland.
Directive (EU) 2016/2284 of the European Parliament and of the Council on the Reduction of National Emissions of Certain Atmospheric Pollutants (NEC Directive).

Directive (EU) 2024/2881 of the European Parliament and of the Council of 23 October 2024 on Ambient Air Quality and Cleaner Air for Europe.
Directive 2004/107/EC of the European Parliament and of the Council Relating to Arsenic, Cadmium, Mercury, Nickel and Polycyclic Aromatic Hydrocarbons in Ambient Air.
Directive 2008/50/EC of the European Parliament and of the Council on Ambient Air Quality and Cleaner Air for Europe.
Environmental Protection Act of 27 April 2001. Journal of Laws 2001, No. 62, item 627.
Regulation of 23 December 2022 on Air Quality Standards. Journal of Laws 2022, item 2856.
Regulation of the Minister of Climate and Environment of 11 December 2020 on the Levels of Certain Substances in the Air. Journal of Laws 2021, item 92.
Regulation of the Minister of Energy of 27 September 2018 on Quality Requirements for Solid Fuels. Journal of Laws 2018, item 1890.
Regulation of the Minister of Industry and the Minister of Climate and Environment of 4 November 2024 on Quality Requirements for Solid Fuels. Journal of Laws 2024, item 1618.
Regulation of the Minister of the Environment of 24 August 2012 on Permissible Levels of Air Pollutants. Journal of Laws 2012, item 1031.
Treaty on the Functioning of the European Union. Official Journal of the European Union. Brussels, Belgium: European Union.

Regional Resolutions and City Council Acts

Kraków City Council. (2014). *Resolution No. CXXI/1918/14 of 5 November 2014 on Air Quality Improvement Measures in the City of Kraków*. Kraków City Council.
Kraków City Council. (2018). *Resolution No. XCVIII/2555/18 of 28 March 2018 on Air Quality Improvement Measures in the City of Kraków*. Kraków City Council.
Małopolska Regional Assembly. (2013). *Resolution No. XLIV/703/13 on the Types of Fuels Permitted for Use in the Area of the Kraków Municipality*. Małopolska Marshal's Office.
Małopolska Regional Assembly. (2016). *Resolution No. XVIII/243/16 of 15 January 2016 on the Introduction in the Area of the Municipality of Kraków of Restrictions on the Operation of Installations in Which Fuels Are Burned*. Małopolska Regional Assembly.
Małopolska Regional Assembly. (2017). *Resolution No. XXXII/452/17 of 23 January 2017 on the Introduction in the Area of the Małopolska Region of Restrictions and Prohibitions in the Area of the Operation of Installations in Which Fuels Are Burned*. Małopolska Regional Assembly.

Chapter 3
The Role of Public Awareness in Solving Air Pollution: The Case of Kraków Smog Alert

Mateusz Klinowski

Abstract In the literature, it seems widely accepted that public awareness—understood as knowledge of the problem and its sources—plays a crucial role in shaping effective responses to environmental challenges. This chapter examines the significance of societal knowledge and perceptions of air pollution in driving citizen engagement and policy change, with a focus on the case of Kraków Smog Alert, a grassroots initiative that emerged and operated in Kraków prior to the city's major shift in public policies on air pollution. Drawing on empirical data and a large corpus of documents, the chapter illustrates how civic mobilization and bottom-up initiatives could raise the visibility of the problem, influence public discourse, and pressure decision-makers to adopt appropriate regulatory measures. Particular attention is given to the strategies employed by Kraków Smog Alert to communicate scientific evidence and frame smog as a shared public concern. The findings demonstrate that while enhancing public awareness at the local level can help create momentum for introducing environmental regulations, there is no convincing evidence that it is a necessary condition for the adoption and implementation of particular air-quality policies. The chapter situates the case of Małopolska within the context of current scholarly debates on the role of public awareness in environmental public policies, as well as the challenges of European law and multilevel governance.

Keywords Air pollution · Kraków smog alert · Grassroots environmental activism · Public awareness · Antismog resolutions · Kraków · Małopolska

M. Klinowski (✉)
Department of Law and Administration, Jagiellonian University, Kraków, Poland
e-mail: mateusz.klinowski@uj.edu.pl

M. Stępień, M. Klinowski, *Fighting Air Pollution*, Law and Visual Jurisprudence 17, https://doi.org/10.1007/978-3-032-23909-9_3

3.1 Introduction: The Role of Social Activism and Public Awareness in Policymaking

Existing scholarship offers various attempts to explain how environmental harms become publicly recognized. Also, the role of environmental public awareness in political action has already been studied in the literature. From the perspective of this book. particularly significant is the work by Veronica Herrera (2024), focused on "slow-moving harms." The term refers to problems similar to pollution that exist alongside communities and are typically ignored or accepted as parts of everyday life until, for some reason, they become matters of concern and catalysts for social movements. Herrera, examining three case studies from cities in South America, investigates how issues "that long went unnoticed or were accepted as part of the everyday landscape" became recognized problems, prompting action and policy change. She explores "how citizen-driven efforts can push the state to implement environmental rights protections, and how ideas about pollution as a policy problem become institutionalized" (Herrera, 2024, p. 5). Notably, Herrera conducted ethnographic research based on interviews, observations, and document analysis. Her work can also be understood as a comparative case study, testing the significance of "bonding mobilization" (internal community integration) and "bridging activism" (finding external advocates) for the success of environmental movements. Her study does not specifically address air pollution; nonetheless, it provides insight into various contexts of social mobilization for environmental causes. There are also a number of studies on the emergence of awareness regarding air pollution, including research on the role of the media in shaping public consciousness (e.g., Bakaki et al., 2020; Fabricant, 2023).

Nonetheless, we believe that Kraków constitutes another interesting case that may help draw important conclusions on the extent to which social engagement facilitates policy change. In 2012, the second-largest city in Poland witnessed the emergence of a pivotal citizen-led movement: Kraków Smog Alert [*Krakowski Alarm Smogowy* (KAS)]. KAS, which later evolved into a nationwide Polish Smog Alert [*Polski Alarm Smogowy* (PAS)], transformed public perception of air pollution through innovative communication campaigns and simultaneous engagement in political processes. Its efforts culminated in the adoption of a groundbreaking coal and wood ban in the city, which served as an inspiration for other Polish cities and regions. To this day, KAS/PAS continues its mission, redefined as the consistent implementation of antismog measures across Poland, which remains a largely coal-dependent nation. By characterizing KAS activities and evaluating their effectiveness, we hope to provide a case study that will supplement existing literature on the relationship between environmental legislation and public awareness of environmental issues. At the same time, we find the existing research lacking in several respects.

Research in the field has already documented the development of local smog alerts in Poland, the social composition and communication practices of these movements, and their apparent influence on the increasing political salience of air pollution (Frankowski, 2019; Maltby et al., 2024; Subašić et al., 2024). Nevertheless, this literature leaves several related questions unresolved. First, public awareness, civic mobilization, and the activity of organized advocacy groups are frequently treated as elements of a single process, even though they represent analytically distinct phenomena. A population may possess considerable knowledge about environmental harm without showing signs of collective mobilization. A relatively small activist organization may influence policy despite limited mass participation. Conversely, widespread public concern may coexist with political inaction or the adoption of ineffective measures. Research on proenvironmental behavior has already demonstrated that environmental knowledge and concern do not translate automatically into action because of social, economic, and institutional barriers (Kollmuss & Agyeman, 2002). Additionally, Burstein's (2003) systematic review indicates that public opinion has a substantial influence on public policy and that this influence becomes stronger when an issue is highly salient. However, these findings demonstrate that knowledge of a problem does not automatically produce policy change and cannot be generalized across all issues and institutional contexts without qualification.

Second, studies of environmental activism tend to concentrate on agenda setting and policy adoption. Less attention is devoted to the relationship between awareness and the later stages of the policy process—the design of regulatory instruments, their implementation, their enforcement, and the achievement of measurable environmental outcomes. Yet the political recognition of a problem, the enactment of legislation, and an effective solution to the problem should not be treated as equivalent achievements. A movement may succeed in placing an issue on the political agenda while failing to secure an effective policy response. It may contribute to the adoption of ambitious legislation without being capable of ensuring its implementation. This idea is consistent with the research on policy implementation, where the adoption of legislation is treated as only one stage of the policy process (Wu et al., 2015).

Our initial intuition is that public awareness of the problem and subsequent civic involvement are not factors determining the effectiveness of any particular regulation. Such factors seem to belong to a separate ontological category in the first place. They concern practical knowledge of how to act against the causal background of the phenomenon in question and within the institutional context of political bodies relevant for addressing the problem. Various authors have already demonstrated that the subsequent outcomes of adopted policies depend upon a variety of conditions, including administrative capacity, interorganizational coordination, and credible enforcement (Matland, 1995).

Meanwhile, in the case of KAS, the successful increase of public awareness is often conflated with the alleged successful implementation of antismog resolutions in Kraków and Małopolska. Journalists and researchers seem to believe that KAS campaigns and advocacy played a decisive causal role in the adoption and implementation of both resolutions. Those accounts, we suspect, underestimate the importance of the institutional environment in which activism takes place and distort the actual history of the adoption and implementation of the resolutions.

Legal and political pressure, sheer political opportunity, administrative (in) capacity, and the changing costs of governmental inaction—these are seemingly much more probable reasons for the enactment of environmental policies than any kind of civic involvement. The policy effects in the area of environmental protection attributed to activism may as well result from various factors characteristic of the practice of governance, especially because environmental policy in the European Union is produced through multilevel governance, where local and regional decisions are influenced by national and European legislation and judicial rulings, as well as fiscal arrangements and budgetary constraints. Even the distribution of responsibilities for implementation among different levels of government (national, regional, and local) matters. Hence, even at first glance, there is a plentitude of factors that must be considered when explaining the successful implementation of environmental policy. In fact, in the following paragraphs, we will attempt to demonstrate that these factors provide a better explanation for the content and effectiveness of the antismog regulations in Kraków and Małopolska than public awareness or civic involvement facilitated by KAS.

Finally, relatively little is known about the changing role of environmental movements after their initial regulatory successes. Organizations established to challenge political authorities may gradually become recognized providers of expertise, consultation partners, recipients of public funding, and participants in the implementation of the regulations they helped establish. However, such a transformation may operate twofold. It may increase an organization's access to decision-makers and its ability to shape technical policy. But it may simultaneously weaken the organization's grassroots character, its independence, and its overall capacity to mobilize public dissatisfaction. The history of KAS provides an especially valuable case through which one can examine these questions.

In this chapter, then, we will briefly describe the history of KAS and its public involvement. Our idea is not only to characterize the nature of the movement but also to understand its role in the adoption and implementation of both antismog resolutions passed by the regional parliament of Małopolska. Our principal research question here is: how did public awareness and civic involvement, being a result of the activity of KAS, contribute to the adoption, design, and implementation of antismog policies in Kraków and Małopolska?

This question contains several interconnected dimensions that we would like to explore in the following paragraphs. The chapter examines why organized antismog activism emerged in Kraków at a particular historical moment, despite the much longer presence of severe pollution; through which mechanisms KAS influenced citizens, media, and political decision-makers; how its activity interacted with political interests, reputational concerns, and the increasing public availability of air-quality data; and why the regulatory trajectory of Kraków differed so significantly from that of the rest of Małopolska. It also considers how the role of KAS (and PAS) changed after the adoption of the antismog policies.

It must be noted that the broader Małopolska experience complicates any straightforward success narrative. The strict prohibition of solid fuels adopted for Kraków differed fundamentally from the regulatory model applied to the remainder of the region. Outside Kraków, as already explained (see Chap. 2), the policy relied on the gradual replacement of noncompliant installations, increasing technical standards, subsidies, and decentralized implementation by municipalities. Despite extensive public communication and the initial presence of local smog initiatives, implementation of the 2017 resolution remains slow, deadlines were postponed, and large numbers of highly polluting installations continue to operate to this day. Our case study therefore is even more interesting, as it combines an initial example of successful agenda setting and regulatory innovation with a subsequent record of uneven implementation and limited regional effectiveness.

The chapter advances three related arguments. First, KAS played a substantial role in transforming the public perception of air pollution from a normalized environmental condition into a politically salient public harm that can be prevented. Second, this influence should be understood as catalytic and enabling rather than as a sufficient cause of policy change. The adoption of antismog resolutions in Małopolska resulted from the convergence of many various factors. KAS provided political actors with public justification for otherwise unpopular restrictions. The available evidence does not, however, demonstrate that increased public awareness of the problem or KAS activity alone was either a necessary or a sufficient condition for the reform. Third, the importance of public awareness was specific to certain phases of the regulatory process. It was particularly significant for agenda setting,[1] problem framing, and the political legitimation of restrictive regulation. But it was less capable of ensuring implementation and long-term effectiveness. These later stages depended primarily on the adopted model of regulation, the clarity of obligations, the scale and accessibility of financial assistance, coordination among different levels of government (national, regional, and local), the administrative capacity of municipalities, and credible enforcement. The difference between the strict Kraków prohibition and the model adopted for the rest of Małopolska illustrates how the same public awareness and civic involvement may generate divergent outcomes when translated into different regulatory designs.

The contribution of the chapter is therefore not simply to provide a history of a successful environmental movement. It uses the case of KAS to refine understanding of how activism operates within a multilevel system of environmental governance. It allegedly demonstrates that the actual influence of civic movements may be restricted only to the initial part of the policy process, where the innovative use of media channels and public communication contributes significantly to agenda

[1] To clarify the concepts used in the following paragraphs, agenda setting occurs when air pollution becomes a problem that political institutions are expected to address. Policy design concerns the choice of instruments, obligations, deadlines, exemptions, financial mechanisms, and institutional responsibilities. Policy adoption refers to the enactment of legal acts expressing policy design responding to the set agenda. In turn, policy implementation refers to the administrative and technical process through which adopted legal requirements are translated into the replacement of polluting installations and changes in household behavior. Thus, policy effectiveness refers to implementation and is understood in terms of observable progress toward the policy's declared objectives, particularly the elimination of noncompliant heating installations and the improvement of air quality.

setting. It also demonstrates, however, that the success of agenda setting may conceal weaknesses in policy design and implementation that become visible only over a longer period.

Later chapters, in turn, consider how failures of policy design and implementation may contribute to the qualification of the antismog resolutions as an instance of symbolic law and to the perception of air pollution as an inherently intractable problem.

3.2 Study Design and Sources

This chapter adopts an interpretive socio-legal case study design. It does not seek to measure public attitudes through a representative survey, nor does it attempt to isolate the effect of activism through an experimental or quasi-experimental design. Instead, it offers a historically informed reconstruction of a policy process. The principal empirical basis of the chapter consists of publicly available documentary materials. These include strategic documents adopted by the authorities of Kraków and the Małopolska region, regional air protection programs, antismog resolutions (and their accompanying explanatory memoranda and appendices), official reports on the implementation of air-quality policies, materials published by KAS and PAS, press coverage, and reported air-quality data. These sources were used to reconstruct the chronology of the policy process, identify the arguments advanced by the principal actors, and compare the declared objectives of the adopted measures with their subsequent implementation and observable effects. The analysis is based on close reading and chronological reconstruction rather than on a formal content-analysis procedure.

Such a documentary record is supplemented by notes from informal conversational interviews—in the sense described by Patton (2015, pp. 426–431)—with the three publicly known founders of KAS: Andrzej Guła, Anna Dworakowska, and Ewa Lutomska. These exchanges were not research interviews in the methodological sense, and the interlocutors were not selected to constitute a representative or theoretically differentiated sample. The author's notes, though, are not complete transcripts and do not record every interaction with the relevant actors. These conversations took place on numerous occasions in the course of scientific conferences, public protests, civic events, and consultations concerning the implementation of antismog measures. Some of them occurred while the author of this chapter was serving as the mayor of a municipality in Małopolska and was himself involved in attempts to introduce regional and local measures addressing residential emissions. The author maintained, and continues to maintain, collegial relations with the founders of KAS.

Information derived from such conversations serves primarily to clarify the sequence of events, the origins of particular initiatives, and the participants' own understanding of their actions. Where the chapter relies on such material, it is identified explicitly as an informal conversation, personal communication, or the recollection of the author.

As such, the chapter is not written entirely from the standpoint of an external observer. The author was involved in environmental activism and, as a municipal mayor, participated in discussions concerning the design and implementation of air-quality policies in Małopolska. He attended meetings, public consultations, and public events connected with antismog policy and had direct access to some of the political and administrative processes described below. This insider position provides access to aspects of the policy process that are not fully reflected in official documents. It makes it possible to identify informal relations, political concerns, and practical implementation problems that may otherwise remain invisible. At the same time, it creates clear methodological risks, as personal involvement may introduce bias.

For this reason, the chapter distinguishes between two types of statements. First, there are factual claims supported by legislation, official documents, reports, monitoring data, or contemporaneous press materials. Second, there are the author's interpretations and recollections arising from his own participation in the events. Especially, claims concerning broader political motivations or causal significance belong to the latter category. It is important to remember that such claims are interpretive conclusions and are formulated with an appropriate degree of caution. Nonetheless, we believe that the limitations enumerated above do not invalidate the case study and its conclusions.

3.3 Geographical and Historical Context of Air Pollution in Kraków

The emergence of citizen-led environmental initiative considered by air quality in Kraków was not by a chance. In fact, Kraków was uniquely positioned for such a movement to emerge, given its decades-long reputation as one of Europe's most polluted cities. High concentrations of particulate matter (PM), benzo(a)pyrene (B(a)P), as well as sulfates and nitrogen oxides (NO_x) have been well documented in the city since the late 1960s (Wilczyńska-Michalik et al., 2017). This persistent issue was significantly compounded by the accumulation of several socioeconomic and geographical factors.

(1) Kraków has unique geoclimatic conditions. The city is located at the bottom of the Vistula River valley and is surrounded by hills. This significantly limits horizontal ventilation of the city. During winter seasons, the city witnesses frequent low temperatures as well as atmospheric inversions. All-day inversions could happen during up to 20% of the year, while at night, inversions are present during 86% of the year (Bokwa, 2008, pp. 674–675). In the past, these conditions trapped pollutants and initiated smog incidents.

(2) Owing to its historic nature, the city encompassed thousands of aging, poorly insulated buildings—concentrated predominantly in its center. Most of these buildings typically relied on primitive, inefficient solid-fuel boilers, stoves, and open hearths for room and water heating. The situation was further exacerbated by a prolonged policy stance from authorities, who historically viewed heat supply as a private matter rather than a municipal service. This was also reinforced by a prevailing cultural perception. The attitude of the authorities also contributed to this situation. Generally, heat supply for years has been considered largely as a private matter. Authorities haven't cared about providing inhabitants with the access to the system heat (alternatively, network heat) produced centrally.[2] In 2012 network heat was responsible for 41.5% of energy used for households heating in Poland, while hard coal and wood for 41% and 40%, respectively (Adamczyk et al., 2017: 16318). The popularity of coal and wood for heating among Polish households was due to economic reasons. Coal and wood were the cheapest fuels used for heat production even in 2012 (Adamczyk et al., 2017: 16319). As coal was extensively used for residential heating, its dispersed use in individual buildings for many years was one of the major sources of PM and B(a)P in Kraków and its suburban area. While in the first decade of the twenty-first century there were studies indicating that industries, especially energy plants, were responsible for most of the particulate matter measured in Kraków (e.g., Bokwa, 2008), in the second decade, residential combustion for heat, hot water, and cooking became the major source. Such a shift was caused by a couple of circumstances, but mostly by the introduction of the stricter industrial emissions control after the accession of Poland to the EU in 2004.

(3) After 1945, Poland experienced a planned transformation from a rural to an industrial economy, accompanied by intense state-driven urbanization. Heavy industry was often deliberately located in urbanized areas as part of a larger political and cultural project. For this reason, the communist regime decided to locate the country's biggest steel mill in close proximity to the historic center of Kraków, mainly to manifest a new era in the city's history and to balance the cultural influences of the intellectual elites of the cultural capital of the country. As a result, dramatic aero-sanitary conditions persisted in Kraków from the mid-twentieth century onward. In the 1970s, annual average concentrations of PM10 in the city exceeded 130 μg/m^3, while the highest sulfur dioxide (SO_2) concentrations in Kraków were recorded at the end of the 1980s. Because of these extreme levels of pollution, some authors explicitly called the city and its neighboring area a zone of environmental disaster (e.g., Nowicki, 1993).

[2] It is often assumed self-evident that central heat production by large facilities is cleaner than dispersed heat production—at least as long as it takes combustion. Large facilities (power or heating plants) are required by law to have a certified filter system and use certified, high-quality fuel for their boilers and chimneys. Those facilities, run by public or private companies, also care about economic efficiency and invest in modern technologies to control combustion and emissions to cut costs. Actual measurements demonstrate that in practical conditions, such a central emission source could emit fewer particulates than a single primitive cauldron (personal experience).

Because of high levels of SO_2 in the past, Kraków often struggled with acid rain that destroyed its architectural heritage—a phenomenon typical of industrialized cities in the nineteenth century. Meanwhile, in 1978 the city was included in the United Nations Educational, Scientific and Cultural Organization (UNESCO) List of Natural and Cultural Heritage, so the struggle to rescue historical buildings in Kraków, often fueled by grassroots initiatives, became an important and publicly discussed issue, shaping public perception of the city as plagued by air pollution. This struggle also marked the first time the problem of air quality gained nationwide recognition.

In 1979, Poland—already identified as one of the biggest polluters in Europe—signed the Convention on Long-Range Transboundary Air Pollution (CLRTAP), which was one of the first international agreements aimed at reducing and preventing emissions of transboundary pollutants, mainly produced by industry. It has been ratified by more than 50 countries, initially facilitating collaboration among member countries (by sharing data and strategies for improving air quality) and promoting scientific research and monitoring. Over time, several protocols targeting specific pollutants were signed, supplementing the treaty with effective mechanisms for their control and limitation. As a result, observable declines occurred, primarily in acid rain and smog episodes triggered by long-range transport. In the case of the energy production and industry sectors, however, the most important was the 1999 Göteborg Protocol, which required parties to reduce emissions of SO_2, NO_x, volatile organic compounds (VOCs), and ammonia (NH_3).

Poland's accession to the European Union in 2004 was the strongest impulse for the modernization of the national economy, especially its polluting sectors. EU law is far more stringent on pollutant emissions, and Poland was obliged to harmonize its internal legal system with it. For example, Directive 2001/80/EC on large combustion plants (LCPD)[3] introduced strict limits on SO_2, NO_x, and dust emissions. It forced Polish power plants to install costly flue-gas desulfurization and denitrification systems, which were key to reducing acid rain. The later directive—Directive 2010/75/EU on industrial emissions (IED)[4]—became the main tool for controlling industrial emissions in the EU, forcing industry to regularly upgrade facilities to meet increasingly stringent emission standards. Finally, Directive (EU) 2016/2284[5] established national obligations to reduce emissions of SO_2, NO_x, ammonia, VOCs, and fine dust (PM2.5). These directives were transplanted into Polish national law mainly through the Environmental Protection Law of 2001.[6] The act introduced a

[3] Directive 2001/80/EC of the European Parliament and of the Council of 23 October 2001 on the limitation of emissions of certain pollutants into the air from large combustion plants, OJ L 309, 27.11.2001: 1–21.

[4] Directive 2010/75/EU of the European Parliament and of the Council of 24 November 2010 on industrial emissions (integrated pollution prevention and control), OJ L 334, 17.12.2010: 17–119.

[5] Directive (EU) 2016/2284 of the European Parliament and of the Council of 14 December 2016 on the reduction of national emissions of certain atmospheric pollutants, amending Directive 2003/35/EC and repealing Directive 2001/81/EC, OJ L 344, 17.12.2016: 1–31.

[6] Ustawa z dnia 27 kwietnia 2001 r. Prawo ochrony środowiska, Dz.U. 2001 nr 62 poz. 627.

permit system for industrial emissions and a framework of fees and penalties for environmental use and exceedances, creating economic incentives to reduce pollution.

Alongside regulatory pressure, the restructuring of Polish industry (a shift from heavy industry to machine production, product assembly, and logistics), the introduction of new technologies, and a mere decrease in production due to economic turmoil associated with the transformation to a free-market economy generally contributed to the significant reduction of air pollution in Poland. Such a reduction was clearly visible in Kraków, too. For example, steel production in the steel mill in Kraków Nowa Huta dropped from 7 million tonnes of steel per year in the late 1970s to 1.7 million tonnes per year in 1990 (Bokwa, 2008, p. 675).

At the end of the first decade of the twenty-first century, annual concentrations of SO_2 and PM in Kraków decreased by 70–80% compared with those in the early 1970s. Between the 1960s and the 1990s, the number of days with fog in the city center dropped from about 120 to 20. Increasing concentrations of PM were observed beginning around 2001, with SO_2 usually staying below the allowed limits while PM10 remaining permanently above them. Chemical analysis of PM10 in Kraków revealed concentrations of B(a)P exceeding the target level of 1 ng/m^3 in air by 50–250 times (Bokwa, 2008).

(4) With industrial emissions gradually declining, the residential sector emerged as the primary source of air pollutants in Poland at the turn of the twenty-first century. Solid fuel combustion in residential heating remained responsible for the majority of particulate matter (PM) emissions as late as 2014—a trend that has largely persisted since. (In Poland, building emissions are commonly referred to as low emissions, defined as emissions originating from sources no higher than 40 meters; see Adamczyk et al., 2017). According to the national monitoring network, annual mean limit values were exceeded in 36 zones for PM10 and 24 zones for PM2.5, out of a total of 46 designated air quality zones.[7] Furthermore, benzo(a) pyrene—B(a)P—concentrations exceeded EU thresholds in 42 zones. On a national scale, individual space heating was estimated to contribute 88%, 86.5%, and 98% to the annual mean exceedances of PM10, PM2.5, and B(a)P, respectively.[8]

In 2008, hard coal was the dominant fuel for heat generation in Poland, accounting for 75.8% of the total output. The remainder comprised heating oil (7.7%), natural gas (5.6%), biomass (4.8%), and other fuel sources (6.1%) (URE, 2010). In 2004–2008, small consumers were the third-largest users of hard coal in Poland, after power plants and combined heat and power (CHP) plants, as well as industry and construction. Coal consumption in this sector accounted for 13% of the country's total coal consumption. For the coal-mining industry, despite its large

[7] Air-quality zones in Poland are established by the Regulation of the Minister of Environment of August 2, 2012, on zones for air-quality assessment, Dz.U. 2012 poz. 914.

[8] Główny Inspektorat Ochrony Środowiska, Jakość powietrza w Polsce w latach 2013–2014 w świetle wyników pomiarów prowadzonych w ramach Państwowego Monitoringu Środowiska [Air quality in Poland in the years 2013–2014 in the light of the results of measurements conducted by the State Environmental Monitoring], Warszawa 2015.

dispersion, small customers were a significant recipient, as over 25% of the industry's revenues came from this sector (GUS, 2010).

The increasing contribution of residential emissions to poor air quality in Kraków became apparent at the end of the twentieth century. Air pollution—systematically measured in the city since 1966—for decades has demonstrated a strong seasonal pattern, with maximums in winter and minimums in summer. As industrial production levels are more or less constant throughout the year, this could only be attributed to weather conditions (atmospheric temperature inversions and wind stagnation) or residential coal combustion for heat, which is strongly correlated with low temperatures. Additionally, precise measurements conducted in different areas of Kraków demonstrated that the highest levels of SO_2 were noted in the center of the city, presumably due to residential combustion of poor-quality coal containing sulfur. By the end of the twentieth century, the variance in SO_2 concentrations between different parts of Kraków had practically disappeared. Because industrial facilities are restricted to specific industrial zones rather than evenly distributed, the SO_2 uniformity demonstrated that industry alone could not account for the widespread pollution, thereby conclusively confirming the dominant role of residential emissions.

(5) Across Poland, including Kraków, the impact of residential emissions escalated for another key reason: the progressive deterioration of coal quality available to individual consumers. As stringent emissions standards and permit systems were implemented for industry, large energy producers bought up high-grade coal to minimize compliance costs and optimize operations. Consequently, superior coal was effectively swept from the market through long-term corporate contracts. Individual consumers and their fuel suppliers—primarily small retailers—were left with no choice but to rely on mining by-products and production waste. Until 2018, coal supplied to the residential sector contained a high proportion of low-quality fuels, such as coal sludge, flotation concentrate, fines, and coal waste—estimated at 30–40% of the market—with households purchasing over 75% of these products. Despite their high mineral dust, ash (up to 40%), and sulfur content (up to 1.2%), these fuels were widely purchased due to their low price and guaranteed availability. This issue was most acute in Śląsk and Małopolska—the regions with a direct proximity to coal mines. Because coal quality standards for domestic use were nonexistent prior to 2018, virtually any extracted material could be marketed as household fuel, regardless of its poor composition, low calorific value, and high emissions profile.

Later, to catch up with growing demands from the residential sector, imports of low-quality coal from abroad also began. Between 2000 and 2020, coal imports to Poland increased significantly. In 2000, they reached approximately 1.5 million tonnes, while in the record-breaking year of 2018, they reached approximately 20 million tonnes. About 70–74% of imported coal came from Russia, but it was also imported from places like Colombia, Australia, Indonesia, and South Africa. The share of imported coal in the market reached approximately 20% of residential consumption in the peak year of 2018. Most of the imported coal consisted of fractions with low calorific value and high sulfur and ash content. For global exporters, Poland has become a place they could sell even waste, if only it had an appropriate appearance and color.

Finally, three additional factors deserve mention.

(6) At the beginning of the twenty-first century, the structural condition of many residential buildings, especially in Kraków's historical center, was severely degraded. Their state was already poor prior to the political transition, as the communist regime (1945–1989) had consistently neglected the maintenance of nationalized properties. Consequently, many buildings lacked adequate thermal insulation and relied on obsolete solid-fuel systems. Across Poland's residential sector, heating was primarily supplied by grate furnaces characterized by outdated technology, low thermal efficiency (25–60%), and a total absence of dust-abatement equipment (Stala-Szlugaj, 2011). Even relatively modern installations often exceeded their operational lifespan. Compounding the issue, local authorities lacked the financial resources required to renovate and refurbish the municipal housing stock, while the privatization process was stalled by complex legal and property ownership disputes. Together, these structural and administrative obstacles significantly exacerbated Kraków's air pollution crisis.

Poor structural conditions in residential buildings and inefficient heating systems were not unique to Kraków; rather, they were prevalent across Poland. Consequently, air pollution driven by low-efficiency combustion—characterized by high emissions and excessive coal consumption—was a nationwide issue. Kraków's distinctiveness lay in the sheer scale of the problem, given its dense concentration of aging buildings, which was further compounded by its challenging topography.

(7) The fact that old types of heating devices were still in use and that their technical state was often bad opened a route for further worsening of the aero-sanitary situation in Polish cities. Many property owners, motivated by rising prices of good-quality coal, started to use plastic and paper waste as supplementary fuel for heating their homes, amplifying the toxicity of residential emissions beyond conceivable limits. Small cities, where public authorities had no practical means to control residents, became places where breathing during winter was almost impossible for weeks. As there were no sensors in those places to record the quality of air, the situation was ignored for many years by local authorities, regional and national regulators, and public opinion.

The problem of residential waste being used for heating was a public secret in Poland. The results of tests on ash samples suggest that up to 30% of Polish households heated by solid fuels burned various types of waste, including plastics from residential product packaging.[9] As this secret gradually became more publicized, and with growing public dissatisfaction and concern, it began to be considered by decision-makers as an important reason for proposing effective removal programs for manually operated stoves and boilers that made waste combustion possible. In that case, waste burning and the growing public disapproval of such practices, as well as of political inaction, were certainly among the factors that explain the formulation of proposals to ban solid-fuel installations or to replace inefficient ones with more automated devices that make waste burning impractical.

[9] Ekspert: spalanie śmieci w Polsce jest problemem społecznym, Serwis Nauka w Polsce—naukawpolsce.pl, 21.10.2016.

(8) In the literature, the question of waste burning is often explained by energy (fuel) poverty (e.g., Bharadwaj et al., 2026). A similar explanation has recently been proposed in Poland as well (e.g., Chmielewski et al., 2022). There are many operational definitions of fuel poverty, based on, for example, household income, individual capabilities (e.g., maintaining appropriate indoor temperature), or the technical state of the building. In Polish scholarship, the phenomenon has been scrutinized in detail by Lewandowski et al. (2018). Studies from China link poverty with increased contribution to indoor and ambient emissions and increased exposure (e.g., Yun et al., 2020), although the causal relationship is usually understood as two-way, since poor air quality also significantly increases energy poverty (Li et al., 2024).

The transition from the planned economy of the communist regime into the market economy of the 1990s resulted in difficulties for families with lower incomes. These families, often from vulnerable groups, usually inhabited old communal buildings in the historic centers of Polish cities. While electric energy prices were still regulated by the state, solid fuel for individual customers was not, making heating theoretically unaffordable for many families (families compensated for the high prices of heating by cutting other expenses and significantly downgrading the quality of their living). At the beginning of the twenty-first century, the problem started to gain political salience. Although the problem was observable in everyday life, it was mentioned for the first time in official documents only in 2009. The Polish Prime Minister addressed the problem in his inaugural speech only in 2017 (Frankowski, 2019).

From that time on, fuel poverty became a topic of government political communication. As an argument for antismog policies, its role was more complex. For reformists, it was used as a reason for the subsidized removal of solid-fuel installations operated by financially disadvantaged families, while the mining lobby continuously presented coal as the most affordable solution for a significant part of Polish society. Depending on the perspective, therefore, fuel poverty could be an argument for energy transformation from coal-based inefficient heating to low-emitting or zero-emission sources, as well as, paradoxically, for preserving outdated and cheap coal-dependent technologies.

There are authors who suggest (e.g., Frankowski, 2019) that fuel poverty was a significant cause of air pollution in Poland, as well as one of the reasons for the adoption of more effective policies to address the problem in the years 2015–2016. Of course, the inability to buy better-quality fuel or to retrofit one's own house or apartment influences emissions to *some* extent. However, waste burning and solid-fuel burning—the more direct causes of air pollution—are not necessarily consequences of energy poverty. Needless to say, pollutants were emitted across the whole territory of Poland independently of the actual financial situation of inhabitants. Also, the estimated number of Poles living in energy poverty was 12.2% (1.3 million households) (Rutkowski et al., 2018), while pollutants were emitted by the majority of households since most residential buildings used solid-fuel heating systems. Additionally, more than twice as many households, as already mentioned, burned waste. So the numbers do not add up to support the fuel-poverty hypothesis. It seems, then, that something other than poverty and low income is responsible for the use of solid fuel and waste for heating.

Several studies suggest that cultural perceptions and customs are important factors that should be taken into consideration by policy planners dealing with the problem of air pollution in Poland (e.g., Włodarczyk & Herczakowska, 2025). We observed that individuals are often culturally attached to coal and wood as their sources of energy, which are locally accessible and thus more reliable than natural gas and electricity. Surveys conducted in Poland in recent years confirmed these observations (e.g., NIK, 2025), as reluctance toward energy transition to cleaner sources of heat turned out to be the consequence of a general lack of trust in new technologies and the costs of their use, as well as in long-term government commitments and promises of financial support for households removing coal- or wood-based inefficient installations. Furthermore, waste burning was often perceived as a pragmatic option due to a lack of awareness—or outright dismissal—of toxic emissions, which were frequently discounted as environmental propaganda. For these reasons, although energy poverty is an important issue, it was neither the root cause of Kraków's air pollution nor the primary motivation for reform. The other structural factors discussed were far more direct and significant.

Figure 3.1 illustrates our proposed conceptual model for the causes of air pollution in Kraków.

All of the circumstances described in this section constitute a complex network of successive or simultaneous causes of poor air quality in Kraków.

Although the situation in Kraków seemed somewhat special, similar factors were usually at play in other parts of Poland. Polish cities had (and actually still have) the worst air quality in the EU. In 2011, as many as six out of ten European cities with the biggest number of days exceeding the daily mean limit value for PM10 (50 μg/m^3) were located in Poland. In 2012, Poland recorded the highest annual mean B(a)P concentrations of any European country, three times higher than the next country (Czech Republic) on this infamous chart. Nonetheless, the highest annual mean PM2.5 concentrations that year were measured in Kraków. For these reasons, the city was identified as the third-most polluted agglomeration in the European Union, regularly exceeding air-quality limits for 150 days annually, sometimes as much as eight times (WHO, 2016).

As these statistics were finally popularized in the 2010s by the Polish and international press, they became one of the major reasons for postulating a policy shift in Małopolska (see below).

Meanwhile, our analysis demonstrates two interesting circumstances. First, the character of air pollution in Kraków and Małopolska in the first decades of the twenty-first century changed—localized industry as a major source of air pollution was replaced by the dispersed residential-building sector. Second, the changing character of the problem of air pollution (the change in its main source), due to previous attempts to tackle it (i.e., the successful introduction of emission standards for industry), actually made the problem more difficult to solve. We will elaborate on this idea in the next section.

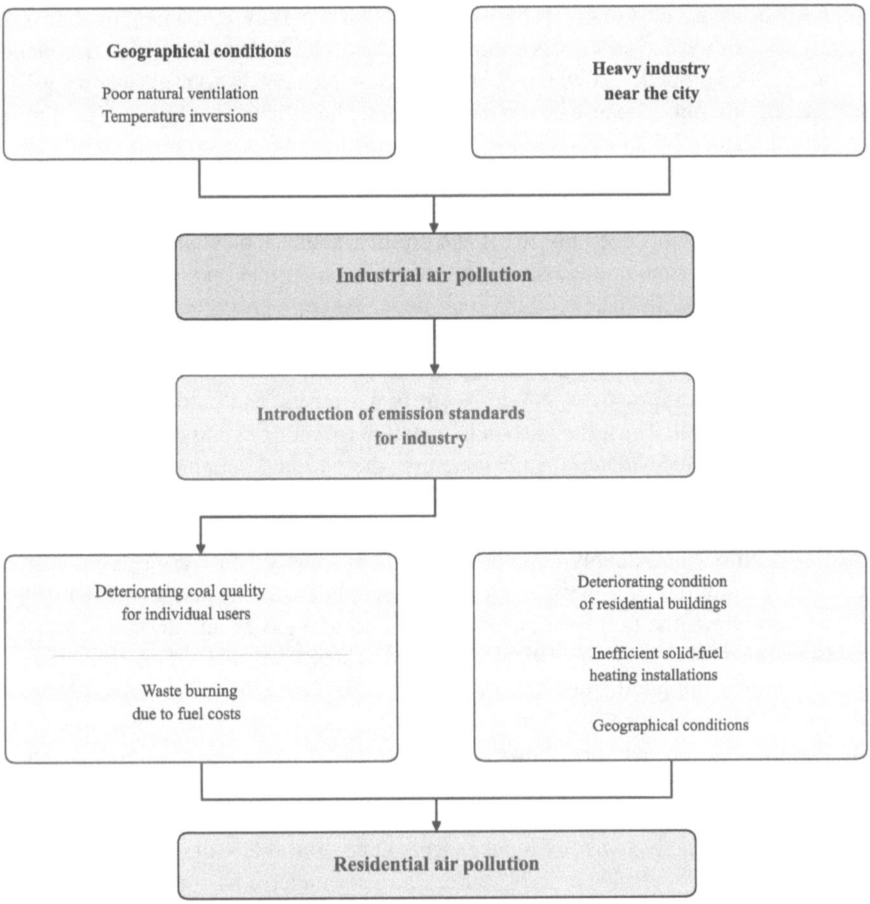

Fig. 3.1 Causality of air pollution in Kraków

3.4 Socioeconomic and Political Obstacles to Addressing the Air Pollution Problem in Kraków

For many years, severe air pollution in Kraków was largely accepted as a normal condition. This normalization of the environmental threat by the political class and the general public alike posed a significant initial obstacle to attempts to change the situation. The communist regime did not offer many opportunities for protest, especially because state-managed industry was the main source of pollutants, and industrialization was presented by state propaganda, not without justification, as a source of social and economic progress. This fostered a degree of public acceptance of pollution, as well as reluctance to challenge the status quo. Pollution was viewed as a necessary consequence of modernization, despite its considerable costs. To illustrate the point, between 2014 and 2020 alone, air pollution is estimated to have imposed an annual cost of €60 billion on the Polish economy, equivalent to approximately 13% of the nation's gross domestic product (GDP) (Health and Environment Alliance, 2025). For Kraków, the economic consequences of poor air quality were substantial, not only because of the risks to public health but also because acid rain directly threatened the city's historic heritage. At the end of the twentieth century, when Kraków gradually became a popular tourist destination, reputational costs also began to be taken into account.

But it was Poland's deep historical and political reliance on coal that represented perhaps the most fundamental structural barrier to significant policy change in the area of air quality. In the literature such dependence is characterized as a socio-technical and political-economic lock-in (see, e.g., Unruh, 2000; Brauers & Oei, 2020). Kuchler and Bridge (2018) argue that coal in Poland is also intrinsically woven into cultural practices, energy-security narratives, and culturally embedded imaginaries of coal. Thus, the lock-in in question extends beyond energy consumption alone to include material infrastructure, the national economy, and political mechanisms. Household practices surrounding coal—its purchase on local markets, transport, storage, combustion, and even the use of ash on icy sidewalks and streets—also became deeply embedded in Polish society and were reinforced by national celebrations of miners' work and pride in Poland's abundant coal deposits. At the same time, the turbulent introduction of natural gas as an alternative household-heating fuel during the 1980s generated widespread distrust of this energy source, largely imported from Russia and thus vulnerable to sudden price changes and political instability. Many families invested in gas heaters as the state expanded the gas distribution network; however, sudden price increases prompted a rapid return to coal as a cheaper and, most importantly, locally supplied fuel. These historical and cultural particularities made anti-smog policy especially difficult whenever its core objective was to reduce dependence on coal—the main source of pollution. In fact, several scholarly sources directly underscore the complex socio-economic structure of the air pollution problem in Poland. Culture and widespread public reliance on coal—historically a cheap and accessible fuel—have been identified as important sources of political and economic resistance to change (see, e.g., Citkowska-Kimla, 2019). Anti-smog policies therefore challenge not only powerful vested interests, such as the mining lobby, but also, and equally importantly, entrenched cultural patterns, beliefs, and perceptions.

Additionally, as mentioned earlier, stricter industrial emission standards made the problem of air pollution even harder to address. In reaction to market pressures for efficiency and regulatory pressure to lower pollutant emissions, Polish heavy industry and the energy production sector underwent a relatively rapid process of modernization. This transformed the nature of the air pollution problem in places like Kraków, as the emissions from the residential sector started to dominate the landscape as well as the profile of pollutants.

As heavy industry reduced its direct environmental impact, the role of the domestic sector became increasingly visible, even to the naked eye. Pollution became more localized and immediate: it was produced not by distant factories and tall chimneys, but by residential chimneys in ordinary neighborhoods, in close proximity to people's homes.

The issue of pollution thus ceased to concern only a few institutional coal users and became much more politically complex—as the number of relevant stakeholders increased dramatically, including a large share of the city's inhabitants, who were also voters. Any potential solution therefore had to account not only for economic interests but also for a complex set of political, social, and economic trade-offs.

Regulators usually have greater freedom to impose financial burdens on companies, as they are market actors primarily oriented toward financial returns. Imposing even smaller burdens on individuals is more difficult, because their motivations are not purely financial, their well-being is itself a regulatory concern, and, ultimately, they are voters who influence which policies are adopted and by whom. Taken together, these factors made air pollution much more difficult to tackle.

As the character of air pollution changed, so did the way ordinary citizens experienced it in everyday life. As pollution increasingly came to be perceived as local and immediate, affected citizens became more receptive to a political narrative that the situation was unacceptable and required intervention. This change in everyday experience was not, by itself, sufficient to generate civic mobilization, let alone meaningful policy change. Comparable pollution driven by residential sector affected large parts of Poland, yet radical policy change occurred only in Kraków. Clearly, something more was at play in the city. The prevailing narrative in scholarship and the popular press attributes this shift to the emergence of an innovative grassroots organization that changed public perceptions of air pollution and mobilized political elites to adopt a local prohibition on the use of solid fuels.

3.5 The Genesis of Kraków Smog Alert (KAS)

In the fall of 2012, the politically and culturally normalized air pollution in Kraków became a source of personal frustration for a small group of concerned friends, including Andrzej Guła and his wife, Anna Dworakowska. Their primary impetus stemmed from a profound personal concern over Kraków's air pollution levels and its adverse effects on their children's health. In an informal conversation with the author, Guła recalled that one day, he began studying and collecting data on air quality and realized that, despite the fact that during winter months the atmosphere in Kraków is actually poisonous, it is a common practice at schools and kindergartens to bring children outside for walks to breathe "fresh air." Guła started meeting with local politicians to draw their attention to the problem and to regulate a practice he considered dangerous. His idea was to establish a citywide air quality alert system to warn citizens and schools during severe pollution events, ensuring children could be kept indoors.

The informal group growing around Guła and Dworakowska quickly recognized the burgeoning potential of social media, particularly Facebook, as a useful tool for information dissemination and public mobilization. They called themselves "Krakowski Alarm Smogowy (KAS)" (English: Kraków Smog Alert). At that time in Poland, Facebook was a popular platform for political activism, as posts with social and political content were not yet artificially limited by algorithms. Consequently, their initial posts, which shared real-time air-quality data and highlighted alarming concentrations of dangerous particles, quickly attracted hundreds of followers. Although some authors see the adoption of Facebook by KAS as pivotal for its later success (e.g., Lillevik, 2019), fostering direct public engagement through social media was a matter of necessity, since the group, in the beginning, was small and had no other tools at its disposal. The use of Facebook enabled a rapid increase in visible online mobilization. This was particularly important for KAS because the movement initially lacked the organizational infrastructure and resources of an established advocacy group. The early history of the movement resembles the mechanism studied by Bennett and Segerberg (2012), which is characteristic of actors lacking an established membership structure. Such actors rely on digital media to enable the circulation of personalized political content and to reduce the costs of involvement and participation for their potential members.

From the beginning, KAS assumed that the primary cause of air pollution in Kraków was residential coal burning. Such a claim was controversial since it contradicted well-entrenched popular opinions and perceptions of smog as a phenomenon produced by distant industry, not by ordinary people (see Waldholz, 2018). It was those perceptions that particularly led to the social apathy that characterized Poland before—if you cannot do anything about it, you should take air pollution for granted. Understanding that air pollution could be eliminated by one's own actions constituted a major step for the entire movement. Consequently, their second assumption was even more polarizing: only by enacting stringent regulations would it be possible to substantially improve air quality in Kraków.

From a scholarly point of view, the KAS strategy—founded upon those two controversial claims that contradicted popular views—can be interpreted as a process of diagnostic, prognostic, and motivational framing (Benford & Snow, 2000). The movement identified residential combustion as the principal source of the problem, presented restrictive regulation as a feasible remedy, and proposed civic mobilization as a necessary and potentially effective path to change. In this sense, KAS did not merely disseminate information but developed a causal story (see Stone, 1989) that, by bypassing established cultural perceptions and patterns, redistributed responsibility and redefined available policy alternatives. According to this framing, smog was not an indispensable consequence of economic progress but rather a symptom of social and technological backwardness—one that could be addressed through civic mobilization and subsequent local policy.

In 2013, Guła and his friends launched their first major public campaign. Gigantic posters depicting individuals wearing oxygen masks appeared across the city, urging people to sign a petition addressed to the region's political elites, prompting them to introduce bans on solid fuel in Kraków. The campaign was designed to disrupt the process of public consultation on the update of regional air-quality policy. Such consultations were required by law when updating air protection programs—policy documents adopted for areas where the target limits of pollutants under the EU 2008 Air Quality Directive[10] had not been met. These programs had to set out measures appropriate for reducing excess pollution, as well as include a diagnosis of the problem, with proposed corrective actions, their estimated costs, and expected environmental effects.[11]

The first air protection programs were created in Poland in 2003 and 2004. Between 2003 and 2010, such programs were developed for all provinces. Conducted analyses revealed that these programs were primarily drafted to address PM10 and B(a)P exceedances caused by residential combustion. The most polluted provinces were Małopolska, Dolny Śląsk, and Śląsk (Schönfelder, 2011). Nonetheless, in 2010, the limit and target values for PM10, PM2.5, benzene, benzo(a)pyrene, nitrogen dioxide, and arsenic dioxide were not met in 45 out of 46 air-quality zones in Poland (Adamczyk et al., 2017). Expert assessments of the programs published in 2015 demonstrated that they were often too general, not specifying the sources of air pollution in the zones, the required corrective actions, or their costs (see Adamczyk et al., 2017: 16322). With monitoring of the implementation of corrective actions also lacking, one could reasonably assume that those programs were introduced only to fulfill the formal legal requirements of the 2008 Directive but were ineffective by design.

In fact, many of these frameworks identified so-called "low-emission reduction programs"[12] as the primary corrective measure; however, these were merely local government initiatives enacted through local council resolutions. Their main objective was to provide citizens with subsidies to replace inefficient heating systems with newer technologies. Those local programs were usually small in scale and did not lead to any significant improvement in aero-sanitary conditions.[13]

The first action plan for Kraków and the rest of Małopolska region was passed in 2009 and did not include a ban on solid fuels. Its catalogue of possible interventions was rather limited to guarantee lack of resistance from voters in large numbers using solid fuels for heating. In 2013, the plan was scheduled for an update, and KAS used this opportunity to push for a radical policy shift. The group organized a series of rallies, marches, and public appearances accompanied by striking visuals and direct messaging. These actions were not merely informational but were designed to be emotionally resonant, aiming to break through public apathy and political inertia. Such a communication strategy was consistent with the concept of social amplification of risk. According to Kasperson et al. (1988), the perceived urgency of a hazard

[10] The Directive 2008/50/EC of the European Parliament and of the Council of 21 May 2008 on ambient air quality and cleaner air for Europe (OJ L 152).

[11] The specific content was described in the regulation of the Minister of the Environment—Rozporządzenie Ministra Środowiska z dnia 11 września 2012 r. w sprawie programów ochrony powietrza oraz planów działań krótkoterminowych, Dz.U. 2012 poz. 1028

[12] In official documents translated to English also as *low-stack emission abatement plans*.

[13] It all came down to the budget. For example, both Krakow and Wadowice (a small city with 20,000 inhabitants located close to Krakow) had their programs of low emissions reduction, and both cities were devoting a similar share of their budgets to that goal. Yet Krakow was able to subsidize the replacement of hundreds of installations per year, whereas Wadowice tens.

depends on the amplification provided by media and institutions, including grassroots organizations. The creation of "moral shock" is often required to overcome stalemate and apathy.

The appeal to emotions was particularly critical in addressing air pollution—a phenomenon long taken for granted in Poland, whose severe health implications were routinely dismissed. It was plausible that purely rational arguments or data alone might have been insufficient to provoke widespread action. KAS seemingly recognized the importance of effective, emotion-based public communication that could facilitate "moral shocks." This approach paid off well. One of the most defining moments was a symbolic funeral procession in October, when masked residents marched to the regional assembly to deliver a coffin to lawmakers who were reluctant to ban solid fuel combustion.

KAS's actions finally brought success. Although reluctant at the beginning, the local parliament voted for the ban on solid fuels in Kraków in November 2013. Such an act was considered revolutionary—without a doubt a turning point in the history of the problem in Poland.

The success of the communication strategy adopted by KAS was consistent with existing studies on the role of emotions in changing public policies and agenda setting (see, e.g., Jasper, 2011). Sustained media attention to the problem, thanks to the constant supplementation of emotional content by KAS, increased the salience of air pollution and made it more difficult for local and regional politicians to ignore (e.g., McCombs & Shaw, 1972).

The following year, the local council in Kraków passed a resolution[14] demanding that the city's president (mayor) implement a number of countermeasures, including an alert system with publicly available visual information on pollution levels and official recommendations to stay at home during periods of severe pollution. Principals of educational institutions (schools, preschools, and nurseries) were also instructed to restrict or prohibit children's presence in open spaces if air-quality standards in Kraków were "significantly exceeded." Other proposed actions included banning heavy trucks from entering the city, offering free public transport for passenger-car owners, intensifying street cleaning to reduce dust fallout, and strengthening controls to curb waste combustion.

As public perception of air pollution had already changed completely, city officials began to implement each of the proposed measures. The alert system, including public street displays and public transport screens, was introduced first, combined with free public transport during smog days and restrictions on school activities. In the following years, as the Polish parliament gradually amended the law, Kraków consistently implemented other actions from the resolution, including restrictions on entry to the city center for certain categories of vehicles (see below). However, introduction of the alerting system was the immediate and most important

[14] Uchwała Nr C/1550/14 Rady Miasta Krakowa z dnia 26 marca 2014 r. w sprawie kierunków działania dla Prezydenta Miasta Krakowa dotyczących działań krótkoterminowych wynikających z przekroczenia norm zanieczyszczenia powietrza.

consequence of the adoption of the 2014 resolution, since from that moment on, official smog alerts became an indispensable part of city life during winter.

The restrictions imposed in schools—and even the preceding discussion about introducing them—changed how parents and teachers perceived air pollution. For many of them, the decision to restrict their children's outdoor activities was the first occasion on which they reflected on the levels of pollutants in the air. As repeated pollution alerts began to limit pupils' outdoor activities, smog finally became part of the daily conscious experience of many Kraków residents. The importance of such everyday experiences has already been emphasized in the scholarly literature (e.g., Bickerstaff & Walker, 2001).

Parents were not the only group affected. It is therefore noteworthy that the third founder of KAS, Ewa Lutomska, was a sports teacher at one of the city's schools. Smog episodes affected her work much more directly than they did many other professions, as a significant proportion of her classes took place outdoors.

Guła continued his activism at the national level. He used his personal contacts with national-level decision-makers working at the National Fund for Environmental Protection and Water Management (Narodowy Fundusz Ochrony Środowiska i Gospodarki Wodnej) to initiate an informal working group on a subsidy program for removing and replacing the least efficient and most polluting solid-fuel heating installations. Those early discussions evolved into the first national subsidy program designed to support cities dealing with air pollution, known as "Kawka" (Crow). Despite the success of its earlier editions, due in particular to the high level of financial support offered—up to 90% of the investment costs associated with removing and replacing coal-burning installations—the program was discontinued at the end of 2015 by the new ruling coalition of populist and far-right parties, in what amounted to a symbolic reversal of green policies targeting coal.

The regional parliament, however, still governed by a coalition of liberal parties, continued to pursue the progressive anti-smog agenda. Although in August 2014 the Provincial Administrative Court in Kraków ruled that the 2013 resolution was unlawful, it had become difficult to reverse the course already set by the public protests organized by KAS. Moreover, a more decisive anti-smog policy had become politically advantageous, as around the same time Poland faced the threat of substantial financial penalties from the European Commission. We will return to this topic shortly.

Meanwhile, in 2015, the national parliament, in which the liberal coalition still held a majority, amended the Environmental Protection Act,[15] and Andrzej Duda, the newly elected president from the populist party and himself a resident of Kraków, signed the amendment into law, thereby creating a direct legal basis for the adoption of anti-smog regulations at the regional level. The legislative initiative came from a group of Civic Platform MPs and was led by Tadeusz Arkit, an MP from Małopolska. The amendment consisted of a handful of articles explicitly empowering regional

[15] Ustawa z dnia 10 września 2015 r. o zmianie ustawy—Prawo ochrony środowiska, Dz.U. 2015 poz. 1593.

parliaments to regulate the types of installations and fuels permitted in their territories. The absence of such explicit statutory authority had been one of the main grounds on which the administrative court invalidated the initial coal ban in 2014.

The amendment's swift passage—it was introduced on 23 February and signed into law by the new president on 6 October—was possible because the Civic Platform held a parliamentary majority at the time. The absence of a presidential veto, in turn, reflected a regional political consensus and civic pressure rather than the president's personal commitment to a more progressive air-pollution policy. This interpretation is further supported by Andrzej Duda's later public statements, in which he repeatedly criticized EU climate and energy policies—including regulations concerning energy-efficient light bulbs—and defended the continued widespread use of coal and other solid fuels in the residential sector.

As a result, the regional parliament of Małopolska voted for two separate resolutions in 2016 and 2017 (see Sect. 2.3.2). The resolutions banned certain types of solid fuels—mostly coal—and certain types of installations—mostly outdated primitive cauldrons—and were accompanied by a public promise of extensive subsidy programs for cauldron removal and house insulation. All these measures were in accordance with KAS proposals. In the following years, both resolutions were successfully defended in court.

As the pioneering efforts of the group in Kraków garnered national attention—serving as an inspiration for other communities across Poland—KAS evolved into a broader national movement, "Polski Alarm Smogowy (PAS)" (English: Polish Smog Alert). In many Polish cities, similar initiatives began to emerge, and almost all regional parliaments started developing their own versions of anti-smog resolutions, albeit usually less ambitious than the one adopted in Małopolska. By 2018, as many as 89 civic initiatives in different parts of Poland had been identified as smog alerts,[16] that is, informal, independent, non-profit grassroots movements, typically composed of members of the urban middle class and concerned with the problem of air pollution (Frankowski, 2019). At first glance, the comparatively limited influence of these local initiatives might appear to explain why the policies adopted elsewhere were generally less ambitious than those promoted by KAS in Małopolska. Many of these local smog alerts were small, sometimes consisting of little more than a single person running a Facebook profile. We believe, however, that there is a better explanation: contrary to the mainstream narrative, civic involvement and rising public awareness were not, in fact, the major drivers of air-pollution policy reform in Małopolska. There are several reasons for this view.

First, despite overenthusiastic press coverage of the role of civic involvement and grassroots campaigns in changing officials' approach to air pollution in Kraków and Małopolska, actual civic involvement in smog alerts was not that big. KAS was visible, indeed, thanks mainly to clever communication campaigns that resonated in Polish and even international media, but quantitative studies revealed that only

[16] Later, that number started to shrink as more and more people turned away from the movement because of social dissatisfaction with the insufficient results of antismog activism (see below).

6.6% of Kraków's residents engaged with KAS's online content on social media. Typically, social engagement with content published by local smog alerts involved fewer than 4% of the residents of a given city or town (Frankowski, 2019). In reality (that is, in real life rather than online), civic involvement was even much lower. The period of "intensified" engagement in antismog activism in Poland was also rather short. The same analysis demonstrated that the peak of civic involvement was in the winter of 2016/2017, whereas half of the provinces voted on their resolutions in 2018 or later. Social involvement in the subject, therefore, was clearly not harmonized with actual policy change. This, of course, suggests that the former was not the cause of the latter.

Interestingly, even in Małopolska—where the antismog movement was presumably the strongest—besides Kraków, only one community actually petitioned the regional parliament to introduce a solid-fuel ban on its territory during the policy shift.[17] Apparently, local politicians remained insensitive both to the actual levels of pollution and to the growing public awareness of the problem, measured by the number of likes below the emotional posts shared on social media of local smog alerts. If only public engagement constituted a motive for politicians to act in the region, one would expect a different result.

This corresponds with the course of a meeting organized by the regional authorities with the mayors of municipalities in Małopolska regarding the implementation of the EU-cofunded program, which was intended to support and supplement the implementation of antismog policies in the region.[18] Although the meeting coincided with the peak of nationwide smog alert activity, initially only one of the mayors present (from Wadowice) explicitly declared support for cofunding air protection and antismog measures.[19] The situation became dire, since without this single voice of reason, the whole program would have been canceled due to the lack of support from Małopolska's political class.

Another study that provides a hint on the significance of smog alerts—this time for shaping awareness of ordinary people in Poland—is the report published by the Polish Economic Institute (Śliwowski et al., 2020). According to the findings, only one-third of responders recognized residential combustion as the actual source of air pollution, almost 40% believed that Poland has the cleanest air in Europe, and homeowners, to a large degree, still morally and socially accepted behaviors contributing to air pollution, despite realizing their health consequences (20% personally accepted pollution from burning dirty fuel, and almost 40% used ineffective

[17] That was Wadowice in 2017, the small city where one of us served as a mayor at that time. The regional parliament, overtaken by the populist party majority, has not answered the petition to this day, ignoring its duty to address the problem of air pollution through appropriate (effective) measures.

[18] The name of the program was "Integrated Project LIFE," and we described it in another chapter of this book.

[19] The account is based on the author's notes and recollection as a participant in the meeting organized by the Marshall of Małopolska in 2015.

furnaces). As the authors of the report underscored, complex behavioral patterns are quite resistant to information campaigns.

Moreover, more recent studies demonstrate that awareness of the problem of air pollution in Poland remains moderate and varies geographically and temporarily—it is higher in winter as well as in more affected regions (Nazar & Niedoszytko, 2022). The most troubling conclusion is that even among physicians, knowledge of the health consequences of air pollution is only moderate. The study confirms that in the case of air pollution, public awareness depends more on direct personal experiences than on factual data and information campaigns in the press.

Taken together, this evidence strongly suggests that KAS and other local smog alerts had only a limited influence on public awareness of the problem, let alone on the behaviour of political elites or their willingness to act. Social engagement was actually confined to Kraków, and after the initial moment in 2014/2015, it quickly disappeared. Therefore, we believe that available evidence supports the claim that, contrary to the popular narrative, the policy shift in Kraków and Małopolska was driven not by innovative activism but by a set of circumstances that have not been mentioned so far. We now turn to them in the following sections.

3.6 The City International Reputation at Stake

If civic engagement and social activism were not responsible for the adoption of antismog resolutions in Kraków and Małopolska, then what was? What other factors mobilized the political elites of the city and region, first, to come up with an ambitious political agenda and, then, to adopt progressive measures after years of inaction? In fact, there are several circumstances worth mentioning as probable drivers of the resolutions. One is the growing significance of Kraków and Małopolska as an international travel destination.

The role of rapid tourism growth in the region is usually overlooked in discussions about the dynamics of air pollution policies. However, a relatively weak currency (Polish złoty), good services, decent living conditions, a rich network of hotels and holiday apartments, and the presence of low-cost flight operators—enabled by massive investments in the local airport and subsidies from the regional and central governments—elevated tourism into one of the major drivers of the region's economy. Low-cost airlines arrived in Kraków in 2004, and thanks to them, passenger traffic increased fivefold between 2003 and 2007. In 2007, over 3 million passengers used the services of the local airport (Kurek & Faracik, 2008). The tourism sector's contribution to Kraków's economy has grown significantly since the beginning of the twenty-first century. In 2014, Kraków was visited by 7.6 million tourists, 2.5 million of whom were foreign. City officials estimated that tourism accounted for 10% of the city's economy, with indirect effects generating about 10% of the jobs in Kraków, translating into approximately 40,000 positions (Ogórek, 2015). Similar figures appeared in subsequent industry reports. Taking indirect and induced effects into account, the tourism industry generated an estimated PLN

5.295 million in GDP for Kraków in 2016, accounting for 8.27% of the city's total GDP. That same year, tourism was expected to generate 28,970 jobs in Kraków. With multiplier effects, this figure increased to 40,551 jobs. Tourism accounted for 10.14% of employment in the city's overall economy (MOT, 2017).

The growing importance of tourism in the city's economy was also the consequence of Kraków's rising position in various industry rankings since the beginning of the twenty-first century. In the second decade of the twenty-first century, the city began to appear at the top of these rankings, surpassing more renowned tourist destinations in Spain and Italy. This created a feedback loop that resulted in a boom.

As Kraków's position as a tourist destination grew internationally, its continuous presence on the list of the most polluted cities in the EU became a problem.

In the 2010s, Kraków (and Poland in general) was often featured in the international press as the European capital of air pollution. Even minuscule Polish cities gained international attention as they surpassed the pollution levels measured in China's capital, Beijing. For example, the small town of Skała, located south of Kraków and having fewer than 4000 inhabitants, made headlines in *The Financial Times* at the end of 2016 (Huber, 2016). As the fear that air pollution could be weaponized by Kraków's competitors on the global tourism market surfaced in the press, the push for a new political agenda on air pollution started to build up, uniting public and private concerns. Decision-makers started to perceive bad reputation as an obstacle for future economic growth, while private investors viewed it as a potential risk to investments.

Press coverage from that period indicates that concerns about the city's reputation were an important factor in prompting public officials to take more decisive action on air pollution (see e.g., Casey, 2013). Such a reputational mechanism is plausible in light of existing research, as air pollution affects destination image and perceived travel risk, while city branding increasingly functions as an element of urban policy and economic development strategy (see, e.g., Becken et al., 2017; Gu et al., 2024).

3.7 Delay in the Implementation of the EU Air Quality Directive

In 2013, the province of Małopolska was governed by a democratic conservative-liberal coalition, which was dominated by the party "Platforma Obywatelska (PO)" (English: Civic Platform). The same coalition was ruling the country. The city of Kraków, in turn, was led by its long-time president, identified with the mainstream left but effectively ruling with the support of the same liberal party (PO) that held power in both the province and the country. This created a political opportunity for the realization of a more liberal and progressive agenda in the area of environmental protection.

Such an agenda, by the way, became a political necessity. The reason for it was the delayed implementation of the EU 2008 Clean Air for Europe (CAFE) Directive.[20] Under the directive, Poland was obliged to adopt effective policies to lower air pollution. We mentioned already that despite the adoption of air protection programs in all Polish provinces by regional parliaments, the values set by the directive for specific pollutants were almost nowhere met. The ineffectiveness of those regional acts became apparent in the 2010s, even for the European Commission. What was worse, Poland's ineffective air pollution governance began to take its toll on the entire EU. From 2011 to 2012, an increase of 2.4% in B(a)P emissions in the EU-28 was reported, and the countries contributing the most were Poland (24%), Romania (21%), and Germany (18%) (EEA, 2014, p. 27). In consequence, the European Commission referred Poland to the Court of Justice of the European Union and requested for financial penalties—first in 2011 and then again in 2015.

On 10 December 2015, the European Commission announced that it had referred Poland to the Court of Justice of the European Union over persistently high levels of particulate matter, following a reasoned opinion sent to the Polish government in February 2015. The Commission stated that Poland had failed to comply with the 2008 CAFE Directive, as the daily limit value for PM10 had been persistently exceeded in 35 of the country's 46 air-quality zones for at least five years, includingin 2014. Moreover, in nine zones, the annual limit values had also been persistently exceeded. The Commission clearly indicated in its complaint that excess PM10 pollution in Poland was predominantly caused by low-stack emissions from household heating and that measures taken so far by regional parliaments to limit this pollution were insufficient. It further pointed to the lack of effective measures in air-quality protection programs adopted at regional and local levels, as well as the inappropriate transposition of the directive into national law, which made the enforcement of air protection deliberately complicated.[21] This constituted a strong political message, as the threat of severe financial penalties loomed over the Polish political class. For decision-makers, it became apparent that the European Commission expected Poland to address the problem of air pollution in a novel way.

As the Commission decided to refer Poland to the Court of Justice of the European Union (CJEU) over its failure to comply with the CAFE Directive, the government became concerned that an adverse judgment could expose the country to substantial financial penalties and jeopardize access to EU funds needed to finance major infrastructure investments then underway. This concern was expressed at different levels of government, and the Ministry of Environment signaled that, unless regional parliaments adopted more decisive measures in the next round of updates to their air protection programs, any financial consequences borne by the

[20] The Directive 2008/50/EC of the European Parliament and of the Council of 21 May 2008 on ambient air quality and cleaner air for Europe (OJ L 152), which is often referred to as the Clean Air for Europe (CAFE) Directive.

[21] As a result, the European Court of Justice (ECJ) has ruled against Poland on 22 February 2018 for persistently breaching EU air-quality limits.

state could ultimately be passed on to regions and municipalities.[22] For local governments in the most polluted regions and cities, this prospect was particularly serious. Their persistent failure to achieve the required improvements in air quality left them especially vulnerable if the central government were to introduce a mechanism for allocating responsibility for financial losses resulting from Poland's noncompliance with the Directive.[23]

EU legal pressure is a well-characterized mechanism in the area of environmental policy and governance (Ladi, 2005). Usually, it is understood as an external political-opportunity mechanism that alters the costs of governmental inaction (Jack, 2011). Certainly, this was the case for Poland.

The appearance of KAS was thus a good occasion for politicians to depart from the long-standing political consensus that had resulted in ineffective legislation. Civic online mobilization and high-profile protests were then instrumentally used as arguments in political debates in the local parliament to dismantle political opposition, mainly from conservative parties.

Therefore, existing evidence, specifically the chain of events just mentioned, strongly suggests that the shift in air-quality policies observed in Poland after 2015 was mainly the consequence of legal action undertaken by the European Commission, whereas social activism, involvement, and growing public awareness epitomized by KAS were only supplemental.

Politicians in Małopolska had also tried earlier to use antismog activism to achieve short-term political goals. When Kraków was bidding to host the 2022 Winter Olympics in 2013, city officials used the problem of air pollution to help justify the substantial public expenditure required by the planned event. During the public relations (PR) campaign financed by the city, the Olympics were advertised with the claim that they were actually the best way to tackle air pollution.[24] In fact, experts and activists were convinced that the event would rather impair antismog policies, as huge funds would be redirected to cover the lavish expenses the Olympics organization entailed. Although the whole political class reached a consensus and was determined to hold onto the idea of Winter Games in Kraków, a grassroots movement named "Krakow Against the Olympics" appeared in 2013 to protest against it. The initiative managed to persuade the city council to conduct a

---

[22] The account is based on the author's recollection of informal conversations with officials from the Małopolska region and their concerns voiced during formal meetings at that period of time. In the years 2014–2018, the author held the position of mayor of a small and heavily polluted city near Krakow and was involved in the proceedings that finally led to the adoption of the 2017 antismog resolution.

[23] On the day when the 2016 resolution for Krakow passed in the regional parliament of Małopolska, Vice Marshall Wojciech Kozak mentioned financial threat, alongside health costs, as the major reason for the implementation of the solid-fuel ban. He estimated that the amount of fines would amount to PLN 4000 million (EUR 930 million)—see Dominika Wantuch, Uchwała antysmogowa przyjęta! Zakaz palenia węglem i drewnem w Krakowie od 2019 r., Wyborcza, 15.01.2016.

[24] The twisted rationale behind the claim was that if the Olympics were to be held in heavily polluted Kraków, the central government would be obliged somehow to improve air quality to avoid international embarrassment.

local referendum in 2014, which finally terminated the idea. During the referendum campaign, the movement's leaders sued the president of Kraków over false claims about the role of the Olympics in combating air pollution. KAS joined the campaign and gave testimonies regarding their understanding of effective antismog policies in Małopolska.

Our considerations seem to be consistent with studies on civic involvement in Poland in that period. In particular, Maltby et al. (2024) examined whether policy change in Poland was driven primarily by objective pollution levels and information about them, which could increase public awareness, or whether activist groups both raised awareness and exerted direct pressure on policymakers to address the problem. The study demonstrated that local public awareness of air pollution was largely independent of the presence and activity of smog alerts. This suggests that the contribution of activism to policy change operated less through raising public awareness and more through its direct or mediated influence on policymakers. Through effective communication campaigns, KAS garnered the interest of the national press, which in turn increased political attention to the issue. Whether policymakers would have acted in the absence of such support remains unresolved.

Before we move further, however, it is important to note that although the majority of provincial parliaments adopted a series of antismog resolutions inspired by the example of Małopolska, the issue of delayed implementation of the CAFE Directive was not resolved, and air pollution remained a problem almost everywhere in the country. The Polish government's arrears became an issue discussed by the European Commission again in 2018 (Olszewski, 2018). Finally, in 2025, Poland was again referred to the Court of Justice of the European Union by the European Commission for failing to ensure effective access to justice for individuals and NGOs seeking either to require public authorities to adopt an adequate air quality plan or to challenge the legality or adequacy of already adopted plans.[25]

3.8 The EEA Report on Premature Deaths in Poland

Two additional circumstances appear to have been relevant to the adoption of antismog resolutions in Małopolska. In 2014, the European Environment Agency (EEA) published a report on the state of air quality in Europe. The report identified Poland, alongside Bulgaria, as one of the EU Member States with the highest mean PM concentrations associated with the residential sector. On page 55, it contained a table presenting estimates of "premature deaths attributable to PM2.5 and O3 exposure in 2011 in 40 European countries and the EU-28." For Poland, the estimated number was 42,412 deaths. By comparison, the total number of premature deaths in the EU-28 was estimated at 430,219 (EEA, 2014, p. 55).

[25] See the official press info at https://ec.europa.eu/commission/presscorner/detail/lv/ip_25_1509.

The report received extensive coverage in the national press and was used by KAS in its advocacy for the coal ban in Kraków and elsewhere. It provided activists with a powerful science-based argument that was difficult for representatives of the coal trade and mining interests to contest in public debate. More recent research likewise suggests that the official quantification of the health costs associated with domestic combustion, presented by an authoritative EU institution, was "important in generating awareness of the scale of the problem" (see Maltby et al., 2024, p. 1340).

The same study also identifies access to "hyperlocal (...) networks of sensors" as another important factor in building public awareness of air pollution in Poland (see Maltby et al., 2024). This constitutes the second factor relevant to our analysis and is considered in the following section.

3.9 Local Sensors and Visualization of Air Pollution

Air-quality assessments and monitoring in Poland were carried out by the Regional Inspector of Environmental Protection, an institution subordinate to the minister responsible for the environment and consisting of a main office and 16 provincial inspectorates. Before 2000 in Poland, there were as many as 100 certified measurement stations operated by the inspectorates, and the growth of the monitoring network was rather slow. Until 2010, the number of stations had not even reached 200. As those stations were located primarily in big agglomerations and industrial areas, awareness of poor air quality among the general population was rather limited.[26]

The development of the network outside of agglomerations was also hindered by resistance from local politicians, who were reluctant to reveal the actual scale of pollution in their communities. It was convenient for them to pretend that air pollution was a feature of big cities like Kraków, where the problem was already highly publicized.[27] The mass appearance of affordable air pollution sensors was a game-changer, as it democratized measurement, taking it out of the hands of politicians. This finally opened the eyes of the people, who now realized the scale of the problem.

While the concern over smog became more prevalent in public discourse in Poland, a group of colleagues and marathon runners faced the everyday dilemma of

[26] While the official monitoring network was constantly developed by the government, it now consists of almost 400 sensors operated by the inspectorate.

[27] Sometimes that resistance took grotesque forms, like in the case of the mayor of Sucha Beskidzka (a small town in Małopolska), who cut the electric cable of the monitoring station to sabotage measurements in order to hide the poor state of the atmosphere in his touristic town. According to the conversations we held during official meetings, among the strongest smog deniers were mayors from mountain resorts and spa towns, concerned about the reputational losses of their communities if public opinion learned the true scale of air pollution. Actually, the air in places historically visited by patients with respiratory problems was more toxic than the air those patients breathe at home.

planning outdoor training sessions in ways that would minimize their exposure to polluted air. They quickly discovered that inhabitants of Kraków lacked access to current and reliable data regarding air pollution levels. As they were also students at the AGH University of Science and Technology in Kraków, they had the capability to address the problem through a technical solution. The idea of building a scalable network of low-cost sensors emerged, and soon after, Airly—a company headquartered in Kraków—was born to commercialize it.

The final product consists of the following components integrated into the comprehensive system: (a) a distributed network of sensors capable of measuring in real time concentrations of particulate matter (PM2.5 directly, PM1/PM10 interpolated), alongside atmospheric parameters such as air temperature, pressure, and humidity, and sending those measurements via the Global System for Mobile Communications (GSM) protocol to the server; (b) a dedicated web platform and mobile application that serve as intuitive interfaces for data visualization and public access; and (c) a system of advanced algorithms to generate 24-hour air-quality forecasts based on collected data. Currently, Airly has achieved substantial market penetration in Poland, operating a dense and widespread network of over 2800 sensors across the country.[28]

The general idea behind the product was to enable individual users to buy a relatively cheap yet reliable sensor and take part in citizen data gathering, contributing to the general effort of raising awareness of the local pollution problem. The free app provided data access to anyone, whether they own a sensor or not, allowing the network to grow, primarily in Kraków. Meanwhile, in other places, inhabitants gained the power to check pollution hour by hour and street by street. The information on air quality was presented on users' mobile phones or computers as colorful overlays of aerial maps. This enabled citizens to directly "see" pollution and its dynamics through its visual and spatial representation.

Airly sensors completely changed the social perception of air pollution in Poland. They made possible comparisons between urbanized city; industrial, suburban zones; and the countryside—for the first time providing proof that the countryside could be much more heavily polluted than city centers. The sensors helped pinpoint the actual sources of pollution (individual buildings, often in suburban areas). They helped citizens verify the actual effectiveness of antismog measures adopted by politicians. All of this evidence was highly persuasive, thanks to the language of visual information. Existing scholarly sources underscore that the expansion of low-cost sensing not only altered the spatial resolution and accessibility of air-quality information but also increased residents' involvement in the problem through participation in the production and interpretation of environmental evidence (Gabrys, 2014; Rai et al., 2017).

As air pollution was becoming an important issue in public debates at that time, people craved information on air quality. Decision-makers, on the other hand,

[28] The primary source for information on Airly, its history, and its products is its company's website at https://airly.org/en/.

looked for justification for stricter regulations. Many municipalities, even small towns, started commercial partnerships with Airly, encouraged by wide media coverage of the pollution problem, indicating the lack of education and reliable information on the actual levels of pollutants. This resulted in the development of rather sophisticated networks of sensors, on many occasions integrated, for example, with local procedures for pollution-level warnings.[29] Interestingly, the transformation from a central network of high-cost monitoring stations to low-cost dispersed sensors is a trend that had been foreseen over a decade ago (Snyder et al., 2013).

Airly introduced its product on the market in 2016, so it had no direct influence on the policy shift in Kraków and Małopolska; however, it definitely helped change public perception elsewhere, as in the following years, antismog resolutions were adopted by other regional parliaments. The authorities in 14 out of 16 regions in Poland passed appropriate regulations without significant opposition, mainly due to popular agreement on the occurrence of the problem. Existing studies demonstrate that public understanding of air pollution is shaped primarily by personal, localized experience (e.g., Bickerstaff & Walker, 2001).

Airly sensors clearly played a role in the implementation of the antismog resolutions. Airly helped establish long-lasting popular support for the resolutions by making people aware of the scale of air pollution in the region. Moreover, the sensor network made it easier to recognize that a substantial share of the remaining air pollution in Kraków originated outside the city, which helped sustain public support for the anti-smog policy despite its initially limited visible effects. In defense against critics, supporters of the ban could therefore argue that persistently high pollution levels in Kraków did not necessarily indicate policy failure, as they were partly attributable to atmospheric transport from neighboring municipalities.[30] This argument, prevalent in debates at that time, definitely helped the municipal authorities further enforce the ban.

3.10 Discussion of the Causality Behind the Adoption of the 2016 and 2017 Resolutions

During the first half of the 2010s, a significant change in the public perception of air pollution occurred in Kraków and Małopolska. Severe pollution had been documented for decades, but it had not previously resulted in regulatory measures comparable to the resolutions ultimately adopted for Kraków in 2016 and for the

[29] A good example of such integration was Wadowice, a relatively small municipality of 38,000 inhabitants near Krakow, where Airly sensors were installed in elementary schools (and other public buildings) in the city and ten neighboring villages to also provide visual information on air quality and was integrated with the early warning system to protect pupils from pollutants.

[30] It is interesting to note that the visual information on pollution provided by Airly was sufficient to support the ban (to dismantle the arguments of the critics) but, at the same time, was not enough to nudge people outside Krakow to remove their solid-fuel installations.

remainder of Małopolska in 2017. Explaining this change requires an account of how the long-normalized condition became politically salient and how particular regulatory responses became suddenly conceivable.

The available material excludes a monocausal explanation. In our opinion, the policy shift resulted from the interaction of several circumstances, none of which was sufficient in isolation (see the table).

Causes for the policy shift in Małopolska in 2016–2017	
1	European Commission actions against Poland, especially the complaint before the EU Court of Justice in December 2015 (caused mobilization among decision-makers at the national and regional levels)
2	Emergence of "Krakowski Alarm Smogowy," its galvanizing campaigns, and clever political lobbying (gave decision-makers justification for proposing otherwise unpopular regulations)
3	The European Environment Agency Report 2014 on premature deaths attributable to air pollution in Poland (caused moral panic in the press and the general public, albeit limited to the more educated part of society, mostly inhabitants of bigger cities)
4	Emergence of the low-cost sensor network, giving access to reliable real-time data on air pollution (allows even ordinary people to "see" the quality of air in their own vicinity, transforming air pollution from an abstract issue into a concrete one)

The abovementioned factors were not simply additive, and their significance, according to our observations, depended largely on their interaction. For example, KAS communication proved more effective because politicians had become more receptive to its arguments as EU pressure increased the need for a visible policy response. The significance of KAS campaigns for public perception of air pollution grew because of the publicization of new scientific evidence on health risks and the appearance of easily accessible visual data on localized air pollution. Access to those data, in turn, became important through the awareness produced by communication campaigns facilitated by KAS, which underlined the need for up-to-date information on air pollution. Finally, publicly available reliable data on pollution in the vicinity helped the public to assess the effectiveness of the policy responses proposed by politicians.

The resulting explanation on the adoption of antismog resolutions in Małopolska is conjunctural: the policy shift emerged from a configuration of mutually reinforcing conditions rather than from one dominant cause. In other words, we argue that the configuration of circumstances outlined above provides a plausible explanation for the adoption of the 2016 and 2017 resolutions. It remains uncertain, however, whether the emergence of KAS was a necessary component of that configuration.

The involvement of KAS was definitely not a sufficient condition for the adoption of the 2016 and 2017 resolutions. But are there any reasons to believe it was a necessary one?[31] Based on a reconstruction of events from previous paragraphs, the

[31] It is important to note, however, that the appearance of KAS was presented as necessary for facilitating a policy shift by the president of Krakow himself: "Before 2012, residents weren't particularly interested in this topic. Only that year proved to be a turning point: posters appeared

causal role of KAS can be described in several ways. First, the organization contributed to problem framing: it identified residential solid-fuel combustion as a major preventable source of pollution and presented regulatory intervention as morally necessary. KAS also acted as an interpreter of expert knowledge, translating it into messages and visuals relatable to the broad public and appealing to their concerns. Perhaps even more importantly, KAS generated media amplification enough to affect the political agenda. Sustained media attention of the problem made it more difficult for public authorities to continue to ignore it. Wide coverage of events organized by KAS also enabled the organization to engage directly in policy advocacy. Its founders communicated formally and informally with officials and participated in consultations to promote specific regulatory instruments, then defended them publicly. In doing so, KAS performed a legitimating function for antismog policies since its campaigns allowed decision-makers to present restrictive regulations as an appropriate response to civic demands. It is important to remember that restricting the use of coal and wood imposed real costs on households and interfered with practices previously considered by many as private choices. Political actors, thus, had strong incentives to avoid such restrictions.

Although all these processes clearly demonstrate the importance of KAS in the adoption of antismog resolutions in Kraków and Małopolska, one may still question whether the emergence of KAS was a necessary causal condition for it.

Public awareness cannot be treated simply as an independent cause situated between environmental conditions and political decisions. Rather, it is produced by various actors within the broadly understood political process, including media, nongovernmental organizations, and state institutions. The activity of KAS was entangled in that process. However, to assume that politicians simply followed public opinion is naivety. Activism alters the political environment without necessarily becoming the principal motivation of decision-makers.[32] Our case study seems to provide us with a good argument for that claim.

The number of people whose decisions were fundamental to passing both antismog resolutions by the regional parliament of Małopolska is quite limited. Based on the author's participant observation, the whole process of formulating, passing, and enacting the resolutions was controlled by a few individuals, and most of them were politicians acting for political reasons. For them, air pollution was not a problem in its own right but rather a means to other ends. Such instrumentalization was especially visible in the case of the Vice Marshall of the Małopolska province, Wojciech Kozak, who became the face of the antismog resolutions—especially the second one—when his party [Polskie Stronnictwo Ludowe (PSL)] was part of the ruling coalition in the regional parliament. A couple of years later, in 2022, when

in Krakow, journalists took a keen interest in the topic, and people began participating in demonstrations. This mobilized officials and politicians to take action"—an interview with Jacek Majchrowski by Patryk Salamon, LoveKrakow.pl, 22.10.2021, https://10lat.lovekrakow.pl/aktualnosci/jacek-majchrowski-wymienilismy-ponad-45-tysiecy-piecow-i-wydalismy-na-ten-cel-blisko-340-mln-zl_43257.html.

[32] For similar conclusions, see Maltby et al. (2024).

the regional parliament was already under the control of the populist party [Prawo i Sprawiedliwość (PiS)], he voted to postpone the entry into force of the 2017 resolution he had "so vigorously" promoted before, helping PiS effectively dismantle its binding force. The liberal press and, of course, KAS regarded that decision as a betrayal of the cause (Fijak, 2022). From the perspective of cabinet politics, however, the decision can be understood as an attempt to balance the expectations of the electorate with the demands of emerging political alliances.

Also, the president of Kraków, Jacek Majchrowski—who in 2013, quite surprisingly for the public, supported unconditionally the citywide ban on coal—was, in the following years, quite reluctant to enforce regulations, relying more on financial nudges, information campaigns, and even social ostracism facilitated by KAS against violators of the ban than on administrative measures.[33] As a consequence, even to this day, there are a certain number of illegal installations operating in Kraków, effectively polluting the atmosphere in the city. For a long time, the slow pace of replacing inefficient installations in neighboring communities (constituting the metropolitan area of Kraków) served as a convenient excuse for not dedicating too many city resources to enforcement, as poor air quality could be explained by the transport of pollutants from the surrounding communities of Kraków.

These two personal examples demonstrate, at least to a certain extent, that even the ban on solid fuels in Kraków can be interpreted primarily as an instance of symbolic legislation rather than evidence of genuine concern among local policymakers about air quality and its consequences. Political support for the antismog resolutions from regional decision-makers was therefore contingent and reversible. Even the subsequent adoption in 2016 and 2017 of the two divergent antismog resolutions by the same regional parliament can be interpreted as evidence of the continuing influence of political constraints. Namely, media visibility of KAS campaigns and civic mobilization expressed through local alerts did not translate into a prohibition on the use of solid fuels throughout the province. The latter resolution may in fact then be understood as a step back in tackling air pollution. Nonetheless, KAS contributed to both resolutions, and the level of public awareness of the air pollution problem seemed to be even greater in 2017 than in 2016 or 2015. In our opinion, this demonstrates that in the case of both resolutions, there were other factors, besides social activism and public awareness, that turned out to be decisive in determining the content of the adopted regulations. Actually, the experience of local antismog initiatives—i.e., other smog alerts that emerged after KAS in other cities, towns, and provinces—demonstrates that public awareness campaigns and civic

[33] At the beginning of 2020, it is half of year after the 2016 resolution came in force, still there were 2850 illegal solid-fuel installations in Krakow, but the president explicitly declared that because of the ambiguity of the national law, he would not exercise his powers to remove them by force, thus enforcing the ban—see the response to the interpellation of city councilor Łukasz Gibała given by the mayor of Krakow on 20 February 2020, document OR 03.0003.1622.2020. At the beginning of 2021, still approx. 900 illegal solid-fuel installations remained in Krakow—see the response to the interpellation of City Councilor Łukasz Gibała given by the mayor of Krakow on 5 March 2021, document OR 03.0003.2696.2021.

involvement may exist without producing regulatory measures equivalent to the Kraków prohibition.

Available evidence suggests that KAS should be described most accurately as a contributing cause for the adoption of both resolutions but not a necessary condition in the causal sense. It is not possible to claim that no policy change would have occurred without the movement. On the other hand, without the increasing pressure associated with Poland's noncompliance with EU air-quality obligations, KAS campaigns might have produced even greater awareness without any regulatory outcome. The organization's influence was thus catalytic, as it enabled the adoption of certain regulations at a specific moment in a specific region. Without KAS, policy change in Kraków and Małopolska would probably have occurred anyway; however, the timeline and the prohibitive force of the measures actually adopted are matters of discussion, since KAS was not merely an ornamental accompaniment to the decisions of regional politicians. KAS influenced how the problem was understood by them and the public, which solutions entered the political agenda, and how restrictive regulation could be justified. Notably, this interpretation of the role of KAS—and of the public awareness it helped to generate—is consistent with research showing that the political consequences of social movements depend on a broader configuration of conditions, including the structure of political opportunities, rather than directly on the scale of public mobilization (e.g., Amenta et al., 2010; Meyer, 2004).

3.11 Evaluation of the Effectiveness of the 2016 and 2017 Resolutions

The adoption of the two separate resolutions, reflecting two different philosophies of environmental legislation, gave us a unique occasion to compare both types of regulation. Under the 2016 resolution for Kraków alone, the use of solid fuels for heating has been prohibited since 1 September 2019. The 2017 resolution, in turn, was originally scheduled to take effect on 1 January 2023 with respect to the least efficient heating installations; however, in September 2022, the Małopolska regional parliament decided to postpone the deadline until 1 May 2024.[34]

We propose two different quantitative criteria for estimating the effectiveness of both resolutions: (a) the measured air quality in both regions (in Kraków and in Małopolska beyond Kraków) and (b) the number of inefficient solid-fuel installations operating in territories where the resolutions were adopted. These criteria are, of course, not independent of each other, but we will consider them separately for the sake of our argument.

---

[34] Uchwała Nr LIX/842/22 Sejmiku Województwa Małopolskiego z dnia 26 września 2022 r. w sprawie zmiany uchwały Nr XXXII/452/17 Sejmiku Województwa Małopolskiego z dnia 23 stycznia 2017 r.

Let us start with the measured levels of pollutants. The analysis published by KAS gave us a first glimpse of the situation. Using official data from the network operated by the state's environmental inspectorate, experts compared the dynamics of air pollution between 2012 and 2020 in Kraków and in areas outside of the municipality, finding that the annual mean concentration of PM10, PM2.5, and B(a)P in PM10, as well as the number of days exceeding daily PM10 concentrations, dropped significantly faster in Kraków (Kleczkowski & Kotarba, 2020). The mean concentration of PM10 during heating seasons decreased by 45.42% in Kraków, whereas in the rest of the province, only by 28.73%. Analogously, measured PM2.5 fell by 43.76% in Kraków and 32.15% in the rest of the province. What is more important, in the period 2014–2020, there was a huge 41.5% decline in the mean concentration of B(a)P in Kraków during heating seasons, whereas in the remainder of the province, it rose significantly by 14.4%.

Such a result, in our opinion, could be interpreted as a consequence of a set of circumstances. The obvious one is the relative ineffectiveness of the 2017 resolution for Małopolska. For example, although the national government, under pressure from KAS/PAS, introduced, in 2017, regulations preventing the official sale of new inefficient installations (see below), such products were still offered in Małopolska for years. Hence, many newly constructed homes were equipped with high-polluting installations despite the fact that it was illegal to use them. Apparently, people—rightly so—did not believe in the effective enforcement of the antismog regulations, especially since prominent politicians of the ruling party (PiS) were constantly assuring their voters in state media that coal was the "national treasure" and its combustion was part of the nation's identity. In 2017, even the sitting Minister of Health, Konstanty Radziwił—by the way a medical doctor—called air pollution "a little more theoretical than real danger." These and similar statements by PiS politicians[35] were strongly criticized by KAS/PAS,[36] yet they appear to have resonated with parts of the public, with consequences that were reflected in air-quality measurements. Moreover, there were no regulations establishing emission standards for room heaters (fireplaces, stoves, and furnaces). As a result, approximately 100,000 such devices were legally sold in Poland each year, with a substantial share of these sales occurring in the mountainous areas of Małopolska.[37]

The study also found that, throughout the period examined, the number of days on which PM10 concentrations exceeded the 50 μg/m^3 limit was higher in Kraków than in the rest of the province. However, this number declined consistently each

[35] The President of Poland, Andrzej Duda, announced at COP in Katowice that Poland will mine coal for hundreds of years. Despite the EU climate policy, Minister of Environment Henryk Kowalczyk identified the source of the concentrations of PM10 during Polish winters, with the sand from the Sahara Desert allegedly transported to Poland by wind from overseas.

[36] https://polskialarmsmogowy.pl/2017/01/bulwersujaca-wypowiedz-ministra-zdrowia-list-otwarty-polskiego-alarmu-smogowego/.

[37] It is important to note that we qualify the lack of "background" regulations required for the 2017 resolution to be effective or the risk of weak enforcement as design flaws of the resolution itself—as decision-makers should take all of those factors into account in the early stages of planning of the new regulations.

year in Kraków, whereas in many other parts of Małopolska it remained stable or declined more slowly. The higher number of days exceeding the limit in Kraków was attributed to the greater density of emission sources, associated with the city's higher population density. Additionally, the authors pointed out that pollutants were transported into Kraków from neighboring municipalities.[38]

Further studies confirmed these conclusions. For example, Kicińska and Jawdyńska (2025) calculated the mean concentrations of PM2.5, PM10, nitrogen dioxide (NO_2), SO_2, and ozone (O3) in Kraków in the years 2010–2021 using data from four stationary sensors belonging to the network operated by the environmental inspectorate. The measured PM10 levels in Kraków exceeded the annual mean limit value (40 μg/m^3) for the whole period. Although they had been decreasing continuously between 2010 and 2019, the quality of air improved significantly from 2019 when the solid-fuel ban came into force. From 2019 through to the end of the studied period, PM10 values were within the legal limits set by the 2008 Directive—both during winters (in the heating seasons) and on an annual basis. By contrast, the PM2.5 annual mean value exceeded the legal limit (20 μg/m^3) in each year of the analyzed period, though a downward trend was evident.

In 2010–2021, the measured annual concentrations of SO_2 were within the limit value (20 μg/m^3), although there was a large difference between the heating and nonheating seasons, which decreased over the period. It is also worth noting that the highest SO_2 concentration (18 μg/m^3) was observed during the heating season of 2011/2012, while the lowest SO_2 concentration (5 μg/m^3) was recorded in 2020 and 2021.

B(a)P levels were dramatically exceeded in the studied period. During the 2010/2011 heating season, the measured B(a)P was 20 times higher than the target value (1 ng/m^3). Yet B(a)P concentrations decreased over the whole period, with the most rapid drop occurring between the 2015 and 2016 heating seasons. During the heating seasons of 2020 and 2021, B(a)P concentrations were the lowest ("only" four times higher than the target value). Therefore, data for both SO_2 and B(a)P strongly suggest the effectiveness of the solid-fuel ban in Kraków.

The adoption and implementation of the ban have yielded indisputable results in Kraków's air quality. According to Kicińska and Jawdyńska, annual concentrations of B(a)P decreased over 10 years by more than 60%, SO_2 by more than 50%, and PM10 and PM2.5 by approximately 40%. During heating seasons, the reduction was much stronger, reaching 71.5% for the most problematic pollutant, B(a) P. Kraków was also the city where average B(a)P concentrations decreased the most over the period, surpassed only by Wrocław (64% reduction); however, that agglomeration has a smaller population and more favorable geographic conditions.

The improving quality of the aero-sanitary conditions in Kraków was also evident in the number of days when the legal limit for the mean concentration of PM10 (50 μg/m^3) was exceeded. Initially, this number was almost always greater than the permitted 35 days. From 2015, when there were almost 100 such days in Kraków, a

[38] It was estimated by the numerical modeling that metropolitan transport of pollutants was responsible for 45% of measured PM10 concentrations in 2018.

clear downward trend can be observed, with 2020 being the first year in which the number of exceedance days approached the permitted maximum of 35.

More recent data confirm the conclusions drawn from the described analysis. The mean 24-hour concentration of PM10 in Kraków decreased from 72.1 μg/m^3 to 33.8 μg/m^3 during the heating seasons of 2014/2015 and 2022/2023, while in the rest of Małopolska, it fell from 50.7 μg/m^3 to 30.6 μg/m^3. The mean annual value of B(a)P in Kraków decreased from 8 ng/m^3 in 2010 to 1 ng/m^3 in 2024 (the highest concentration recorded on any sensor within the city). In Sucha Beskidzka (a typical small town situated in the mountains of Małopolska), it decreased from 19 ng/m^3 in 2012 to 5 ng/m^3 in 2024.[39]

As we can see, there was an 87.5% reduction in the highly problematic pollutant B(a)P in Kraków and only 73.7% in Sucha Beskidzka. Additionally, the reduction in PM10 was stronger in Kraków (53%) than outside of the city (39.6%). What is more important, though, is that the target value for B(a)P was not achieved in Sucha Beskidzka, and nowhere else in Małopolska, but was achieved in Kraków.

However, there are also studies whose authors continue to associate air quality in Kraków with substantial health risks, estimating that both non-carcinogenic and carcinogenic risks significantly exceeded acceptable levels. Based on data from the air monitoring system operated by the Regional Environmental Protection Inspectorate in Kraków, they found that, although air quality in Kraków improved over the 2005–2020 period, winter conditions showed relatively little improvement and measured PM2.5 concentrations exceeded the World Health Organization (WHO) recommended value of 25 μg/m^3 on a daily basis (Traczyk & Gruszecka-Kosowska, 2020). From this perspective, even the effectiveness of the 2016 resolution remains open to question when assessed in terms of absolute air-quality improvements and associated health risks. Its effectiveness should therefore be understood as relative rather than absolute. With this reservation in mind, it is reasonable to conclude that the 2016 resolution for Kraków—i.e., the total ban on solid fuels—was more effective than the 2017 resolution for the rest of Małopolska. This conclusion becomes even more plausible when the second criterion proposed for assessing the effectiveness of the anti-smog resolutions is considered: the actual number of high-emission heating installations replaced.

The resolution for Kraków banned solid-fuel combustion altogether and provided for a relatively short transition period before the ban took effect on 1 September 2019. The municipal government not only initiated the legislative process for the ban but also supplemented the law with intensive information campaigns directed at the city's inhabitants and with generous subsidies (in some periods covering up to 100% of the investment value). Subsidies for replacing installations prohibited under the 2016 resolution were financed from the budgets of the municipal, provincial, and central governments.

[39]According to data from the General Inspectorate for Environmental Protection in Poland, presented on the website of the Marshall Office of Małopolska, https://powietrze.malopolska.pl/program-ochrony-powietrza/efekty-realizacji/.

The 2017 resolution, dedicated to the rest of the territory of Małopolska, introduced a rather complicated set of bans—differentiating between different categories of solid-fuel installations (based on their emission class) and different categories of solid fuel. The idea was to gradually incentivize individuals to replace their outdated heating systems, beginning with the worst ones. The transition period was therefore relatively long—for some types of installations extending until the end of 2026—while the replacement of heating installations received only limited financial support from the state, regional, and local authorities, typically covering 30–50% of the investment costs.

As we mentioned earlier, the two resolutions reflected competing "philosophies" of addressing policy problems such as air pollution: a command-and-control approach and an approach based on economic incentives, respectively. The design of the 2017 resolution also appears to have rested on the assumption that, well before the restrictions came into force, changes in energy and fuel markets would encourage households to comply with the policy. The subsidies offered to those who removed their old heating installations were understood merely as an additional incentive to act. An alternative interpretation, however, is that the design of the regulation also reflected political calculations aimed at maintaining support among the rural electorate in Małopolska, which tended to resist proposals for more stringent regulation, including a ban on solid fuels.

After several years, the divergent outcomes of the two approaches became increasingly visible in the rates at which high-emission heating installations were removed in Kraków and in the rest of Małopolska. These differences were also reflected in measured pollutant concentrations within the areas covered by the two regulatory regimes. According to available data, between 2016 and 2020, 18,898 solid-fuel heating installations were removed or replaced in Kraków alone.[40] However, according to official information, approximately 900 such installations remained in the city in 2021.[41] Additionally, between 2013 and 2015, when the possibility of introducing a ban on solid-fuel combustion was first publicly discussed, as many as 7854 installations were removed (Marshall Office, 2022, p. 4). These figures allow two additional percentages to be calculated. The first represents the proportion of solid-fuel installations removed in Kraków between 2016, when the ban was adopted, and 2020, shortly after it entered into force in September 2019. The second represents the proportion removed over the broader period of municipal policy beginning in 2013, when the ban was first proposed. The resulting figures are very similar: 95% and 96.7%, respectively.[42]

---

[40] In 2021, an additional 21 were removed. After 2021, the removal of cauldrons continued, albeit the number of removed installations for each year did not exceed ten, so this seems to be irrelevant for our analysis.

[41] Response to the interpellation of City Councilor Łukasz Gibała, given by the mayor of Krakow on 5 March 2021, document OR 03.0003.2696.2021.

[42] Our calculation follows this scheme: rate of replacement = (number of installations removed in all years in the given period) / (number of installations removed in all years in the given period + 900 installations still left to be replaced in 2021). The first ratio: 18,898/18,898 + 900. The second ratio: 7854 + 18,898 / 7854 + 18898 + 900.

A key element of the measures implemented by the Kraków authorities was the provision of financial support for furnace replacement, covering 100% of residents' expenses in most cases. The city council adopted this program in 2014.[43] Additionally, the city authorities prepared a protection program for people experiencing energy poverty due to increased heating costs resulting from a permanent change in the heating system. This program was implemented between 2014 and 2022.[44]

Thus, Kraków had a coherent, results-oriented, low-emission policy that included a ban on solid-fuel use, first introduced in 2013 and then reiterated in a 2016 resolution. A large percentage of the target for replacing high-emission installations was achieved precisely because of this consistent, long-term policy. In addition to the clear signal for action constituted by the ban, residents were provided with generous financial incentives, which eliminated resistance to bearing the increased costs incurred by the prohibition. Given the combination of consistent communication, clear regulatory signals, and generous subsidies, the high level of implementation of the 2016 resolution is readily understandable. Likewise, it is not surprising that similar results were not replicated in the rest of Małopolska.

According to official estimates, initially there were approximately 436,700 high-emission installations planned for removal in Małopolska outside of Kraków (EEA, 2022). Data provided by the Office of the Marshall of Małopolska (Marshall Office, 2025, p. 2) indicate that for the period 2017–2022, about 68,046 installations were removed and replaced. In the period 2017–2024, it was approximately 96,642 installations, and in the period 2013–2016—preceding the adoption of the 2017 resolution—it was an additional 5358 installations. Hence, those numbers translate to the ratio 15.6% represents the effectiveness of the 2017 resolution from the moment of its adoption by the regional parliament to the planned date of implementation (the end of 2022). The ratio 22% represents the effectiveness of the resolution to this day, including replacement realized to the end of 2024. Finally, the ratio 23.3% tells us something about the general effectiveness of antismog policies in Małopolska, expressed in consecutively amended air protection programs of 2013, 2017, 2020 and 2023. Obviously, it is weak, as approx. 334,700 installations still wait to be removed in the region.[45]

The more direct and independent data that have become available just recently not only confirm, to a large extent, the estimations presented above but also appear to be quite devastating for one's evaluation of the 2017 resolution and the general antipollution policies implemented in Małopolska. These data were derived from

---

[43] Uchwała Nr CXXI/1918/14 Rady Miasta Krakowa z dnia 5 listopada 2014 r. w sprawie przyjęcia Programu Ograniczania Niskiej Emisji dla Miasta Krakowa.

[44] Uchwała Nr XC/1355/13 Rady Miasta Krakowa z dnia 20 listopada 2013 r. w sprawie przyjęcia lokalnego programu pomocy społecznej w postaci Lokalnego Programu Osłonowego dla osób, które poniosły zwiększone koszty grzewcze lokalu związane z trwałą zmianą systemu ogrzewania opartego na paliwie stałym na jeden z systemów proekologicznych.

[45] It should, of course, be considered that the 2016 regulation is already in full force from September 2019, while the 2017 regulation introduced an incomplete ban from the middle of 2024. Yet the timetable of each resolution was also deliberately chosen as part of the policy, so its influence on the ratio is not an independent factor but rather should be regarded as one of the circumstances that determine the effectiveness of the regulation.

the new database organized at the national level—a central register of building emissions (CEEB).[46] As of June 2024, the database was 78% completed, indicating 255,366 solid-fuel cauldrons still for removal in accordance with the 2017 resolution, as well as 268,662 room heaters, including heating appliances such as fireplaces, stoves, kitchen ranges, and even tile stoves.

The total number of devices that should be decommissioned under the current resolution is still 524,028, despite the fact that the deadline for its implementation expired at the end of 2022 (later postponed by 1.5 years). This figure also includes devices that must be decommissioned by the end of 2026, but they represent only a minority of the problem described here (131,498 devices compared to 123,868 that should have been removed long ago and 268,662 high-emission room heaters). Bearing in mind that the data contained in the database still do not cover all households in Małopolska, the effectiveness of the measures taken so far is simply dramatically low. More importantly, it seems that when air-quality programs in Małopolska were developed, the number of solid-fuel installations in the province was seriously underestimated, as the actual number of high-emission appliances indicated in the CEEB is larger than the number initially assumed by decision-makers (436,700).

The quality of data in the CEEB turned out to be a problem itself. On many occasions, local communities complained that centrally gathered data did not represent the actual situation because of the faulty design of reporting and data structure. These allegations regarding the CEEB's functioning were confirmed in a report by the Supreme Audit Office (NIK), which pointed to problems with data reliability due to, for example, the duplication of the number of heat sources reported in a given location (NIK, 2025). At the same time, however, the latest data show that air pollution levels have increased across Poland, including in Małopolska, over the past two years, suggesting a genuine increase in the number of high-emission heating appliances rather than an apparent increase resulting solely from inaccuracies in the CEEB data.[47] Also, the NIK report leaves no doubt about the failure of antismog policies in Poland, including Małopolska, pointing to the low implementation of the antismog resolutions across the country. According to NIK calculations, replacing high-emission heat sources in Poland will take up to 24 years (NIK, 2025).

Furthermore, by choosing not to introduce a ban on solid fuels in Małopolska, decision-makers seemingly ignored the scale of the high-emission installations market. Meanwhile, from 2013 (the beginning of the development of the current antismog policy in the province) until mid-2018, (when regulations regarding solid-fuel appliances were introduced at the state level[48]), approximately 12,000 new

[46] Centralna Ewidencja Emisyjności Budynków, avaiable at https://zone.gunb.gov.pl/pl.

[47] IQAir's World Air Quality Report shows that the annual average concentration of PM2.5 fine particulate matter in Poland in 2025 reached 15.4 μg/m^3, which is higher than in 2024 (14.8 μg/m^3) and 2023 (14.1 μg/m^3)—see IQAir (2026).

[48] See Regulation of the Minister of Development and Finance of August 1, 2017, regarding requirements for solid-fuel boilers, Dz.U. 2017 poz. 1690. More on this topic in the following subsections.

solid-fuel-burning appliances were sold in Małopolska, 80% of which were relatively cheap, low-efficiency units that did not meet any emission standards (Lochno, 2017, p. 22). These appliances not only replaced older devices of the same type but were also installed in newly constructed buildings and even replaced lower-emission boilers. Research conducted among the residents of Małopolska showed that they were eager to switch from low-emission sources to high-emission alternatives due to the short investment return period (2–4 years) (Lochno, 2017, p. 23). Another important factor was the sense of personal independence from outside energy sources, which was absent in the case of the use of network solutions (gas, electricity, district heating). So—again—scholarship confirms that socioeconomic (and cultural) factors were important for the successful implementation of air pollution policies. Unfortunately, they were largely ignored in practice. Meanwhile, public awareness of the scale of the problem and its health consequences was not so crucial, apparently.

Interestingly, all those socioeconomic factors were enumerated as a significant problem in the justification for the Air Protection Program for Małopolska, passed in 2017. The document even stated that without clearly formulated prohibitions, "the remedial measures taken may prove insufficient" in "eliminating low-quality fuels and boilers that do not meet established emission parameters" (Lochno, 2017, p. 23). Unfortunately, there is more to the story. In the same document, there was an analysis of potential scenarios represented by different public policies to be adopted in Małopolska (Lochno, 2017, pp. 148–180). The analysis explicitly stated that only the adoption of a solid-fuel ban similar to the one in Kraków would lead to the improvement in air quality required under the CAFE Directive. It said, without such a ban, "the required air quality levels will not be achieved by 2023."

Nonetheless, for political reasons, the regional parliament (assembly) of Małopolska was unable to vote for the only effective scenario indicated in its own policy analysis, deliberately choosing a solution that was less effective and less reasonable (in the context of existing knowledge about the health consequences of air pollution). The 2017 resolution was thus ineffective by design, insofar as it incorporated instruments insufficient to achieve the declared air-quality targets.[49]

Needless to say, the regional authorities did not provide citizens with adequate financial support in the form of subsidies for the removal of inefficient installations. As we mentioned, the subsidies available at that time covered only 30–50% of the direct expenses associated with the installation of new equipment (not to mention improvements in the thermal insulation of a building), and the amount of money

[49] Although we do not have evidence to establish an intention on the part of individual policymakers to cause failure.

dedicated to them was far below their actual needs, covering only a small percentage of potential requests.[50]

According to EEA (2022), the estimated cost of replacing solid-fuel installations in Kraków (25,182 coal and wood devices replaced in 2012–2019) was approximately €76 million. The number of installations that had to be replaced in Małopolska (excluding Kraków) was estimated at 436,700, and we already know this was probably a huge underestimation. Using the cost of a successful replacement in Kraków as a reference point, the estimated amount of funds required to effectively implement the 2017 resolution was €1.318 million.[51] Taking into account the figures indicated on the official website of the Marshall Office (€625.5 million) as the value of investments in antismog policies in the years 2017–2024,[52] Małopolska has so far provided approximately 47.5% of the sum required for the successful implementation of the resolution. This estimate is very optimistic, though, because the indicated sum of €625.5 million included not only the cost of replacing inefficient installations—more or less, half of this amount was spent on other tasks, such as the thermomodernization of buildings.[53] Paradoxically, the 2017 resolution relied on financial incentives as a central element of its regulatory design, while providing too little financial support for those incentives to operate as genuine incentives in practice.

---

[50] The question of whether the removal and decommissioning programs are themselves an efficient way to address the problem of air pollution is usually also not analyzed in depth during policymaking. The rationale of boiler removal or replacement programs was studied in Adamczyk et al. (2017) via the life-cycle assessment (LCA) methodology, including the environmental impact of the production, removal, and then utilization of different types of boilers against gains in the reduction of emissions or the use of fuel. His analysis proved that coal-fueled boilers have the highest environmental impact among various types of installations available; however, the most economically viable option was allegedly the installation of a boiler fueled with large pieces of wood.

[51] The proportion used to calculate the result was 25,182 – €76 million / 436,700 – € x million. By the way, these estimations seem to be in accordance with the official estimation of the implementation of the 2017 resolution calculations provided by its authors (PLN 4.800 million to 2023). During public debates in 2016, slightly different numbers were presented. It was reported that there were 24,000 solid-fuel boilers and 4000 fireplaces in Krakow. The cost of replacing those installations was estimated at PLN 475 million (EUR 110.5 million)—see Dominika Wantuch, *Uchwała antysmogowa przyjęta! Zakaz palenia węglem i drewnem w Krakowie od 2019 r.*, Wyborcza, 15.01.2016. Those numbers do not change much in our argument, though, as the gap in financing rises as much as to 36%.

[52] The official website of the Małopolska office states that PLN 2.69 billion has been allocated for the period 2017–2024 for the removal of old solid-fuel boilers and furnaces, the thermal modernization of buildings, and the installation of renewable energy sources—see https://powietrze.malopolska.pl/program-ochrony-powietrza/efekty-realizacji/.

[53] The lack of financial support for replacing high-emission coal and wood-burning stoves was evident at the local level as well—in each municipality in Małopolska. The programs offered by the central government and the Małopolska local government to cofinance the thermal modernization of houses and the replacement of furnaces involved such small amounts of money that simple extrapolations indicated that the 2017 resolution would be implemented in about 36–71 years (depending on the percentage share of public funds in the replacement costs)—see Klinowski (2018).

Having all this in mind, in contrast to the earlier resolution for Kraków, it is impossible to consider the 2017 resolution for the rest of Małopolska as a case of successful implementation of an environmental policy. It failed to achieve its objectives under either of the criteria used in this analysis: improvements in air quality and the rate of replacement of high-emission heating installations. Indeed, the number of such installations in Małopolska appears to have increased in recent years, despite the millions of euros invested in addressing the problem. It seems that those funds were simply wasted.

Moreover, antismog policies in Małopolska are in retreat, as the rate of decommissioning old heating appliances in the region has been decreasing since 2022. This coincides with the amendments introduced that year to the antismog resolution for Małopolska, which postponed the final date of its adoption by 1.5 years. This supposedly sent a clear signal to the population of the province that antismog regulations would not be seriously enforced in the foreseeable future. As a result, a quite dramatic change in air quality was observed at monitoring stations in Skawina and Zabierzów (both commuter communities of Kraków). In Skawina, while the maximum daily PM10 concentration in 2023 was 85 $\mu g/m^3$, in 2024, it was as much as 142 $\mu g/m^3$. The same was true in Zabierzów—99 $\mu g/m^3$ in 2023 and 145 $\mu g/m^3$ in 2024. The number of days with exceeded daily PM10 concentrations in Zabierzów increased from 26 in 2023 to 32 in 2024.[54]

The decline in air quality across communities in Małopolska could be observed even before the dismantling of the province's antismog regulations by the populist party PiS. Namely, the average annual concentrations of PM10 dust in Tarnów decreased between 2017 and 2020, then subsequently rose again (Lochno, 2023, p. 7). In Zakopane, they fell significantly between 2014 and 2019 (from 49 to 25 $\mu g/m^3$), then stopped improving at least until 2022. In Sucha Beskidzka, concentrations consistently rose from 2017 to 2022, while in Gorlice, they improved in 2018–2020, before rising again, and so on (Lochno, 2023, p. 8). Additionally, data regarding the mean PM10 concentrations between the heating seasons of 2014–2015 and 2024–2025 show that the reduction in particulates is significantly stronger in Kraków (53%) than in the rest of the province (41%) (Marshall Office, 2025, p. 4).

Those figures demonstrate that the 2017 resolution was problematic in itself: either the philosophy of financial incentives and nudges was not a good choice for the job, or the socioeconomic context prevented the resolution from producing its intended effects. As both explanations are not mutually exclusive, the indisputable success of the solid-fuel ban in Kraków speaks in favor of the thesis that the 2017 resolution—and its underlying philosophy—was a bad choice. The subsequent manipulations around the regulation by populists in 2022 only further undermined its effectiveness.

Sadly, similar phenomena are observed in other provinces of Poland, where regional parliaments adopted ineffective policies modeled on the 2017 resolution, avoiding the obvious lesson of the solid-fuel ban in force in Kraków. As a

---

[54] https://smoglab.pl/kopciuchy-obwarzanek-krakow-2025/.

consequence of these policy failures, it is estimated that after almost a decade of political, organizational, and financial efforts to tackle the problem of air pollution, 3.5–4 million households in Poland still use solid-fuel boilers, primarily coal, to heat their homes.[55] This represents nearly one-third of all households in the country and demonstrates the utter failure of the country's strategy toward the problem.[56]

Contrary to optimistic media coverage and mainstream scholarship underlining the transformative role of public awareness and civil engagement, public inertia persists to a large degree. Some Poles still do relatively little to improve air quality by eliminating the sources of pollution. Nearly half of respondents whose houses are heated with noncompliant boilers report having no plans to change their heating source (Śliwowski et al., 2020). At the same time, 84% of furnace inspections conducted in Poland in 2019 revealed no irregularities, with only 7% resulting in fines, which points to a significant enforcement gap (Śliwowski et al., 2020).

Both implementation and enforcement gaps are caused by a confluence of factors: insufficient resources (financial, human) at the municipal level, where the implementation of antismog resolutions and control take place; a lack of political will; and noncompliance by the public due to socioeconomic reasons. These factors persist despite relatively high public awareness and political salience of the air pollution problem, challenging simple models that treat public awareness as a sufficient condition for effective environmental action.

3.12 Limitations of the Comparison Between the 2016 and 2017 Resolutions

The coexistence of two substantially different antismog resolutions within the same region creates a valuable opportunity to compare alternative approaches to regulating residential emissions. The subsequent differences in the pace of appliance replacement and air-quality improvement provide us with relevant evidence for assessing the relative effectiveness of these two regulatory models or philosophies. This comparison must, however, be interpreted with caution.

Kraków and the rest of Małopolska are not directly comparable units differing only in the content of their respective resolutions. Both regulatory models were

[55] Estimations by Polska Izba Gospodarcza Sprzedawców Węgla [Polish Chamber of Commerce of Coal Merchants], see https://pigsw.pl/.

[56] At the beginning of the 2020s, there were visible symptoms of improvements in air quality in Poland. The number of zones in Poland exceeding WHO guidelines for particulate matter decreased from 38 (out of 46) in 2012 to 25 in 2021. This change was universally attributed to the shift in public policies that took place in Poland (Clean Air Fund, 2023) and not to general trends we mentioned earlier, like decreasing industrial activities, modernization of the economy, and improving the condition of buildings. However, the measurement demonstrating decreasing air quality in Poland in recent years may justify the idea that it is more appropriate to assume that the prior improvement of air quality took place despite the strategies adopted in Poland, rather than thanks to them.

introduced in different social, economic, infrastructural, administrative, and geographical environments. Their outcomes reflect not only the legal requirements themselves but also the conditions under which those requirements were implemented. Those conditions limit conclusions about the causal effect of a solid-fuel prohibition that could be derived from the case.

The first limitation concerns the asymmetry of the compared territories. Kraków is a single, densely populated metropolitan municipality with a relatively integrated administrative structure. The remainder of Małopolska consists of numerous municipalities that differ considerably in size, population density, settlement patterns, financial resources, energy and heating infrastructure, administrative capacity, and exposure to air pollution. Some are urban or suburban municipalities located within the Kraków metropolitan area; others are small towns or predominantly rural communities.

The implementation of the regional resolution depended on the activities of many local authorities with unequal resources and differing political priorities. Kraków, by contrast, implemented the 2016 resolution through a single municipal administration with a clear political commitment and financial resources far greater than those available to any other local authority in Małopolska. At the same time, smaller municipalities frequently lacked sufficient personnel to process applications, conduct inspections, and enforce the antismog resolutions.

Differences between the outcomes of the resolutions may therefore reflect variations in the structure and capacities of the institutions responsible for their implementation, not the substantive superiority of one legal instrument over another.

Temporal differences constitute another complication, as the regulations were not adopted and implemented at the same time, and the deadlines contained in the Małopolska resolution were subsequently postponed. The two regimes were therefore exposed to slightly different economic and political circumstances during their crucial implementation periods. Changes in energy prices, inflation, the availability of heating appliances, and public subsidy programs, as well as factors such as political attitudes toward coal, could have affected the rate of replacement.

Baseline differences are equally significant. Kraków and the rest of Małopolska did not begin the implementation process with identical heating structures, access to energy networks, housing conditions, or levels of public awareness. In some areas of Kraków, residents could connect buildings to district heating or gas networks. In rural and dispersed settlements, such alternatives were often unavailable or economically impractical. Replacing a solid-fuel appliance therefore required different levels of investment and imposed varying recurring costs on households in the two territories. The social distribution of these costs also matters. Households differ in income, access to credit, ability to obtain subsidies, and capacity to undertake complex renovation work. What is feasible for an owner of a property in one of the most attractive Polish cities may be considerably more burdensome for a low-income household in a poorly insulated rural building. Differences in the implementation of the resolutions may therefore reflect material constraints rather than anything else.

It is important to note that even postponing the deadline of the 2017 resolution had a behavioral effect lasting beyond the formal extension itself. We have already mentioned that it signaled that the authorities were unwilling to enforce the regulation consistently and that further postponements remained possible. Such a signal could reduce incentives for households to replace installations before being compelled to do so. In this respect, the implementation of the 2017 resolution was affected not only by its original design but also by subsequent political decisions concerning its credibility.

Finally, the use of measured air quality as an indicator of regulatory effectiveness introduces additional difficulties. Concentrations of particulate matter and benzo(a) pyrene depend not only on residential emissions but also on meteorological conditions such as wind, temperature, or atmospheric inversions. Weather variations distort short-term comparisons since a relatively warm and windy winter may produce lower measured concentrations even when the structure of heating systems has changed a little. On the other hand, a colder winter characterized by frequent atmospheric inversions may produce poorer results despite substantial progress in the replacement of appliances. For this reason, it may be disputable to treat annual air-quality measurements as a direct indication of the performance of the antismog resolutions.

The second indicator—i.e., the number of noncompliant installations—is questionable as well, especially in light of the mentioned doubts regarding the data gathered in the CEEB. Moreover, the number of appliances corresponds with total emissions over a particular territory only to a certain degree, as different types of boilers, stoves, and fireplaces have different usage patterns and emission characteristics.

The indicators of effectiveness chosen for the comparison, though related, are clearly not interchangeable. The removal of appliances constitutes a direct implementation output of the resolutions, whereas lower pollutant concentrations constitute an environmental outcome. A resolution may generate a high number of replacements without immediately producing improvement in measured air quality. Conversely, air quality may temporarily improve for reasons unrelated to the direct output of implementation.

For these reasons, the comparison between the two resolutions undertaken in this chapter should not be understood as a definitive causal test proving the advantage of a prohibitive approach over a less strict response to the problem of air pollution. Nevertheless, despite the limitations, the comparison remains analytically valuable. First, it suggests the need and the direction for further research on the causal effectiveness of antismog regulations and pins down boundary conditions for more adequate tests. Second, the divergent implementation records of both resolutions in Małopolska provide important evidence about the institutional requirements of effective antismog policy. In particular, the differences in the effects of the two resolutions suggest that regulations relying on gradual voluntary adaptation and weakly enforced technical standards are vulnerable to delay, strategic noncompliance by residents, insufficient financing from the government, or even changing political moods. Public awareness and the promise of financial subsidies may prove insufficient where enforcement is uncertain, administrative responsibility is dispersed, and political authorities repeatedly weaken the credibility of implementation.

The comparison therefore, even if it does not determine the absolute effectiveness of the resolutions, strengthens the broader argument of this chapter—that effective environmental regulation depends not only on a single factor, whether it be public awareness of the problem or even formal adoption of certain legal standards, but also on a broad set of interrelated circumstances at play during the process of adoption and implementation of regulations. We believe it is because of the composition of that set and the complexity of the relationship between its members that environmental problems often seem to be difficult to address in an effective manner, as subsequent attempts to deal with the issue turn out to be less effective than was assumed. And it is probable that because of this complexity, decision-makers—constrained by time and analytical capacity—often choose legislation that is deliberately ineffective but serves as an alibi, assuming that an effective solution to the problem is hard to figure out. We will come back to these ideas in the following chapters.

3.13 Further KAS/PAS Campaigns and Their Impact

The apparent failure of the antismog resolutions in recent years should not overshadow the initial success that KAS helped to facilitate. Specifically, Kraków's pioneering coal ban served as a critical policy precedent and a point of reference for other Polish cities and regions. However, although the ban's successful implementation provided tangible proof of concept that such bans were culturally and politically feasible, no other cities followed Kraków in its stringent policy. Solid-fuel bans, albeit in more lenient and extended versions, were approved in over 20 additional towns and cities across Poland. Yet the full implementation of these bans, even a decade later, remains ongoing and incomplete.

Kraków introduced a general prohibition on the combustion of solid fuels, whereas the resolution adopted a year later for the remainder of Małopolska relied primarily on technical emission standards, the gradual removal of noncompliant appliances, differentiated deadlines, and financial incentives. It was this latter resolution that became a policy prototype, propagated through diffusion mechanisms similar to the ones identified by Shipan and Volden (2008). Antismog regulations inspired by the 2017 resolution for Małopolska were passed in almost all (14 out of 16) Polish provinces. Unfortunately, those regulations are still rather symbolic measures, as their influence on the real situation is marginal. For example, even in the closest vicinity of Kraków, in its metropolitan area, the process of removal of high-emission installations, which still exist in large numbers despite the illegality of their operations, significantly slowed down.[57] In other parts of Małopolska and beyond, the situation is even more dramatic (NIK, 2025).

[57] According to the author's recent conversations with the officials from the communities forming the metropolitan area of Kraków, at the beginning of 2026, there were still 7665 appliances not compliant with the 2017 resolution. Those appliances should not be used after 1 May 2024, and

Meanwhile, the initial success achieved by the Krakowski Alarm Smogowy led to the formation of a national organization—an umbrella for a couple of tens of local clean air initiatives. "Polski Alarm Smogowy" (PAS) (English: Polish Smog Alert), funded by the same group of people as KAS, became a lobbying entity and an expert think tank, drawing upon the expertise of professionals from various fields and focused on the long-term increase of air quality across Poland, not only in Małopolska. The organization has garnered international recognition, notably through its nomination for Prince William's Earthshot Prize in 2023. The organization's involvement was focused on the following topics: (a) stricter regulations for the quality of coal combusted in the residential sector, (b) stricter regulations for emissions from solid-fuel cauldrons and boilers, (c) a central and mandatory registry of emission sources in buildings, and (d) nationwide subsidies for households for removing and replacing emission sources and for undertaking thermomodernization of buildings.

One of the legal acts designed to regulate aero-sanitary conditions was the Act of 25 August 2006 on fuel-quality monitoring and control.[58] Although it stated that fuels combusted for energy production must meet quality standards for the purpose of environmental and human health protection, no such requirements were specified for solid fuels. Initially, solid fuels were not even mentioned in the act! Moreover, regulators, working clearly in favor of the mining industry, deliberately adopted a legislative technique of referring to lower-level normative acts to effectively postpone the introduction of a regulation that could result in blowback from the politically influential industry, while at the same time creating a false image of the adoption of antismog measures that could be presented to the European Commission as a successful implementation of the CAFE Directive. In fact, the minister responsible for economic affairs, referred to in the act, did not, for many years, issue any regulation on coal—the most important fuel in Poland. This made it possible to offer as fuel virtually any sort of material that came out of mines and had a dark color.

A separate problem consists of the fact that the Polish unregulated market was open to importers bringing to the country unsorted coal that is often of low quality. Between 2000 and 2020, coal imports to Poland increased 7.5-fold, primarily due to declining coal production by residential mines and the limited availability of residential coal of the desired quality. At the same time, hard-coal mining costs in Poland ranked among the highest in the world (Derski, 2020). This, along with the demand gap, created favorable conditions for increasing coal imports. In 2000, Poland imported coal mainly from Russia (51% of total imports) and the Czech Republic (42%). By 2021, Russia's share of total coal imports to Poland had risen

their continued functioning is illegal. Another 7830 should be removed before 2027. Those numbers illustrate how difficult the implementation of the 2017 resolution is, despite the apparently high levels of initial public awareness and civic involvement in the communities neighboring Krakow. To what extent it is due to the faulty design of the resolution or to the structural or institutional conditions in the area of Małopolska outside of Kraków is a matter of discussion.

58 Ustawa z dnia 25 sierpnia 2006 r. o systemie monitorowania i kontrolowania jakości paliw, Dz.U. 2006 nr 169 poz. 1200.

to 86%. The introduction of sanctions and an embargo on Russian coal in 2022 forced the country to diversify its supply sources. By 2024, Kazakhstan (51% of imports) and Colombia (39%) had become dominant import destinations.

Through sustained advocacy, amplified by extensive media coverage, PAS helped secure support within the PiS-led government for the introduction of long-delayed fuel-quality standards. This influence appears to have been facilitated by PAS's personal contacts with several key officials in political circles close to Prime Minister Mateusz Morawiecki. At the same time, the government was launching a national subsidy program for the replacement of solid-fuel heating installations, which it presented as a major instrument for improving air quality in Poland. PAS argued that, without regulations governing coal quality, substantial public subsidies for replacing heating installations risked being ineffective, as the continued use of poor-quality fuel could undermine the air-quality improvements expected from eliminating high-emission sources.

The process of introducing required regulations was slow, however, and was additionally interrupted by geopolitical turbulence. The first success was the amendment of the 2006 act in 2018. That new act introduced a definition of solid fuel used in the residential sector and created a legal basis for the determination of the quality of such fuels.[59] Once again, however, responsibility for regulating the issue was delegated to the competent minister—this time, the minister responsible for the energy sector. Additionally, the new act strengthened the state's control over imports, supposedly limiting the possibility of bringing to Poland unsorted energetic coal of low quality. The minister's regulation was issued the same year,[60] defining the legal requirements for solid fuels, such as granulation, humidity, sulfur and ash content, as well as energy value.

The regulation initially proved to be a major disappointment, as it permitted the sale of mining waste, which it was intended to eliminate. The worst coal dust and coal waste could be sold until 30 June 2020. This occurred despite adverse opinions from the PAS and the Ministry of the Environment, both of which were completely ignored. The regulation also permitted the sale of coarser coal with high sulfur (up to 1.7%), ash, and moisture content. This meant that even emission class 5 boilers, which were designated as target installations in the antismog resolutions adopted throughout Poland, were unable to meet emission standards when fueled with such products. Additionally, no quality requirements were specified for wood pellets, although on the market at that time, pellets containing plastic granules were available for purchase. In turn, one of the more technical regulations specifying the template for the certificate required for the sale of solid fuels also deliberately omitted the obligation to disclose sulfur content. PAS also intervened in this matter, but its criticism was, of course, completely ignored.[61] When we add to this the fact that,

[59] Ustawa z dnia 5 lipca 2018 r. o zmianie ustawy o systemie monitorowania i kontrolowania jakości paliw oraz ustawy o Krajowej Administracji Skarbowej, Dz.U. 2018 poz. 1654.

[60] Rozporządzenie Ministra Energii z dnia 27 września 2018 r. w sprawie wymagań jakościowych dla paliw stałych, Dz.U. 2018 poz. 1890.

[61] https://polskabezsmogu.pl/normy-jakosci-paliw-stalych/.

under pressure from the mining industry, the government allowed the sale of lignite to individual customers until mid-2020—even though its combustion was prohibited by antismog resolutions yet it continued to be sold—we get a complete picture of a legislative patchwork that significantly undermined the effectiveness of provincial public policies to combat air pollution. No wonder the act and the subsequent ministerial regulations were dubbed as a "waste of time" also by the Supreme Audit Office (NIK), which inspected the newly established system for the monitoring and quality control of solid fuels (NIK, 2020).

Thanks to public criticism and constant pressure from PAS, and in response to weak progress in air-quality improvement, the act of 2006 was amended again in 2022, and the power to regulate the quality of coals was moved to the Ministry of Climate and Environment. The regulations of 2022[62] and 2024[63] gradually introduced stricter norms for solid fuels but still did not prohibit the sale of the worst categories. Quite shockingly, despite the fact that air pollution in Poland remains dramatic, the ban on trade in the worst fuels is scheduled only for mid-2027 in the case of lignite, mid-2029 for coal dust, and mid-2031 for other lower-quality coal-like products (so-called cubes, nut coal, pea coal—terms referring to product granulations).

Unfortunately, geopolitics has also recently left its mark on national public policies addressing smog. In July 2022, the Ministry of Climate and Environment suspended coal-quality standards for 60 days due to energy market turmoil related to the ongoing war in Ukraine, and then again for another 60 days. In September 2022, the Polish parliament (Sejm) passed a law allowing the government to suspend coal-quality standards for up to 2 years. The suspension period ended on 1 January 2024. This means that for almost 2 years, lowest-quality fuels were once again allowed to be sold in Poland. Unfortunately, these fuels were burned unchecked throughout the country across the residential sector, contributing to a halt and, in many places, a reversal of progress in improving air quality.

Another area addressed by the organization was the lack of regulations on emission standards for cauldrons and boilers. While the average life cycle of a typical Polish coal cauldron is around 10 years, for a long time there had been no institution capable of inspecting or certifying installations in households. As a consequence, the poor technical conditions of solid-fuel installations operating in Poland and the technological retardation of boilers offered on the residential market, often by small local producers, contributed significantly to the high concentrations of pollutants measured in the air. PAS made efforts to ensure that the government adopts the necessary regulations to close this gap. Thanks to advocacy and lobbying, emission requirements for solid-fuel boilers were finally adopted in 2017, making the sale of boilers other than those permitted under antismog resolutions illegal from 1 July

[62] Rozporządzenie Ministra Klimatu i Środowiska z dnia 23 grudnia 2022 r. w sprawie wymagań jakościowych dla paliw stałych, Dz.U. 2022 poz. 2856.

[63] Rozporządzenie Ministra Przemysłu oraz Ministra Klimatu i Środowiska z dnia 4 listopada 2024 r. w sprawie wymagań jakościowych dla paliw stałych, Dz.U. 2024 poz. 1618.

2018.[64] Unfortunately, the regulation issued by the minister responsible for energy was so sloppily drafted that loopholes in it allowed for the continued sale of non-classified appliances, resulting in tens of thousands of polluting boilers being installed in subsequent years. As there was no control system established by new regulations, the sale of illegal appliances went virtually unpunished. Only under public pressure did the government attempt to tighten the market in the following years.

Also, the implementation of the subsidy program had been plagued by setbacks, and problems continue even to this day. The program was introduced in 2018 to fill the gap left by the careless dismantling of the previous "Kawka" program in 2016, which was cancelled by the new populist government (mainly PiS) to protect the interests of the mining sector. The program offered subsidies covering up to 40% of the financial costs of replacing heat sources and undertaking comprehensive thermal modernization (70% and 100% in the case of financially disadvantaged families). From its inception, the program struggled with problems related to overly complicated application procedures and insufficient funding. This led to a low level of achievement of its goals. In October 2021, after 3 years of implementation, an audit conducted by the Supreme Audit Office (NIK) found that the program had achieved only about 4% of its target, clearly identifying the causes of this failure (NIK, 2021). It even seemed as if the process of application was also deliberately difficult, since the government was reluctant to devote appropriate funds to finance energy transformation that could damage the interests of the mining lobby.

PAS has consistently monitored and assessed changes to the program, highlighting its deficiencies and advocating for its more efficient and accessible implementation. As the decommissioning of polluting installations remained unsatisfactory, PAS publicized the problem, repeatedly criticizing the program's implementation and pace. Official data from the CEEB register indicate that in the fall of 2024, as many as 2.8 million boilers that did not meet the requirements of the antismog resolutions still operated in Poland, and 30% of buildings were not adequately insulated. According to PAS's estimates, the program achieved only 27% of its target. In 2024, the program was finally put on hold after the new prodemocratic government revealed the scale of financial fraud within its operations.

It is worth noting that PAS advocacy for a ban on the sale of low-quality coal, stricter limits on sulfur content in coal, and more stringent emission standards for solid-fuel heating appliances—all of which were important for improving air quality in Poland—encountered significant resistance from the powerful coal industry, as well as from local producers and distributors of solid-fuel heating equipment. PAS campaigns were frequently attacked in the press and on social media, where they were described as "environmental rage activism" or even "ecoterrorism."

Lately, KAS/PAS played an instrumental role in advocating for the adoption of low-emission zones (LEZs) in Warszawa (2023) and later in Kraków (2024, 2025),

[64] Rozporządzenie Ministra Rozwoju i Finansów z dnia 1 sierpnia 2017 r. w sprawie wymagań dla kotłów na paliwo stałe, Dz.U. 2017 poz. 1690.

which became the first such regulations in Central and Eastern Europe. The organization also called for further amendments to the national electromobility law in order to secure public support for the LEZ rollout. However, LEZs recently became another highly contentious issue, and the local council in Kraków voted to lower the threshold of permitted emissions for cars owned by residents in order to secure political and popular support. The concessions did not prevent the LEZ from remaining a politically contentious issue, and the president of Kraków was ultimately removed from office in a referendum in May 2026, after approximately two years in office. An exit poll conducted during the referendum identified the LEZ as the most frequently cited reason for participating in the vote. This may partly reflect the comparatively restrictive design of Kraków's LEZ, which imposed substantially stricter vehicle-emission requirements than the initial scheme introduced in Warsaw.[65]

Such political resistance to antismog measures indicates changing public awareness of the smog problem in Poland. The results of voting in Kraków demonstrated that KAS/PAS have lost their influence on public perception of the problem. The case also signals that public perception of environmental problems is neither linear nor monotonic, and it cannot be assumed that public awareness and involvement in solving them will grow. The case of air pollution in Poland demonstrates that public engagement quickly fades, and public awareness of the problem evolves and can come into conflict with political salience previously built on public awareness. Exploring this dynamic is interesting in itself and should be the subject of future studies.

While PAS was advocating for necessary regulations at the national level, KAS continued its efforts to broaden public awareness of the air pollution problem, mainly outside of Kraków. The success of the 2017 resolution depended heavily on public involvement, as it largely relied on individual willingness to comply with its provisions. For this reason, KAS once more turned to a strategy of civic mobilization, focusing its efforts especially on commuter municipalities neighboring Kraków. This was reasonable, as those suburban areas are densely packed with individual houses using solid fuel for heat generation, and the transport of pollutants from those communities to the city was proven to hinder improvements in air quality in the region's capital. KAS presented a strong position claiming that the high levels of pollution still measured in the city were the direct product of the negligence of political leaders in the municipalities surrounding Kraków. That message was further reinforced by new scientific studies showing that Kraków's unfavorable geographical location, combined with pollution transported from neighbouring municipalities, contributed to the persistence of poor air quality in the city (e.g., Danek et al., 2022).

With hopes of shifting public perception and fostering citizen engagement once more, KAS launched the "Mobile Lungs" (*Mobilne Płuca*) campaign, consistent

[65] Twenty-eight percent of respondents answered that the adoption of LEZ in Kraków was the reason for their attendance at the recall voting—see Ogólnopolska Grupa Badawcza, & Stan360. (2026, 24 maja). Exit poll: Referendum w sprawie odwołania Prezydenta Miasta Krakowa oraz Rady Miasta Krakowa [Badanie sondażowe przeprowadzone dla Polsat News].

with the public engagement philosophy previously adopted by the organization. It features a 2-meter model of human lungs, crafted from white fabric, which "breathes" polluted air through special fans. Often, over a couple of days, the white fabric would visibly darken to gray or even black as dust particles accumulate, allegedly mimicking the detrimental effects of pollution on the human respiratory tract.[66] The campaign was also accompanied by precise air-quality measurements in communities lacking continuous monitoring by the environmental inspectorate. Initially, these measurements were conducted using a professional monitoring station that was placed in selected communities in Małopolska. After the first measurements in 2015 revealed extremely poor air quality at the initial monitoring site in Skała near Kraków, KAS found it difficult for some time to persuade other communities to host its stationary monitoring equipment.[67] Because of this, measurements continued with mobile sensors installed in a car, which did not require permissions from local governments or any close cooperation.

The Mobile Lungs campaign was extensively showcased, touring 63 Polish towns and cities for 14 days each and generating significant media attention. In the 2023–2024 winter season alone, it garnered an impressive 1300 media mentions, reaching over 14 million people (Clean Air Fund, 2023). Beyond merely raising awareness, the campaign was designed to encourage citizens to apply for government subsidies to transition to cleaner heating systems. However, evidence does not demonstrate that the campaign's considerable media reach translated into measurable behavioral or political mobilization, as air quality in Małopolska has continued to deteriorate. According to our observations at the time, the plastic-lung installations, although visually attractive to the press, appeared to be perceived by many members of the public primarily as a curiosity and did not appear to generate significant social or political mobilization.

KAS also tried to counter the apparent political and social apathy reflected in the declining rate of replacement of inefficient heating installations. The "Initiative 600" campaign—referring to the 600 days remaining for the replacement of high-emission appliances—and the "dirty burners" counter were further attempts to draw public attention to widespread non-compliance with the 2017 resolution and to encourage action. Although the resolution was originally supposed to take effect on 1 January 2023, the rate at which banned heating installations were being replaced in municipalities around Kraków declined significantly, in some cases approaching levels recorded before air pollution had become a prominent subject of public

[66] For a more detailed description of other campaigns and actions by KAS/PAS, see Zabka (2024).

[67] For that reason, the measuring equipment was located in the main square of Wadowice and was only moved in 2019 to Wieliczka when the newly elected mayor from PiS won the elections on the wave of skepticism against progressive public policies regarding air pollution represented by KAS. Before the removal, for several years, the station produced a stable stream of data proving the further deterioration of air quality in Wadowice, despite the 2017 resolution being passed in the regional parliament. Clearly, this legislation, despite public messaging that it achieved success in combating pollution, had only marginal influence in towns, even those relatively close to the provincial capital.

debate. In the area concerned, the number of devices replaced annually fell from 2691 in 2022 to 1460 in 2024. At the same time, over 10,000 illegal boilers and stoves remained in operation (Krakowski Alarm Smogowy, 2025). These figures suggest that the behavioral effects of the heightened public awareness associated with KAS activities had weakened substantially over time. More broadly, they reveal the limitations of a long-term strategy relying heavily on public awareness and civic mobilization to secure compliance with anti-smog regulation.

The limited effects of KAS's later awareness campaigns are consistent with research showing that information and favorable attitudes are insufficient when compliance with regulations entails substantial private costs and when institutional arrangements provide weak or uncertain incentives for behavioral change (e.g., Kollmuss & Agyeman, 2002; Matland, 1995). However, to be precise, there are places in Małopolska and Śląsk where air quality has significantly improved. An example of this is the city of Rybnik, where—as a result of local smog alert activity over the course of 10 years—the number of smog days decreased from 130 (in 2010) to 16 days (in 2023) (Clean Air Fund, 2024). Unfortunately, in other cities, local politicians were reluctant to take any decisive action, and residents did not attempt to exert any pressure, clearly accepting the *status quo* that has persisted for many years. A state of apathy has returned to Poland.

The reasons for people's insensitivity to air pollution are complex, and it seems that outside of the specific context of Kraków in 2012–2015, KAS was simply unable to connect with popular cultural perceptions and the hierarchy of needs. On the other hand, our case study could also be interpreted as a strong argument for the claim that the strategy of economic incentives underpinning the 2017 resolution has generally not worked, and even the high salience of the problem and loud media campaigns have not been able to nudge people to participate in the collective action required to achieve the environmental effects assumed by that strategy. In that case, KAS's efforts were irrelevant as it was unlikely that the 2017 resolution would bear fruit. One may also assume that the persistent obstacles faced by KAS and PAS in their advocacy reflect the complex interplay of political, economic, and social factors in Poland's clean air transition. KAS/PAS and the clean air agenda have simply encountered political resistance from the powerful coal industry, which undermined their efforts. Resistance from officials acting in favor of strong sectoral interests highlights that air pollution is not merely an environmental or public health issue but rather a complex theme deeply intertwined with Poland's political economy.

It is also worth mentioning that KAS and PAS, in a sense, fell victim to their own success. As their founders became recognized as experts and important voices in the debate on the side of civil society, they started to appear on different advisory boards for political and administrative institutions, effectively—in the eyes of some of the supporters and followers from local alert branches—losing their independent status as well as the privilege of openly expressed criticism.[68] Government grants helped

[68] Author's informal conversations with smog alarm supporters in Małopolska in the years 2018–2020.

the organization to professionalize, but they also deprived it of its ability to name problems sharply. From its inception, the movement's founders defined themselves as apolitical so they could exert sustained, non-partisan pressure on local and regional authorities, irrespective of their political affiliation. Such a postulate, in time, lost its validity as the movement's members became involved in the functioning of various public institutions and started to play the role of official partners for politicians and authorities. As KAS leaders became frequent participants in formal and informal meetings, including public panels, media rooms, and conference banquets sponsored by politicians responsible for maintaining ineffective public policies, they turned out to be convenient partners for decision-makers rather than watchdogs. As a result, the civic energy surrounding the idea of antismog revolt was lost to a large extent, and many smog alerts ceased their activities.[69] The later trajectory of KAS/PAS clearly resembles processes described in the literature as professionalization and institutional activism. These processes may provide movements with access to decision-makers and resources to continue functioning while also limiting their tactics and creating tensions with grassroots supporters (Pettinicchio, 2012; Staggenborg, 1988). By evolving to better fit this new role, grassroots organizations like KAS are destined to professionalize, gradually engaging in so-called transactional activism, as defined by Petrova and Tarrow (2007). Such a mode of activism is, of course, not accepted by those who see it as a contradiction to genuine civic participation.[70]

Nonetheless, KAS/PAS stand as a compelling model for environmental activism, even despite the fact that their exact roles in the process of adoption and implementation of the antismog regulations in Poland are still disputed. Surely, KAS/PAS succeeded in their general mission of bringing air pollution to the forefront of environmental debate in Poland. Notably, a handful of smog activists were instrumental in shaping a policy response at the regional level and beyond. Because high-profile antipollution campaigns gained the attention of a national audience, they created media dynamics in which both citizens and political leaders started to perceive pollution as a problem that required attention and certain reforms. Yet it is not clear to what extent KAS activities were necessary for a progressive shift in air pollution policies. The causal chain that led to that shift and the role of KAS and public awareness in general should be a matter for further study. It looks like environmental movements in resource-dependent economies face a more complex challenge than just raising awareness or enacting laws; they must also engage in a long-term struggle to reshape national economic priorities and political narratives, addressing both environmental and socioeconomic concerns.

[69] We checked which smog alerts included in PAS are still active. We used an interactive map of smog alerts in Poland, available on the PAS website. According to the map, out of 58 local initiatives listed, only 24 (50%) were still active (= posting on their social media). In the case of the ten initiatives (17%), there is no longer any online trace of their activity in the mid-2025. See https://polskialarmsmogowy.pl/lokalne-alarmy-smogowe/, accessed 01.06.2025.

[70] It is interesting to note that the history of PAS/KAS apparently contradicts the trajectory that some studies presented as characteristic of citizen-led activism; see, e.g., Subašić et al. (2024).

3.14 Limitations of the Study and Final Remarks

This chapter should be read as an interpretive reconstruction of a complex policy process rather than as a definitive causal evaluation based on experimental or quasi-experimental evidence. The case study presented here is obviously subject to several limitations. These limitations do not invalidate our conclusions but rather define the degree of confidence in our claims. As discussed earlier, the Małopolska region is structurally diverse. The territory outside Kraków includes densely populated suburban municipalities, medium-sized towns, mountain resorts, former industrial centers, and dispersed rural communities. These areas differ substantially, so it is unlikely that a single policy produced a uniform regional effect, especially when its implementation depended heavily on the decisions and capacities of individual municipalities—a characteristic challenge of multilevel governance.

A further limitation arises from the difficulty of separating the effects of anti-smog law from other factors affecting air quality, mainly weather. The spatial transport of pollution creates an additional problem. Ideally, the evaluation of regulatory effects would employ weather-normalized emission or concentration models. The present chapter, however, relies on existing monitoring data and reports and does not conduct such modeling. Another source of variation that our study does not control for is structural factors like energy prices, inflation, changes in household income, the technical state of residential buildings, and levels of industrial emissions.

The source material—especially the author's personal notes, memory, participation in the adoption and implementation of the 2017 resolution, and informal contacts with members of KAS—also requires caution. Recollections and contemporaneous notes are necessarily selective; they are not complete transcripts of meetings or a systematically collected interview corpus. Claims based on such material are useful for reconstructing participants' perspectives and generating plausible interpretations but not for conclusively establishing facts.

Finally, the chapter's causal conclusions are limited by the absence of a strict counterfactual scenario. It is impossible to observe what would have happened in Kraków or in Małopolska if KAS had not emerged, if the European Commission had not intensified legal pressure, or if the regional parliament had adopted a different regulatory model. We are unable to compare directly the actual policy trajectory with an otherwise identical case in which only one causal factor was absent.

The comparison between Kraków and the remainder of Małopolska provides some counterfactual leverage because the two territories adopted different regulatory approaches within the same national and regional legal environments. But as we already mentioned, it is not, however, a controlled comparison. The two territories already differed before the resolutions were adopted, and these prior differences influenced both the choice of policy instrument and its subsequent implementation.

The lack of a strict counterfactual is particularly important for assessing the role of KAS. Evidence indicates that the organization, in the first place, influenced problem framing and the political legitimation of restrictive measures. It does not demonstrate conclusively that no comparable policy change would have occurred in the absence of KAS. EU legal obligations or changes in national legislation in response to growing health evidence might eventually have generated some form of intervention. Therefore, to our minds, it is reasonable to conclude that KAS influenced the timing, form, and ambition of the response, rather than constituting an indispensable cause of the observed policy shift.

We expect that many readers will assume that our case study provides rather weak grounds for a precise estimation of the effects of regulatory instruments (or regulatory models) designed to tackle air pollution in a different national or regional context. The case of Małopolska and Kraków could be treated as a universally replicable model only when contextual differences are accounted for in an appropriate way. This could be a very difficult—if at all possible—task. However, acknowledging these limitations is consistent with the purpose of an interpretive socio-legal case study. Hence, we believe that the conclusions derived from it are valuable for scholars interested in environmental public policies.

This chapter identifies a distinction that is central to the argument of this book: the political recognition of a problem, the adoption of law, and the effective solution to the problem are separate achievements. KAS contributed substantially to the first and helped facilitate the second. The third required conditions that transcend public awareness and civic mobilization. This distinction explains why formally ambitious environmental policies may coexist with weak implementation and limited environmental effects. It also provides a bridge to the institutional analysis developed in the following chapters. Once antismog resolutions had been adopted, the burden of producing practical change shifted to municipal administrations and to the newly created group of eco-advisors.

The same distinction will later inform the analysis of symbolic law and wicked problems. The adoption of legislation may represent genuine political progress while simultaneously serving symbolic functions if authorities fail to provide the instruments necessary for the implementation of adopted policies. We hypothesize that at the moment of the adoption of certain policies, decision-makers may already assume that they are not capable of tackling the problem because of its complexity and thus choose legislation that serves rather reputational goals. Likewise, the multiplicity of actors and complex causal mechanisms involved in antismog policy may encourage the description of air pollution as a wicked problem. The case of Małopolska nevertheless indicates that complexity should not be confused with inherent insolubility of the problem. What appears to be the intractability of the environmental issue may result, at least in part, from political decisions to adopt incomplete instruments, underfunded implementation, dispersed responsibility, and avoidance of the enforcement of unpopular obligations.

References

Adamczyk, J., Piwowar, A., & Dzikuć, M. (2017). Air protection program in Poland in the context of the low emission. *Environmental Science and Pollution Research, 24*, 16316–16327. https://doi.org/10.1007/s11356-017-9233-9

Amenta, E., Caren, N., Chiarello, E., & Su, Y. (2010). The political consequences of social movements. *Annual Review of Sociology, 36*, 287–307. https://doi.org/10.1146/annurev-soc-070308-120029

Bakaki, Z., Böhmelt, T., & Ward, H. (2020). The triangular relationship between public concern for environmental issues, policy output and media attention. *Environmental Politics, 29*(7), 1157–1177.

Becken, S., Jin, X., Zhang, C., & Gao, J. (2017). Urban air pollution in China: Destination image and risk perceptions. *Journal of Sustainable Tourism, 25*(1), 130–147. https://doi.org/10.1080/09669582.2016.1177067

Benford, R. D., & Snow, D. A. (2000). Framing processes and social movements: An overview and assessment. *Annual Review of Sociology, 26*, 611–639. https://doi.org/10.1146/annurev.soc.26.1.611

Bennett, W. L., & Segerberg, A. (2012). The logic of connective action: Digital media and the personalization of contentious politics. *Information, Communication & Society, 15*(5), 739–768. https://doi.org/10.1080/1369118X.2012.670661

Bharadwaj, B., Gates, T., Rose, S., & Vuthaluru, H. (2026). Prevalence of plastic waste as a household fuel in low-income communities of the Global South. *Nature Communications, 17*, Article 50.

Bickerstaff, K., & Walker, G. (2001). Public understandings of air pollution: The 'localisation' of environmental risk. *Global Environmental Change, 11*(2), 133–145. https://doi.org/10.1016/S0959-3780(00)00063-7

Biuletyn URE – Sprawozdanie z działalności Prezesa URE w 2009 r. Nr 3(71). (2010). URE.

Bokwa, A. (2008). Environmental impacts of long-term air pollution changes in Kraków, Poland. *Polish Journal of Environmental Studies, 17*(5), 673–686.

Brauers, H., & Oei, P.-Y. (2020). The political economy of coal in Poland: Drivers and barriers for a shift away from fossil fuels. *Energy Policy, 144*, 111621. https://doi.org/10.1016/j.enpol.2020.111621

Burstein, P. (2003). The impact of public opinion on public policy: A review and an agenda. *Political Research Quarterly, 56*(1), 29–40. https://doi.org/10.1177/106591290305600103

Casey, A. (2013, December 20). People power movements shake up Krakow. *The Krakow Post*. http://www.krakowpost.com/7411/2013/12/people-power-movements-shake-up-krakow

Chmielewski, J., Gietka, M., Wójtowicz, B., Łuszczki, J. J., Gworek, B., & Żeber-Dzikowska, I. (2022). Assessment of rural area residents' awareness of municipal waste incineration. *Journal of Elementology, 27*(3), 611–625. https://doi.org/10.5601/jelem.2022.27.2.2226

Citkowska-Kimla, A. (2019). Poland and the problem of smog – Political action versus social expectations. *Annales Universitatis Mariae-Curie Skłodowska, sectio K – Politologia*, 26(2). https://doi.org/10.17951/k.2019.26.2.127-137

Clean Air Fund. (2023, May 17). *Challenging public perceptions and reforming government programmes in Poland*. https://www.cleanairfund.org/case-study/challenging-public-perceptions-and-reforming-government-programmes-in-poland

Clean Air Fund. (2024, September 6). *How a Polish city became a leader in cutting air pollution*. https://www.cleanairfund.org/case-study/rybnik/

Danek, T., Weglinska, E., & Zareba, M. (2022). The influence of meteorological factors and terrain on air pollution concentration and migration: A geostatistical case study from Krakow, Poland. *Scientific Reports, 12*, 11050. https://doi.org/10.1038/s41598-022-15160-3

Derski, B. (2020, April 22). Dlaczego importujemy węgiel z całego świata? *wysokienapiecie.pl*

European Environment Agency. (2014). *Air quality in Europe — 2014 report (EEA Report 5/2014)*. European Environment Agency.

European Environment Agency. (2022, February 16). *Anti-smog measures in the Małopolska region of Poland.* https://www.eea.europa.eu/publications/managing-air-quality-in-europe/anti-smog-measures-in-the

Fabricant, N. (2023). *Fighting to breathe: Race, toxicity, and the rise of youth activism in Baltimore* (1st ed., Vol. 54). University of California Press. https://doi.org/10.2307/j.ctv2zp50x1

Fijak, M. (2022, September 26). Sejmik bierze na siebie odpowiedzialność za zgony w sezonie smogowym. Kopciuchy zostają do maja 2024. *Smog Lab.* https://smoglab.pl/uchwala-antysmogowa-co-dalej-z-malopolskim-smogiem-dzis-kluczowe-glosowanie/

Frankowski, J. (2019). Attention: Smog alert! Citizen engagement for clean air and its consequences for fuel poverty in Poland. *Energy & Buildings, 207*, 109525. https://doi.org/10.1016/j.enbuild.2019.109525

Gabrys, J. (2014). Programming environments: Environmentality and citizen sensing in the smart city. *Environment and Planning D: Society and Space, 32*(1), 30–48. https://doi.org/10.1068/d16812

Gu, F., Liu, X., Cao, Y., & Wang, Q. (2024). Does haze pollution governance promote the growth of urban tourism economies? Evidence from China's Clean Air Act. *Tourism Economics, 30*(7), 1800–1819. https://doi.org/10.1177/13548166241233624

Health and Environment Alliance. (2025). *Rosnące koszty zdrowotne zmiany klimatu i zanieczyszczenia powietrza – briefing dla decydentów* [The rising health costs of climate change and air pollution – a briefing for policymakers].

Herrera, V. (2024). *Slow harms and citizen action: Environmental degradation and policy change in Latin American cities.* Oxford University Press.

Huber, E. (2016, December 31). Polish city more polluted than Beijing. *The Financial Times.* https://www.ft.com/content/6712dd66-c91d-11e6-8f29-9445cac8966f

IQAir. (2026). *2025 World air quality report: Region & city PM2.5 ranking.* https://www.iqair.com/world-air-quality-report

Jack, B. (2011). Enforcing Member State compliance with EU environmental law: A critical evaluation of the use of financial penalties. *Journal of Environmental Law, 23*(1), 73–95. https://doi.org/10.1093/jel/eqq023

Jasper, J. M. (2011). Emotions and social movements: Twenty years of theory and research. *Annual Review of Sociology, 37*, 285–303. https://doi.org/10.1146/annurev-soc-081309-150015

Kasperson, R. E., Renn, O., Slovic, P., Brown, H. S., Emel, J., Goble, R., Kasperson, J. X., & Ratick, S. (1988). The social amplification of risk: A conceptual framework. *Risk Analysis, 8*(2), 177–187. https://doi.org/10.1111/j.1539-6924.1988.tb01168.x

Kicińska, A., & Jawdyńska, J. (2025). Ban on the burning of solid fuels in domestic furnaces and its impact on air quality – Example of Krakow. *Archives of Mining Sciences, 70*, 3–28. https://doi.org/10.24425/ams.2025.154160

Kleczkowski, P., & Kotarba, K. (2020). *Analiza zmian jakości powietrza w Krakowie oraz Województwie Małopolskim w latach 2012-2020.* Krakowski Alarm Smogowy.

Klinowski, M. (2018, December 17). *Nie ma pieniędzy na walkę ze smogiem. Science (in)action Blog.* https://mateuszklinowski.pl/2018/12/17/nie-ma-pieniedzy-na-walke-ze-smogiem/

Kollmuss, A., & Agyeman, J. (2002). Mind the gap: Why do people act environmentally and what are the barriers to pro-environmental behavior? *Environmental Education Research, 8*(3), 239–260. https://doi.org/10.1080/13504620220145401

Krakowski Alarm Smogowy. (2025, 26 lutego). *Walka ze smogiem w odwrocie? Wymiana pieców w krakowskim obwarzanku zwalnia.* https://krakowskialarmsmogowy.pl/2025/02/26/walka-ze-smogiem-w-odwrocie-wymiana-piecow-w-krakowskim-obwarzanku-zwalnia/

Kuchler, M., & Bridge, G. (2018). Down the black hole: Sustaining national socio-technical imaginaries of coal in Poland. *Energy Research & Social Science, 41*, 136–147. https://doi.org/10.1016/j.erss.2018.04.014

Kurek, W., & Faracik, R. (2008). Selected issues in the development of tourism in Kraków in the 21st century. *Turyzm/Tourism, 18*(1), 65–82. https://doi.org/10.18778/0867-5856.18.1.06

Ladi, S. (2005). Europeanisation and environmental policy change. *Policy and Society, 24*(2), 1–15. https://doi.org/10.1016/S1449-4035(05)70053-9

Lewandowski, P., Kiełczewska, A., & Ziółkowska, K. (2018). *Zjawisko ubóstwa energetycznego w Polsce, w tym ze szczególnym uwzględnieniem zamieszkujących w domach jednorodzinnych* (IBS Research Report No. 02/2018). Instytut Badań Strukturalnych.

Li, X., Smyth, R., & Yao, Y. (2024). Air pollution and energy poverty: Evidence from Chinese households. *The Energy Journal, 45*(6), 1–36. https://doi.org/10.1177/01956574241280797

Lillevik, T. H. (2019). *The fight to breathe – An analysis of the antismog-organization Polski Alarm Smogowy in Poland* [MA dissertation, University of Tromsø].

Lochno, A. (Ed.). (2017). *Załącznik nr 2 do uchwały Nr XXXII/451/17 Sejmiku Województwa Małopolskiego z dnia 23 stycznia 2017 r., Program ochrony powietrza dla województwa małopolskiego. Małopolska w zdrowej atmosferze. Uzasadnienie.*

Lochno, A. (Ed.). (2023). *Załącznik nr 1 do uchwały Nr LXXV/1102/23 Sejmiku Województwa Małopolskiego z dnia 20 listopada 2023 r.*

Maltby, T., Birch, S., Fagan, A., & Subašić, M. (2024). What is the role of activism in air pollution politics? Understanding policy change in Poland. *Environment and Planning C: Politics and Space, 42*(8), 1332–1351. https://doi.org/10.1177/23996544241231677

Marshal Office of Małopolska Region. (2022). *Podsumowanie realizacji Programu ochrony powietrza dla województwa małopolskiego za rok 2021* [Summary of the implementation of the Air Protection Programme for the Małopolska Region for the year 2021].

Marshal Office of Małopolska Region. (2025). *Podsumowanie realizacji Programu ochrony powietrza dla województwa małopolskiego za rok 2024* [Summary of the implementation of the Air Protection Programme for the Małopolska Region for the year 2024].

Matland, R. E. (1995). Synthesizing the implementation literature: The ambiguity-conflict model of policy implementation. *Journal of Public Administration Research and Theory, 5*(2), 145–174. https://doi.org/10.1093/oxfordjournals.jpart.a037242

McCombs, M. E., & Shaw, D. L. (1972). The agenda-setting function of mass media. *Public Opinion Quarterly, 36*(2), 176–187. https://doi.org/10.1086/267990

Meyer, D. S. (2004). Protest and political opportunities. *Annual Review of Sociology, 30*, 125–145. https://doi.org/10.1146/annurev.soc.30.012703.110545

MOT. (2017). *Wpływ ekonomiczny turystyki na gospodarkę Krakowa.*

Nazar, W., & Niedoszytko, M. (2022). Air pollution in Poland: A 2022 narrative review with focus on respiratory diseases. *International Journal of Environmental Research and Public Health, 19*(2), 895. https://doi.org/10.3390/ijerph19020895

NIK. (2020). *Eliminacja z obrotu paliw stałych niespełniających norm jakościowych* (LKA.430.003.2020). https://www.nik.gov.pl/najnowsze-informacje-o-wynikach-kontroli/zmarnowany-czas-w-walce-ze-smogiem.html

NIK. (2021). *Wdrażanie programu priorytetowego "Czyste Powietrze"* (KSI.430.008.2021). https://www.nik.gov.pl/najnowsze-informacje-o-wynikach-kontroli/program-czyste-powietrze.html

NIK. (2025). *Realizacja uchwał antysmogowych* (20/2025/P/24/069/LKR). https://www.nik.gov.pl/plik/id,31538,vp,34684.pdf

Nowicki, M. (1993). *Environment in Poland. Issues and solutions.* Kluwer Academic Publishers.

Ogórek. (2015, March 13). Turystyka generuje 10 proc. PKB Krakowa. To 4,5 mld zł. *Onet.* https://wiadomosci.onet.pl/krakow/turystyka-generuje-10-proc-pkb-krakowa-to-45-mld-zl/9r143rb

Olszewski, M. (2018, March 29). *Polish coal, Polish smog, Polish chaos. Energy transition.* The Global Energiewende. https://energytransition.org/2018/03/polish-coal-polish-smog-polish-chaos/

Patton, M. Q. (2015). *Qualitative research & evaluation methods* (4th ed.). Sage.

Petrova, T., & Tarrow, S. (2007). Transactional and participatory activism in the emerging European polity: The puzzle of east-central Europe. *Comparative Political Studies, 40*(1), 74–94. https://doi.org/10.1177/0010414006291189

Pettinicchio, D. (2012). Institutional activism: Reconsidering the insider/outsider dichotomy. *Sociology Compass, 6*(6), 499–510. https://doi.org/10.1111/j.1751-9020.2012.00465.x

Rai, A. C., Kumar, P., Pilla, F., Skouloudis, A. N., Di Sabatino, S., Ratti, C., Yasar, A., & Rickerby, D. (2017). End-user perspective of low-cost sensors for outdoor air pollution monitoring. *Science of the Total Environment, 607–608*, 691–705. https://doi.org/10.1016/j.scitotenv.2017.06.266

Rocznik statystyczny 2009. (2010). GUS.
Rutkowski, J., Sałach, K., Szpor, A., & Ziółkowska, K. (2018). *How to reduce energy poverty in Poland?* (IBS Policy Paper 1/2018).
Schönfelder, T. (Ed.). (2011). *Analiza możliwości ograniczania niskiej emisji ze szczególnym uwzględnieniem sektora bytowo-komunalnego*. Ministerstwo Środowiska.
Shipan, C. R., & Volden, C. (2008). The mechanisms of policy diffusion. *American Journal of Political Science, 52*(4), 840–857. https://doi.org/10.1111/j.1540-5907.2008.00346.x
Śliwowski, P., Trojanowska, M., & Wincewicz-Price, A. (2020). *Poles and air quality. Social norms as a source of change?* Polish Economic Institute.
Snyder, E. G., Watkins, T. H., Solomon, P. A., Thoma, E. D., Williams, R. W., Hagler, G. S. W., Shelow, D., Hindin, D. A., Kilaru, V. J., & Preuss, P. W. (2013). The changing paradigm of air pollution monitoring. *Environmental Science & Technology, 47*(20), 11369–11377. https://doi.org/10.1021/es4022602
Staggenborg, S. (1988). The consequences of professionalization and formalization in the pro-choice movement. *American Sociological Review, 53*(4), 585–605. https://doi.org/10.2307/2095851
Stala-Szlugaj, K. (2011). Spalanie węgla kamiennego w sektorze komunalno-bytowym – wpływ na wielkość "niskiej emisji". *Rocznik Ochrona Środowiska, 13*, 1877–1889.
Stone, D. A. (1989). Causal stories and the formation of policy agendas. *Political Science Quarterly, 104*(2), 281–300. https://doi.org/10.2307/2151585
Subašić, M., Birch, S., Fagan, A., & Maltby, T. (2024). Activism in the era of democratic backsliding: Explaining the efficacy of the clean-air campaigns in Poland. *Democratization*. https://doi.org/10.1080/13510347.2024.2346109
Traczyk, P., & Gruszecka-Kosowska, A. (2020). The condition of air pollution in Kraków, Poland, in 2005-2020, with health risk assessment. *International Journal of Environmental Research and Public Health, 17*(17), 6063. https://doi.org/10.3390/ijerph17176063
Unruh, G. C. (2000). Understanding carbon lock-in. *Energy Policy, 28*(12), 817–830. https://doi.org/10.1016/S0301-4215(00)00070-7
Waldholz, R. (2018, December 11). Smothered by smog, activists are urging Poland to reconsider coal. *The World*. https://theworld.org/stories/2018/12/11/poland-s-anti-smog-activists-challenge-country-s-addiction-coal
Wilczyńska-Michalik, Wanda & Michalik, Marek. (2017). Air pollution in krakow - A glance into the future from a historical perspective. Acta Geobalcanica. 3. 79-82. https://doi.org/10.18509/AGB.2017.10.
Włodarczyk, E., & Herczakowska, J. (2025). Social dimension of Poland's sustainable energy transition as assessed by residents of the Silesian region. *Sustainability, 17*(6), Article 2707. https://doi.org/10.3390/su17062707
World Health Organization. (2016). *WHO ambient air pollution database*, May 2016. World Health Organization.
Wu, X., Ramesh, M., & Howlett, M. (2015). Policy capacity: A conceptual framework for understanding policy competences and capabilities. *Policy and Society, 34*(3–4), 165–171. https://doi.org/10.1016/j.polsoc.2015.09.001
Yun, X., Shen, G. F., Shen, H. Z., Meng, W. J., Chen, Y. L., Xu, H. R., Ren, Y., Zhong, Q. R., Du, W., Ma, J. M., & Tao, S. (2020). Residential solid fuel emissions contribute significantly to air pollution and associated health impacts in China. *Science Advances, 6*(44), Article eaba7621. https://doi.org/10.1126/sciadv.aba7621
Zabka, J. (2024). Krakow can breathe again. *Transitions*.

Chapter 4
Eco-Advisors: Their Roles and Views

Mateusz Stępień

Abstract Air pollution is one of the most pressing environmental and public health challenges worldwide, including in the European Union. In response, innovative governance instruments have been introduced to support local authorities in implementing and enforcing clean air policies. This chapter examines the role of eco-advisors in Małopolska (Lesser Poland)—a region in Poland—who serve as local officials responsible for providing expertise, raising public awareness, and supporting communities in their efforts to combat smog. Drawing on qualitative and quantitative empirical research conducted in Małopolska, the chapter explores the institutional framework and day-to-day practices of eco-advisors. The findings highlight both the effectiveness and the limitations of this institutional innovation. While eco-advisors have contributed to improving local policy implementation and strengthening citizen engagement, their impact has been constrained by limited resources, structural barriers, and the absence of strong formal powers. The chapter situates the Polish experience within the broader European context of multilevel governance and discusses the potential of intermediary actors to facilitate the implementation of environmental policies at the local level.

Keywords Eco-advisors · Air pollution policy · Multilevel governance · Implementation of EU law

4.1 Introduction: Context and Aims

The dynamics of complex governing structures are often conceptualized through the lens of multilevel governance (MLG). This model is typically understood as a strategy for achieving complex policy objectives by distributing competences both upward and downward from the level of the nation-state while also emphasizing

---

M. Stępień (✉)
Department of Sociology of Law, Jagiellonian University, Kraków, Poland
e-mail: mateusz.stepien@uj.edu.pl

M. Stępień, M. Klinowski, *Fighting Air Pollution*, Law and Visual Jurisprudence 17, https://doi.org/10.1007/978-3-032-23909-9_4

broad inclusivity (Tortola, 2017). In this context, the term governance denotes the enhanced role of nonstate actors (e.g., nongovernmental organizations (NGOs), citizens) in the policymaking process, or at the very least, it signals a mode of governing that diverges from the traditional hierarchical, top-down model. Proponents of MLG regard it as a superior framework for public decision-making, particularly when contrasted with centralized, state-dominated systems (Marks & Hooghe, 2004, p. 16). MLG structures are often described as particularly well suited for addressing cross-boundary problems or issues requiring sustained, long-term commitments, such as air-quality management (Knill & Liefferink, 2007).

Moving from theoretical formulations to practical applications, the policymaking process within EU member states is frequently described in terms of MLG (see Hooghe & Marks, 2001). Air protection policies, in particular, are regulated within such a framework (Knill & Liefferink, 2007; Newig & Fritsch, 2009). Here, MLG can also be understood as a descriptive analytical model of real-world governance practices, wherein decision-making and implementation are distributed across multiple levels of authority and remain open to cross-influences. This highlights both the inherent challenges and strengths of such arrangements and emphasizes the dynamic interactions among different levels of governance—supranational, national, regional, and local—each of which produces decisions of differing scope and nature. All these levels are, to varying degrees, embedded in power struggles among competing actors pursuing their own agendas. However, as some scholars note, the decentralization of competences associated with MLG in environmental governance provides local administrations with a meaningful room for maneuver in addressing problems at the local level and facilitates the incorporation of local knowledge, which in turn enhances the quality of decision-making (Newig & Fritsch, 2009). In reference to the MLG frame, in Poland—a unitary state—the governance process begins with EU air-quality policies and directives, continues through national environmental legislation and regulatory mechanisms, is operationalized by public agencies (e.g., those responsible for air-quality monitoring or administering smog-reduction subsidies), and culminates in a range of decisions made at the regional (e.g., Małopolska Air Improvement Programs (MAIPs)) and the municipal (*gmina*) levels.

The effectiveness of EU air pollution measures under the MLG framework has not yet been comprehensively studied (with the exception of Newig & Koontz, 2013; Gollata & Newig, 2017). Thinking in terms of compliance prevailed within the European legal studies—that is, whether the decisions made at the national or subnational level comply with EU requirements: how air-pollution-related directives are transposed, whether air protection programs are created in a timely manner, and whether information about the air is made adequately available. In particular, the focus has been mainly on transposition, especially on the translation of directives' objectives into specific national legal measures. This is partly because transposition is relatively easy to examine, particularly with regard to the timeliness of transposition measures (Treib, 2014).

Fortunately, new research approaches are emerging that advocate moving beyond the traditional compliance perspective toward identifying the factors that determine, first, the form of legal transposition and, subsequently, the various paths of implementation (e.g., Thomann & Zhelyazkova, 2017; Zhelyazkova et al. 2024). Increasing recognition is being given to what happens at the lowest levels of governance (Bondarouk & Mastenbroek, 2018; Borghetto & Franchino, 2010), including the beneficial role of customized implementation, which "not only affects policy results (output legitimacy), it also provides procedural opportunities to involve societal actors and 'take back control' over distant EU policies (input and throughput legitimacy)" (Thomann, 2019: 2012). This emerging research agenda highlights how legal norms that have been "Europeanized" at the national level are subsequently translated into concrete decisions at the local level—a process shaped by a range of contextual conditions, incentives, and constraints (e.g., Thomann & Sager, 2017). From this perspective, analyses of "EU law in action" pay particular attention to (1) variation among local public actors, particularly in terms of available resources and political commitment; (2) local power and influence networks; and (3) mechanisms for oversight, reporting, tool development, enforcement, and implementation support. This shift in focus underscores the importance of local conditions in determining how local authorities operate in practice—especially in their interactions with citizens, local politics, and interests. Crucially, these authorities play a key role in giving substance to abstract policies and regulations that flow from Brussels through national capitals, shaping their meaning through local implementation.

The case of Małopolska, one of the regions in Poland (see the *Introduction*), illustrates a distinct trajectory in the implementation of a specific segment of EU environmental law. As discussed in Chap. 2, the region has faced—and continues to face—exceptionally high levels of air pollution. The decision to rely on existing legal instruments, particularly the antismog resolution mechanism (regulated under Article 97 of the Environmental Protection Law of 2001—see Chap. 2)—which was not originally intended to serve as a primary tool for combating smog—proved politically expedient for those in power. This approach enabled policymakers to shift responsibility onto regional governments, provided greater regulatory flexibility (and also unequal protection against smog), and allowed for the accommodation of diverse voter preferences. At the same time, it responded—at least to some extent—to rising public concern, growing environmental awareness, and legal obligations stemming from EU membership. However, this strategy may also be interpreted as a way of avoiding direct national-level engagement with one of the country's most pressing societal challenges (see Chap. 2).

Against this backdrop, the Małopolska Regional Assembly adopted Poland's first so-called antismog resolution in 2013, which permitted the use of only two fuels—natural gas and heating oil—for heating within the city of Kraków (besides the heat and hot water provided by the city). In effect, this constituted a ban on the use of coal and wood. However, the resolution was legally challenged and subsequently annulled by administrative courts, delaying the implementation of effective air-quality measures. A revised version of the resolution, adopted 3 years later and maintaining the same regulatory direction, withstood judicial scrutiny and remained legally binding. It was later supplemented by a second, less progressive resolution mandating the phased replacement of heating systems across the rest of the Małopolska region (see Chap. 2).

It should be noted that although, from the perspective of many residents and most experts, the successful adoption of the two aforementioned resolutions came too late, it nonetheless marked a pioneering step within the Polish context. However, the introduction of such measures—for both Kraków and the broader Małopolska region—assumed and required substantial financial and organizational resources. In other words, without dedicated financial support mechanisms (e.g., subsidies for replacing heating systems in Kraków or for changing stoves and improving energy efficiency in homes in the rest of Małopolska), the resolutions would have remained purely symbolic, sharing the fate of many other ineffective environmental regulations. Government programs such as *Kawka* (2013–2018), followed by *Czyste Powietrze* ("Clean Air," launched in 2018) (see Chap. 2), along with other funding sources—including a dedicated municipal program in Kraków that covered up to 90% of investment costs for certain groups of residents—played a crucial role in facilitating implementation. However, managing these funding schemes—alongside the increasing involvement of municipalities in implementing Air Improvement Programs and antismog resolutions—required enhanced capacities, particularly in terms of human resources and local-level coordination. In fact, the very concept of the antismog resolutions, directed to all users of heating installations, presupposed that their implementation would necessitate extensive organizational and coordination efforts at the municipal level. This included sustained interaction with residents, communication and outreach campaigns, and initiatives aimed at informing, educating, and even persuading—all of which were essential to effective enforcement. Over time, it became increasingly clear that obligations imposed on residents—in the absence of financial assistance and robust institutional support—would not only remain unfulfilled but could also generate public resistance. After all, the resolutions impose requirements on hundreds of thousands of recipients—people with different levels of communication skills, varying attitudes toward environmental issues, and widely differing financial capacities.

Against this background, a significant new element introduced to support the implementation of the antismog resolutions (and the related financial programs) was the establishment of a new role at the municipal level in Małopolska: the eco-advisors (EAs)—in many respects, a new profession. When viewed within the framework of multilevel governance in the European Union, the creation and deployment of eco-advisors underscore the critical importance of the lowest level of governance and the necessity of equipping it adequately. Without sufficient human and organizational capacity at the "street level," the effectiveness of the entire policy process cannot be realized.

The implementation of eco-advisors in Małopolska was initiated through the EU LIFE Program, whose updated phase was adopted in late 2013 (https://eur-lex.europa.eu/eli/reg/2013/1293/oj/eng). This iteration introduced "integrated projects" that aim to support authorities in EU Member States in executing environmental and climate strategies at the regional, multiregional, or national level. These projects aimed at enhancing compliance with key EU legislation in six areas: nature conservation, water, air, waste management, climate change mitigation, and adaptation. The rationale behind this framework is rooted in the recognition that EU regulations without effective implementation risk undermining both core values and the Union's tangible influence. Without Małopolska's successful application to this initiative, it is difficult to imagine the changes that have occurred in the region—even if these changes did not fully meet experts' expectations.

The first stage of Małopolska's involvement in the LIFE Program entailed the submission of a proposal to develop a comprehensive view on the role and place of EAs and accompanying promotional activities (start date: 01/01/2015; end date: 30/06/2015). A central outcome of this stage was a consulting firm's report outlining a broad plan to enhance implementation by embedding eco-advisors within municipalities. This plan drew inspiration from the German model of locally employed "climate protection managers" (*Klimaschutzmanager*), supported by federal funds (Deloitte Advisory, 2015, pp. 20–21). These professionals coordinate local climate initiatives and ensure the execution of international, EU, and federal climate legislation at the local level. Typically employed by municipalities, *Klimaschutzmanager* operate as critical links among local administrations, civil society, and the business sector (Zeigermann et al., 2020; see also Buschmann et al. (2022) on their role in adaptation policy).

The second phase involved the successful submission of a comprehensive project proposal entitled *Implementation of Air Improvement Plan for the Małopolska Region – Małopolska in a Healthy Atmosphere* (start date: 01/10/2015; end date: 31/12/2025, later extended). The lead applicant was the Marshall's Office of the Małopolska region, in partnership with several stakeholders, including the Kraków Smog Alarm (see Chap. 3). As the title suggests, the core objective was to operationalize the *Małopolska Air Improvement Program*, a binding regional legal and policy framework outlining specific instruments to combat air pollution. Importantly, the introduction of eco-advisors was conceived as a central mechanism for enhancing the implementation of antismog resolutions.

The project's objectives (see Table 4.1) reflect the underlying logic of the eco-advisors' role. These objectives span three core areas. First, several goals aim to build local administrative capacities necessary for implementing environmental actions at the municipal level (e.g., objectives 1, 6, 7, and 9). These include integrating environmental concerns into municipal planning, improving the practical competencies of local officials, and reinforcing regional cooperation. Second, the project seeks to enhance municipal leadership and eliminate superficial compliance (objectives 2 and 3). These aims respond to known weaknesses in local-level competencies and coordination. Third, the external-facing objectives focus on increasing residents' awareness and public engagement, particularly at the local level (objectives 4 and 5). This includes educating residents and encouraging uptake of financial support schemes. These priorities stem from a critical view of the preparedness of many municipalities to fully implement the Małopolska Air Quality Plan (MAQP) due to both institutional deficits and insufficient political will.

Eco-advisors were envisioned as facilitators of local air-quality policy coordination. According to the project website, they are "responsible for implementing

Table 4.1 LIFE Małopolska objectives

1	The elimination of the barriers created by very low institutional capacities and insufficient implementation of air quality actions at the municipal level by establishing a network of eco-managers;
2	Increasing involvement of municipal authorities from Małopolska in MAIP implementation and subsequent updates of MAIP;
3	Increasing recognition of the significance of air quality management by local decision makers in Małopolska and in other regions;
4	The elimination of the barriers created by low awareness of air quality improvement needs through public education campaigns in the Małopolska region;
5	Building behavioral responses by encouraging inhabitants of the Małopolska region to apply for financial schemes (e.g. grants, soft loans) for the replacement of obsolete solid fuel boilers and thermal retrofitting of houses;
6	The elimination of the barriers created by weak integration of municipal-level planning in the area of energy management and air quality;
7	Increasing the know-how and competences of all local authorities in Małopolska and in other regions;
8	Tightening cooperation within the hotspot (southern Poland, Slovakia and the Czech Republic) by joint activities in emission inventorying and modelling as well as exchange of experiences in the area of air quality improvement; and
9	Effective implementation of a low-stack emission abatement program in Kraków, the first Polish municipality that has introduced a solid fuel ban in the household heating sector.

air-quality initiatives in the region's cities and towns, advising the public on how to stop using old stoves and solid fuel boilers." Notably, neither the original 2009 Małopolska Air Improvement Plan nor its 2013 version included any reference to eco-advisors. A brief mention appeared only in the 2017 revision, which stated: "In municipalities, so-called eco-advisers will be employed. Their task will be to obtain external funding for actions to reduce pollutant emissions and to mobilize residents to participate in these actions. The project is scheduled for implementation from October 2015 to the end of 2023" (MAIP, 2017, p. 40). The 2020 version of the MAIP significantly expanded the description of eco-advisors' responsibilities. These now included advising residents on renewable energy technologies, heating systems, available subsidies, and antismog regulations; conducting environmental education at the local level; and supporting the implementation of national programs such as *Czyste Powietrze* and *Stop Smog* (MAIP, 2020, p. 44). Their primary goal was described as "taking actions to fully and more quickly implement the Małopolska Air Improvement Program" (MAIP, 2020, p. 39). The document also specified the recommended number of eco-advisors per municipality based on population size, as well as per county (MAIP, 2020, p. 47). Counties (*powiaty*) were additionally required to employ a climate eco-advisor responsible for coordinating municipal efforts (MAIP, 2020, pp. 42–46). Importantly, the 2020 plan marked a shift in focus: while earlier documents emphasized securing external funding, the updated version highlighted the eco-advisors' role in directly supporting residents in navigating funding applications—an adaptation to the growing centralization of subsidy programs. This role remained largely unchanged in the 2023 MAIP, which defined eco-advisors' tasks in similar terms (MAIP, 2023, pp. 29–30). Importantly, participation in postgraduate training was initially mandatory for eco-advisors employed under the LIFE Program, as outlined in the consultancy report (Deloitte Advisory, 2015, pp. 47, 59). The first such training was provided by the AGH University of Science and Technology in the 2016/2017 academic year and offered again in 2018/2019.

Eco-advisors are a unique category of civil servants or, rather, public officials. Although they are most often funded through regional budgets—typically supported by the EU's LIFE Program—they carry out tasks at the municipal level and frequently utilize municipal resources. Embedded within local government structures, they work directly on the ground: visiting schools, participating in community events, and engaging with residents on a daily basis. Their deep familiarity with local contexts and the practical challenges of implementing air-quality regulations gives them a distinct vantage point. They hear public concerns, understand residents' needs, and observe whether local authorities foster compliance or undermine it through conflicting messages. They also coordinate information campaigns and witness their immediate effects. In many cases, their assessments are the most accurate—and sometimes the only—source of specific local information. Moreover, their ability to exchange knowledge with peers allows them to provide comparative insights across municipalities. As such, their perspective is crucial for understanding street-level implementation processes, yet it remains largely overlooked. The profession itself is relatively new in Poland and is characterized by a distinctive set of responsibilities and an uncommon institutional position.

Given this broader context, the chapter pursues three interrelated research objectives. The first is to examine the general working conditions, institutional settings, and specific tasks performed by eco-advisors, as well as their self-perceptions regarding their role. These findings serve as a basis for evaluating the eco-advisor model as a potential framework for managing air quality—or, more broadly, other public environmental goods—at the local level. This, in turn, allows for a critical reflection on the model's strengths, limitations, and potential areas for improvement. The second objective draws on the unique vantage point of eco-advisors to provide insight into residents' attitudes toward smog and mitigation efforts. This includes advisors' observations on the public's motivations, knowledge, and dispositions concerning air pollution and the measures applied to address it. In this context, eco-advisors are treated as indirect—but highly informed—sources of information. This approach is justified by their privileged access to community behaviors, offering a valuable complement to self-reported narratives and survey-based data on residents' responses to antismog regulations. The third objective is to analyze how eco-advisors assess the real-world functioning of antismog regulations and related policies, given their central role in implementation. Particular attention is paid to the challenges they identify in the implementation process and their reflections on how the effectiveness of these policies might be enhanced.

4.2 Methodology Applied

To achieve the aforementioned objectives, a two-stage research tool was designed and implemented: in-depth interviews with eco-advisors, followed by a survey developed on the basis of the interviews. This approach combined qualitative and quantitative methods, with the former constituting the core of the research and the latter serving as a complement.

The interviews were conducted in 2022. Participants were selected randomly from a publicly available list of eco-advisors working in the Małopolska region. The implementation of the LIFE Program with respect to eco-advisors began in 2017, when 16 individuals were initially hired. By 2020, the regional Air Improvement Plan mandated that each municipality employ at least one eco-advisor by 30 September 2021. In 2022, the number of eco-advisors exceeded 200; however, this figure fluctuated over the course of the year, and not all active advisors were included in the official online directory dedicated to Małopolska's antismog initiatives. The interviews were relatively short, lasting approximately 1 hour on average. Notably, they were typically conducted online during the advisors' working hours. This arrangement has certain drawbacks, as participants were in their workplaces, potentially near supervisors or surrounded by colleagues (for a discussion of in-depth interviews conducted online but outside workplaces, see Stępień, 2025). Nevertheless, this approach had the benefit of increasing advisors' willingness to participate, as scheduling during working hours is easier than requesting participation during personal time. The main study was preceded by a pilot phase involving three eco-advisors. Somewhat surprisingly, thematic saturation was reached relatively quickly with regard to the emergence of codes and meanings (Hennink et al., 2017; see also empirical studies suggesting that thematic saturation typically occurs after 6–12 interviews: Guest et al., 2006), which led to the decision to conclude this research phase after conducting 17 full interviews.

The interview protocol was based on differentiating among various modalities of effectiveness (communicative, psychological/motivational, behavioral, axiological), applied here to antismog resolutions and more broadly to air-quality policy. Once again, it is worth emphasizing that understanding the perspectives and observations of EAs contributes significantly to grasping the local context of environmental law implementation, as they possess direct knowledge from one-on-one conversations, community meetings, field visits, and inspections. Significantly, most eco-advisors live in the municipalities where they work, which gives them deeper insight into the community. At the same time, this embeddedness may cause some practices to go unnoticed because they are perceived as self-evident. The significance of their perspectives cannot be overstated, though it is also essential to account for their embeddedness in local connections (including power-related ones), which on occasion might cause their ecological accountabilities—notably for air quality—to be balanced with or even subordinated to different commitments. This remains a hypothesis, framed conditionally and narrowly. Still, it is not controversial to suggest that being embedded in a local context offers unique insight while also presenting certain limitations (e.g., an aversion to criticizing "their own" community). It is also necessary to acknowledge the broader context in which the interviews were conducted. Initially, this was the late stage of the COVID-19 pandemic, followed by the Russian invasion of Ukraine; as one advisor [EA 12] put it, "people just don't care. In light of everything happening in the world, that furnace is the least important thing right now."

Moving to the type of data analysis employed, thematic analysis was selected as the primary method for organizing and interpreting the material. This approach was chosen for its ability to "identify, analyze, and report patterns (themes) within the data" (Braun & Clarke, 2006, p. 79). The objective was to map eco-advisors' perspectives on various issues and to extract key themes—concepts that encapsulate core ideas relevant to the research aims and reflect patterned responses or clusters of meaning. Thematic analysis is commonly used to distill extensive and heterogeneous qualitative data into a structured and interpretable format. In this study, following an initial familiarization with the interview transcripts, preliminary themes aligned with the research questions were identified. The transcripts were then reviewed again, and the thematic framework was refined and reinterpreted to develop a clearer and more nuanced understanding of the eco-advisors' viewpoints.

The initial application of thematic analysis only partially fulfilled the research objectives. Due to the nature of the research instrument, it was not possible to assess the influence of municipality size or type on the implementation of antismog resolutions. Furthermore, the interview method did not allow for the development of standardized indicators that would enable a precise comparison of advisors' opinions and observations. The sample used in this first research phase was also not representative. It is likely that individuals who agreed to participate in the interviews were characterized by higher levels of engagement or a stronger sense of professional responsibility—traits that may have made them more inclined to accept the research invitation. For these reasons, a follow-up quantitative study was deemed necessary to complement and extend the qualitative findings.

In the second stage of the empirical research, an online questionnaire was developed and, after a pilot phase, sent to all eco-advisors working in Małopolska at the time the tool was being designed. The survey was conducted in April 2023—invitation emails were sent to 203 eco-advisors representing 182 municipalities (some municipalities employed more than one advisor), using contact information from the official website (https://powietrze.malopolska.pl/ekodoradcy/). A total of 126 eco-advisors completed the entire questionnaire, yielding a response rate of 62%. To maximize participation and minimize survey abandonment, the collection of demographic data was deliberately limited (e.g., questions about gender and age were excluded). This decision was motivated by concerns about maintaining respondent anonymity. Detailed demographic questions could have increased concerns about the possibility of identification, especially given that the community of eco-advisors in Małopolska is relatively small and their contact details are publicly accessible. The collected data were subsequently subjected to statistical analysis.

4.3 The Work and Perspective of Eco-Advisors: A Qualitative Approach

4.3.1 Work Context and Tasks

General Findings

In the in-depth interviews, we asked EAs about the various aspects of their work (e.g., the tasks they perform, the attitude of local authorities, career trajectories). Several general findings merit preliminary mention.

First, the interviews reveal considerable variation among eco-advisors. While some possess educational backgrounds or prior professional experience in environmental fields, the majority have followed administrative career paths, often having previously worked within local government structures. This does not imply that the latter group performs their duties inadequately; however, specialized knowledge related to environmental issues—particularly air pollution—clearly shapes an advisor's approach to the role. In general, therefore, eco-advisors should be regarded not as comprehensive environmental experts but rather as civil servants engaged primarily in bureaucratic and administrative responsibilities, as will be further discussed. Moreover, the interviews highlight significant disparities in both resources and the scope of air-quality initiatives across municipalities. These institutional differences directly influence the operational capacities and effectiveness of individual eco-advisors.

At the time of the study, the core task performed by eco-advisors was managing subsidies for replacing heating systems and conducting thermal retrofitting—particularly by the *Clean Air* program (see Chap. 2). While such assistance is undoubtedly necessary, this practice tends to prevent many of the eco-advisors from adopting more systemic or innovative approaches. That said, it should be acknowledged that much more is happening in Małopolska's municipalities in the realm of air quality than before the eco-advisor initiative was introduced. As one eco-advisor, EA 12, explained, "I worked in the office before, and really… nothing in the field of air protection happened apart from the annual report. All these activities only started after 2016." More broadly, eco-advisors' accounts—likely shaped in part by the constraints of the employed interview scenario—seldom reflect a wider environmental or ecological context. Most respondents focus narrowly on specific air-quality-related tasks, often without a holistic approach to environmental protection, though a few notable exceptions exist (e.g., ED 1 and ED 2). A bureaucratic impasse is also evident: the regional Air Improvement Program sets minimum thresholds for inspections, meetings, etc. While this allows for quantification and reporting, it also constrains innovation and comprehensive thinking. This institutional confinement is further underscored by the limited collaboration with nongovernmental organizations: most eco-advisors do not report engaging with such entities in any meaningful way, although one (ED 3) mentioned cooperation with ClientEarth. Eco-advisors are generally aware of organizations such as the Kraków Smog Alert (see Chap. 3), but they do not maintain ongoing partnerships with them; interactions are infrequent and typically limited to occasional invitations to participate in events.

It is also noteworthy that eco-advisors generally avoided explicit references to local politics. While this was not the primary topic of the interviews—focused on the effectiveness of antismog resolutions—the issue of political will and leadership at the local level remains highly relevant. Literature on local air-quality policy implementation (e.g., in the Netherlands) has debated whether managerial competence or political will—that is, the presence of a clear mandate and prioritization—plays the more decisive role (Bondarouk et al., 2020; see also Bondarouk et al., 2017). In this context, one might suspect that probing the attitudes of local leadership was a sensitive issue for eco-advisors, particularly given that most of the interviews were conducted during working hours, often in the municipal offices where the eco-advisors themselves were based. Only one advisor—ED 2—spoke openly about the significance of political will, offering a positive assessment of the support they received from their local leadership:

> When your boss is determined and doesn't let up, it gives you more energy—it shows that the job matters. If you had a boss who said, "Do it because it's required, because there'll be an audit," then your approach would be different, right? But he's engaged, he applauds you, notices new ways of reaching residents, and when someone in the community says, "That's a great initiative," it changes the way you work. That's the main benefit—when the head cares, the rest of the body cares too, right?

This topic might be better explored through quantitative methods, where guarantees of anonymity and private participation (e.g., through survey responses) may encourage respondents to make more candid reflections.

Comprehensiveness of Support and Proximity

When describing their roles and responsibilities, EAs often emphasized the comprehensiveness of the services they provide. They indicated that residents receive full information and assistance throughout the entire process of seeking environmentally friendly home modernization solutions, as well as in securing and settling funds for such investments. Eco-advisors highlighted their support at every stage—from searching for information, choosing the appropriate funding program, submitting applications, to the final stage of project settlement. This sense of comprehensiveness was underscored by EA 5: "If a resident ends up here, in our municipality, we can help them from A to Z." Other eco-advisors [14, 12, 11] echoed this sentiment: "We pretty much prepare everything for the residents"; "We practically do everything for the residents here at the office"; "[we help] from A to Z.".

Occasionally, as EA 14 explained, this assistance extended beyond typical duties, including accompanying residents to notary appointments (to help resolve legal ownership issues that enable funding eligibility) or even providing help at a construction material depot during fuel purchases. Such efforts, beyond formal obligations, are justified by the desire "to help the least capable individuals who genuinely want to make a change and to facilitate all these procedures for them." EA 2 also remarked, "It's no trouble … to visit them [residents], because I've done that—bringing along a trusted installer to help assess the cost or verify if some charlatan [i.e., an unreliable service provider] gave an accurate quote." These additional actions are supported by the local nature of their work and their close social proximity.

Eco-advisors perceive themselves as closely connected to residents. This proximity operates on two levels. First, it is spatial—they live and work in the same municipalities, typically located in municipal offices that are well known and accessible to local residents. Second, it is social—they are familiar with local conditions, know how to communicate effectively within their communities, and are attuned to the specific social and cultural dynamics of their surroundings. Depending on the size of the municipality, eco-advisors are often regarded as "local people." In most cases, they reported that residents know who they are, what their role entails, and where to find them. As EA 9 noted, "Residents know where they can come … and if someone wants help, they'll definitely get it." This combination of spatial and social proximity, reinforced by public awareness of their function, translates into genuine accessibility. It is particularly valuable for supporting individuals who may lack cultural or technological competencies—for instance, those who struggle with submitting online funding applications.

This proximity and comprehensiveness result in high levels of interaction between eco-advisors and residents. For example, in the context of individual inquiries and consultations, EA 3 reported: "Last year [2021], I received 6,500 phone calls, the same number of emails, and 1,200 in-person visits. Our municipality isn't particularly large, so the number of people and calls really shows the level of interest." Such intensity inevitably generates challenges. EA 2, when asked about the difficulties of his work, responded: "In human interactions, people rarely say 'thank you.' And then they'll smear your name, saying they weren't informed properly." He also mentioned being publicly criticized, particularly by a group that constantly contests everything: "They don't want to help at all, but they'll trash every piece of information we post online or on Facebook. That's their thing—never help, but criticize everything we do." Given the personal nature of their work, it is unsurprising that eco-advisors often become the targets of emotions and frustrations, serving as personifications of imposed regulations. EA 5 described this experience as demotivating. She noted the tendency of residents to blame the municipality—or, effectively, the eco-advisor—for inconveniences related to bans and mandates, which were part of antismog regulations:

> (…) the municipality is seen as the bad guy because it has to enforce ... or ensure that residents replace their boilers. So, residents come in saying, "The mayor is such and such," bad-mouthing the mayor, bad-mouthing the municipality, claiming we're only here to punish, not help. That creates a negative image of the municipality ... because of the anti-smog resolution. Sometimes, I feel overwhelmed by these people, by these opinions, where on the one hand, you want to raise awareness, but on the other, someone gives you negative feedback ... and then your motivation drops.

Another source of discomfort relates to situations where EAs organize events or other initiatives but receive little to no response from residents. EA 2 recounted how, during the COVID-19 pandemic, he proposed a contest for eco-themed short videos with a cash prize: "There were zero or even fewer than zero participants.

When you come up with cool ideas, gadgets, or events and get no response, it really cuts your wings." Working at the local level—especially when trying to move beyond entrenched social practices—carries these kinds of risks.

Informing and Educating

Informational (and advisory) and educational activities are central components of the eco-advisors' role, in terms of both their official tasks and actual practice. While these categories can overlap, the latter is more focused on fostering proenvironmental attitudes, particularly regarding air quality, while the former involves the straightforward dissemination of facts. These eco-advisors' activities can target individuals (e.g., advising visitors, mailing brochures) or larger groups (e.g., meetings with seniors, school visits, local festivals). A different typology distinguishes between content delivered directly by eco-advisors (e.g., at consultations or events) and content distributed *via* mass media (e.g., Facebook, websites, newspapers, radio broadcasts, or posted mail). It is important to note that the study was conducted during the tail end of the COVID-19 pandemic, and many eco-advisors referenced limitations in communication due to the pandemic.

Municipalities already maintain established communication channels with residents, which eco-advisors typically rely on while also supplementing them with additional methods. For example, EA 6 described a typical toolkit:

> Twice this year, residents who use old boilers were sent information about the main obligations under the anti-smog resolution. Notices were published in the local press, posted on the website and social media. We're organizing an outdoor event near the municipal office in early September, with an eco-adviser booth. My colleague and I also distributed leaflets in nearby properties via the postal operator.

There are variations between municipalities in the scale of informational and educational efforts driven by the differences in resources available to support them. Broader initiatives are more likely when there is strong support from local leaders and residents, along with greater resources. One example comes from EA 2, who works in a well-resourced, dynamic municipality (though not a large city):

> We organize eco-picnics and run a campaign called "NAME ANONIMIZED," where we showcase efforts that improve air quality. We collect plastic bottles, caps, and used batteries in schools. Municipalities are rewarded for these actions. We've sown flower meadows, installed insect houses, distributed mini greenhouses to kindergartens … Young people pedal bikes to generate electricity and watch educational films on air quality. We won a recycling machine ("recyklomat"), set up composting bins in the local park, purchased Airly sensors to monitor air quality, and installed educational paths in our local forest. We include anti-smog resolution info with tax notices. I believe residents are aware—both of their obligations and the consequences of pollution.

In this case, the breadth and diversity of activities are striking. Air-quality issues are not approached narrowly; rather, the objective is to cultivate broader environmental awareness. Accordingly, the role of eco-advisors extends well beyond processing grant applications and providing consultations.

When it comes to youth-oriented education, the methods are even more creative and varied. EA 10 noted: "It's definitely easier to reach children and young people than adults—it's easier to run such activities in schools, and the interest is higher. When it's just for adults, there's less engagement." Indeed, young people are a strategic target in eco-advisors' work. Games and play-based methods are frequently used. EA 7 described puppet shows for younger children and mentioned educational maps for kindergartens that highlight antismog landmarks in the municipality. Prior experience and intermunicipal eco-advisor networks contribute to these ideas. Next, EA 1, for example, organized field trips to district heating plants: "pupils gained first-hand experience in a place they rarely visit. The tour of the facility was impactful." Another initiative involved 2-week workshops in mobile educational labs, where students could touch heat pumps and learn how solar panels work. As EA 1 reflected, "I think the impact will last. Their awareness was raised, and they passed some of that knowledge on to parents, grandparents, and friends."

Nearly all eco-advisors highlighted the development of air-quality monitoring and public notification systems as a significant area of progress. For instance, EA 1 described the installation of 21 sensors and LED display boards near transportation hubs. According to his account, every town in the municipality now features a board that communicates real-time air-quality data. These visual tools serve both informational and educational purposes. EA 1 and EA 2 reported that their municipalities had also introduced an emoji-based alert system in schools. This simplified format effectively conveys air-quality levels to children and adolescents. Moreover, EA 2 emphasized the broader impact of such measures: "If a parent sees the board while dropping off their child, and it shows a red face in a gas mask, they'll ask, 'Were you outside today? Why?' These little interactions can have long-term effects." In addition to real-time air-quality updates, the LED boards in public spaces and educational institutions often display information about available subsidies, becoming elements of a broader visual ecosystem. This system subtly integrates environmental awareness into the rhythms of daily life, reinforcing behavioral cues and prompting community engagement.

Official Inspections

Eco-advisors spoke at length about the specifics of conducting inspections related to fuel quality and the installations in which combustion occurs. *Air Protection Improvement Programs* (of 2017, 2020, 2023) require municipalities to carry out a designated number of inspections annually (i.e., planned inspections). In addition, municipalities are reqired to conduct intervention inspections in cases where air quality deteriorates significantly—particularly when particulate matter (PM) 10 levels reach the second or third alert thresholds. A third type of inspection arises from the Eco-intervention System: a mechanism that allows citizens to report suspected violations via a dedicated website or mobile application (https://ekointerwencja.ekomalopolska.pl/app/ekointerwencja/index.html). These reports are made anonymously by indicating the suspected pollution source on a special e-map. Each such submission triggers an inspection that must be conducted within a specific time frame as stipulated by the *Air Protection Improvement Program.*

In any of the three types of inspection, if violations are found and legal sanctions (such as a fine or, later, a court-imposed penalty) are to be applied, police or municipal law enforcement (*Straż Miejska* or *Straż Gminna*) must be involved. In practice, eco-advisors often conduct these inspections jointly with enforcement bodies or independently gather documentation, which is later used by police or municipal guards to issue penalties. While the primary role of inspections is to ensure compliance with antismog regulations, they also represent a form of direct contact between eco-advisors and potential polluters. Key factors in this context include the scale of inspections (particularly the number of eco-interventions), the procedures followed during inspections, the availability of resources for conducting them, the attitudes of eco-advisors and law enforcement officers, and the actual enforcement of sanctions. The extent to which violations are penalized sends a significant signal to the public—especially when fear of sanctions is a major motivator for compliance.

The spatial and social context of inspections is highly relevant. In densely populated areas, inspections are often visible to neighbors, which creates a preventative effect by signaling that anyone might be inspected. EA 11 noted: "residents generally feel that risk, that they might be inspected... because it spreads. If someone's neighbor gets checked, they talk about it—'they're going around and doing inspections'—so I think people have that tingle of concern that they could be next." This reflects the social dynamics of enforcement: awareness of inspections can lead to behavioral change, provided certain conditions are met. Of course, the nature of the inspection itself matters. As EA 13 stated, "we go into a village and inspect a few buildings, and the neighbors see it and realize—we could show up at their place next. And that thought—that we might find something—makes people give up on burning illegal fuels. They know we can show up anytime and uncover illegal burning practices banned by the resolution." Meanwhile, EA 6 mentioned: "our staff did visit the reported residents. They gave warnings and left informational materials, and in one case even collected a sample and sent it for analysis." This lenient approach—favoring education over repression—may be justified in some cases. However, such "softness" also communicates a broader message about the stance of local authorities. Unfortunately, we do not know how informants perceived this leniency. Visibility of enforcement is critical—as both a symbolic signal and a mechanism for influencing behavior—but so, too, are the outcomes of inspections and the institutional will to act.

Importantly, inspections are not conducted in a political vacuum. Municipal authorities in Poland—both the executive (mayors, village heads, city presidents) and the legislative (municipal councils)—are, as a rule, directly elected. Thus, their policies must resonate with the views of a significant portion of residents, including those who are skeptical about air pollution, contest regulatory measures, or oppose financial penalties. One political strategy is to avoid alienating voters who are hostile to air-quality resolutions by practicing "light" enforcement while at the same time offering support to those more cooperative. EA 5 directly referenced the "public image" of municipalities, saying:

> I think it's a complicated issue. On the one hand, we should penalize people… so we carry out inspections. But on the other hand, there's the PR side of things. If the municipality

> hands out too many fines, it will be perceived negatively by residents. That could, for instance, lower support for the current administration.

Similarly, EA 10 noted:

> And certainly, another barrier is that … well, that the municipality itself is expected to carry out inspections. That's not necessarily ideal. Perhaps it would be better if external institutions handled that, because mayors, village heads, or city presidents don't always want to … be the ones punishing their own residents.

Desire to retain or build electoral support limits the political viability of strict, consistent enforcement in many municipalities. The strategy of "soft enforcement"—minimizing fines, applying the lowest penalties, and refraining from follow-up inspections—only makes sense where large parts of the population do not view air pollution as a pressing issue. If the public did prioritize clean air, stringent inspections would bring political dividends.

Some eco-advisors advocated for a situational, case-by-case approach to inspections. EA 3 offered a general reflection:

> I believe each case is particular. The municipal guards have been around for years; they know the social makeup of the community and the unique circumstances of each resident. They should have tools and discretion to tailor the penalties accordingly … I think it's more important to let the guards assess each case individually and give them a broader range of influence over the resident.

However, this strong emphasis on individualization may be criticized, as it potentially undermines the achievement of broader air-quality standards (that benefit everyone). Nevertheless, some situations are difficult to assess. EA 2 recalled that, starting in July 2017, a provision of the antismog resolution prohibiting the use of noncertified boilers took effect in Małopolska (outside Kraków). Aware of the upcoming ban, some sellers offered these boilers at promotional prices, and certain residents—especially older ones—fell into this trap. "So sometimes," EA 2 admitted, "we turn a blind eye. Because what can you say? That you got tricked into buying this boiler two years ago, and now you have to scrap it?" This eco-advisor explicitly stated that no legal action was taken in such cases—an example of moral reasoning prevailing, at least in narrowly defined circumstances, over strict adherence to legal norms.

4.3.2 Eco-Advisors on Residents' Attitudes and Motivations

Motivations for Compliance

Eco-advisors consistently emphasize a notable improvement in public awareness regarding air-quality protection. Achieving this outcome was a key objective of the EU LIFE project implemented in Małopolska and a central task assigned to eco-advisors. Although they articulated varying assessments of the extent of this improvement, they all acknowledged it. At the same time, they repeatedly pointed to significant persisting challenges in this regard. One should also remain mindful of potential constraints faced by eco-advisors when speaking critically about "their" municipality and its residents. Awareness and knowledge alone do not suffice—motivations for compliance (or noncompliance) with antismog resolutions are of equal importance. While the resolutions stipulate sanctions for noncompliance, much of their effectiveness hinges on residents' attitudes, as the initiative for compliance ultimately lies in their hands. Although the introduction of the resolutions was accompanied by extensive information and education campaigns, which were later continued, our understanding of public attitudes remains limited beyond simplistic survey questions. In this context, the interviews with eco-advisors—individuals deeply embedded in their communities and engaged in daily interactions with residents—shed light on the motivations of citizens subject to these regulations. These insights complement the broader literature on proenvironmental behavior, which seldom examines motivations for compliance with specific environmental regulations (e.g., Kollmuss & Agyeman, 2002).

The case of Małopolska outside Kraków is particularly instructive, as the process of phasing out outdated heating sources was still underway at the time of the interviews. Based on the accounts provided by eco-advisors, several distinct types of resident motivations can be identified.

Health concerns constitute one such motivation. Several eco-advisors noted that these concerns were particularly salient among younger, educated individuals with children, especially those who had moved from urban to rural areas (e.g., EA 6). Affirming the presence of health-related motivations, EA 1 linked this trend to broader lifestyle shifts: "a whole package—exercise, healthy eating, environmental awareness ... and now we also care about the air we breathe. Our health has become valuable enough that we pay attention to it, and clean air is part of that." These emerging cultural trends favor an understanding of smog as a health threat and encourage, at minimum, compliance with related regulations.

But how widespread are such motivations? Here, the differences between municipalities are substantial. While EA 1 estimated that nearly half of the residents in their municipality belonged to this group, EA 2 offered a contrasting view: "very few people are aware enough to make the switch [of the heating system] for health reasons." According to their observation, only about 10% were driven by health considerations, adding: "they didn't wait for subsidies; they just replaced their systems because their health mattered most." EA 12, EA 8, and EA 15 reported even lower levels of health-driven motivation. As EA 12 put it, "You could count on one hand the people who switched solely due to environmental awareness or a desire to improve air quality." Thus, health-related motivations do exist but are limited to a narrow segment of society and are more prevalent in certain municipalities.

A particularly frequent theme in the interviews was the perception that fear of sanctions serves as the primary motivation behind residents' decisions to replace old heating systems. Several eco-advisors emphasized that many people comply not out of environmental concern but simply because "you have to do it to avoid fines later" [EA 6]. As EA 1 noted, "the fear of penalties is, to some extent, a motivating factor for residents." EA 2 similarly observed that "people have it in the back of their minds that the regulations will eventually apply to them, that something has to be done about those furnaces." Interestingly, EA 8 expressed a comparable view, pointing out that many residents proceed with replacements not because of awareness that they are harming themselves or others but rather "because they have to, because they're afraid of getting fined, afraid that the municipal police might show up."

Such motivations may stem from either general legalistic attitudes toward the law or residents' perceptions of enforcement—that is, the likelihood and consequences of inspections and their expectations for the future. A few eco-advisors noted that for some residents, the mere existence of a legal obligation sufficed. For instance, EA 5 (like EA 2 and EA 17) said that "residents usually replace it because they know they have to... They pay more attention to the regulation than to the fact that they are actually improving air quality."

Comfort and cost savings also serve as key motivations for compliance. Here, legal regulations align with individual interests. EA 9 explained that residents often prioritize convenience: "if someone has a coal furnace, switching to gas is just easier. And they're usually happy with the change." Older residents, or their children, often seek to eliminate the physical burden of maintaining coal-based systems. As EA 2 put it, "they just don't have the strength anymore to carry coal, shovel it, or go to the furnace room. And they understand that the younger generation won't always be around to help."

Financial incentives also matter. As EA 2 observed, "people do the math—if there are subsidies, they go for it." EA 3 emphasized the alignment of economic and practical benefits: "the main driver is financial. People have realized that installing new gas systems or other compliant heating means savings and less work. Even in rural areas where people used to rely on their own wood, there's a trend now toward installing gas networks because people want the convenience." In such cases, legal prohibitions act as a prompt for modernization, but the decisive factors are personal convenience and economic rationale, not environmental concern.

To summarize, according to eco-advisors, residents comply with antismog regulations for a variety of reasons: concern for personal and familial health, fear of sanctions (including a general sense of legal obligation), or for the sake of convenience and financial benefit. Importantly, few advisors pointed to motivations rooted in environmental or ecological responsibility. Nevertheless, understanding the distribution of these motivations within the population is crucial for designing policies that enhance the effectiveness of such resolutions. This also has implications for communication strategies. As EA 3 noted in relation to their municipality, "you get through to people more easily these days with economic arguments than with health ones." This suggests that economic considerations may be more persuasive in legal justifications and outreach strategies, contributing to the ongoing debate in the literature on whether cost-benefit analyses, particularly financial ones, provide sufficient motivation for environmentally responsible behavior (Steg et al., 2014; Steg et al., 2015; Whitehead & Cherry, 2007).

Social Control

Eco-advisors' accounts suggest that residents across different municipalities display diverse attitudes toward antismog resolutions and environmental issues more broadly. Awareness of the harmful effects of air pollution likewise varies considerably. These differences shape the range of strategies that residents adopt when confronted with a neighbor's polluting behavior. Responses depend not only on individual views about illegal combustion practices but also on local social dynamics—for instance, whether neighbors know each other personally, are related, or share a long-standing presence in the community. Those disturbed by polluting stoves and motivated to act may (1) initiate direct conversation and attempt to persuade the polluter, (2) exert pressure through informal social networks, or (3) report the suspected violation, either by phone (to eco-advisors or municipal services) or anonymously via the online *Ekointerwencja* platform (https://ekointerwencja.ekomalopolska.pl). Taken together, eco-advisors' testimonies provide valuable insight into the functioning of social control, understood here as community-based mechanisms of informal pressure on individuals who violate antismog regulations.

It is important to note that municipalities surrounding Kraków have experienced, and continue to experience, substantial migration from the city. For many, an ideal lifestyle includes a house surrounded by greenery in the rolling hills around Kraków. Numerous individuals have relocated to these peri-urban areas, settling in single-family homes or terraced developments. Often, the newcomers—typically living in buildings equipped with renewable-energy-based heating systems—differ in their environmental attitudes from long-established local communities, frequently composed of extended families and reliant on traditional high-emission stoves. In such cases, violations of air-quality regulations that might otherwise go unreported—either due to shared attitudes or reluctance to report "one's own"—eventually reach the authorities. This raises questions about the long-term impact on neighborly relations and community cohesion. As EA 6 explained:

> There are more and more people moving here from Kraków who come to the countryside specifically to breathe clean air. So, when they see black smoke coming from a chimney—once, twice, three times—they eventually take action, usually by submitting a report. This leads us to conduct an inspection. The resident being inspected starts to realize that the next time might result in a fine, so they start using the boiler differently and often begin considering replacing it altogether. I think they're especially aware of this when new people move into the neighborhood.

Several eco-advisors noted a growing decrease in tolerance for neighbors' fuel-burning practices. EA 6, expanding on the topic of intervention-based inspections, stated: "It all depends on how neighbors react ... What we're seeing is increased 'neighborly' concern about air quality, and that forces polluting residents to be more cautious." ED 9 pointed to a recent shift in attitudes, especially among parents of young children, who had already replaced their heating systems for health reasons:

> Lately, there has been a real change in attitudes. Residents—especially those with small children—who are aware of air pollution issues and have replaced their heating systems for their own health and that of their neighbors, are becoming less tolerant of those who don't

comply with the resolution and still burn prohibited materials. We are receiving more and more reports. In earlier years, such reports were rare.

Thus, not only newcomers but also parents of young children (often overlapping groups) are initiating forms of social control, creating new pressures within communities, and prompting intervention requests that can no longer be ignored. EA 7 highlighted the kind of reasoning that residents often use when filing reports: "I have young children, and my neighbor is polluting—I don't want them to get cancer, and I don't want to get sick either." While these pressures tend to originate from specific types of residents, it is evident that many across the region have become less hesitant to report suspected legal violations—indicating that such hesitations were once widespread.

Social influence often takes subtler forms. Changes made by one household can trigger local trends. EA 8 emphasized that while media campaigns increase awareness of antismog regulations, peer-to-peer influence is often more powerful: "What really matters is what a neighbor tells another neighbor—that's key." If modernization proves successful, early adopters frequently encourage others to follow suit. EA 6 shared an example of residents who "say they would never go back to their old heating system because the new one is so convenient, doesn't require extra effort, and keeps everything clean. Plus, the operating costs are equal to or sometimes even lower than those of the old system." These kinds of stories disrupt old assumptions and serve as motivation for others. In some cases, pressure to replace stoves arises from local conformity and imitation.

In other instances, peer pressure stems from a sense of fairness. A person who has made an investment in cleaner air and incurred costs may resent neighbors who neither contribute nor bear consequences for their polluting behavior. Residents often frame this as a free-rider problem. EA 13 described the emergence of "pressure" (though without detailing its form) in situations where one neighbor had upgraded but others had not:

If my chimney is no longer emitting smoke, I start to see my neighbor's chimney differently. Suddenly it becomes more of a problem than it used to be. Residents who have made the switch, who know they're now more environmentally responsible, tend to pressure their neighbors to do the same—or at least notice the problem and ask the municipality to inspect or intervene.

Such social pressures often flow from younger to older residents. EA 12 emphasized the importance of educating children about smog, noting that it creates long-term ripple effects: "We often hear things like, 'My daughter came home and told me: you can't do this, you must do that differently'. Those are nice signals. Children are noticing—and sometimes they're the ones to bring it up with their grandparents. That's how we reach older generations." Other eco-advisors (e.g., EA 9 and EA 2) similarly highlighted the intergenerational transmission of environmental awareness, observing that "grandchildren telling their grandfathers it's unhealthy [to pollute the air] makes a real difference."

In this way, eco-advisors observed that a single stove replacement can initiate broader local trends. Residents who modernize their heating systems often exert informal pressure on those who lag behind, motivated by a sense of fairness and a desire to sanction free riders—individuals who continue to pollute while avoiding both financial burdens and legal accountability (see Porębski, Klinowski, Stępień 2026). This dynamic may also operate in reverse. As EA 7 noted, some residents justify their own compliance by saying: "If everyone else has replaced theirs, I have to too—otherwise I'll be the only one polluting on the block." As modernization progresses, it becomes increasingly easy to identify noncompliant households. Intergenerational dynamics further reinforce this shift, subtly influencing individuals who might otherwise be less inclined to adhere to regulations.

The ease of filing reports and the rise in modernization create powerful new social dynamics. EA 7 (as well as EA 2, EA 16, and EA 17) explained that the *Ekointerwencja* app allows any resident to "view a map with building numbers and see which ones have been flagged for emissions." As he added, "everyone is afraid of ending up on that map." This serves as a new form of social control. The app and growing reporting culture "lead residents to replace their boilers. If many neighbors already have, and I'm the only one left using coal, then it's obvious I'm the one polluting–so I switch." This is a compelling mechanism of informal enforcement: as more residents replace their systems, noncompliers become easier to identify. Once this critical mass is reached, additional pressures accelerate.

Despite a growing willingness to report violations, certain areas of Małopolska still perceive such actions as morally problematic. Within more traditional mindsets, informing authorities about a neighbor's illegal behavior is often regarded as an act of betrayal—particularly in tightly-knit communities with entrenched social norms. EA 2 distinguished between two categories of residents: those who consistently oppose harmful practices and those who refuse to report—even when personally affected—stating, "I won't report my neighbor, even if he's dumping sewage or using a smelly furnace next door." When asked to elaborate, EA 2 simply responded: "That's just the mentality. You'll have to live next to that neighbor forever, even if he's poisoning you." In such cases, preserving long-standing neighborly relations takes precedence over both individual and collective health concerns. EA 5, echoing this concern, emphasized the need to reshape public perception: "We need to show people that reporting is not betrayal. It's about protecting what belongs to all of us—our shared air." This tension between solidarity and enforcement is reflected in national-level data. According to a 2020 survey conducted by the Polish Economic Institute (PEI, 2020), more than 60% of respondents viewed reporting air-quality violations as morally acceptable. Nevertheless, this leaves a significant minority who continue to perceive such actions as inappropriate—likely shaped by regional, cultural, or historical factors.

The reluctance to report was a recurring theme in the interviews. EA 1 advocated for more intervention-based inspections to replace planned ones, which he argued were less effective. EA 3 called this resistance "a small-town problem." Though he encourages residents to "take a photo or call me when someone is polluting," he admits: "People don't want to do it. They'd rather shut their windows than file a complaint." Fear of retaliation extends to court proceedings as well—if the accused refuses to accept a fine, neighbors may be unwilling to testify. As EA 3 noted, "If there's an *Ekointerwencja*, the accused will immediately suspect who reported them. That's the problem—people don't want to be seen as snitches. But if someone's burning rubber, there's no question it should be reported." This phenomenon reflects a classic social dilemma: individual inaction (e.g., avoiding conflict) leads to a collective harm—deteriorating air quality.

Finally, some residents misuse the *Ekointerwencja* system to pursue personal grievances. EA 7 remarked: "As is often the case in Poland, you get neighborly feuds—reporting someone eight times a week just because you don't like them, even if they're using a gas boiler." In a similar vein, EA 13 noted that "some addresses get flagged over and over again—even though inspections find nothing. One neighbor just wants to make life difficult for another." Such misuse not only diverts municipal resources but also erodes the credibility and deterrent power of inspection mechanisms, potentially diminishing public trust in the enforcement process.

In sum, social control—or its absence—profoundly influences individual decisions about stove replacement and fuel usage. The balance between adopters and laggards, the social composition of these groups, and residents' willingness to report violations all shape how antismog resolutions are enforced on the ground.

4.3.3 From the Perspective of Eco-Advisors: Factors Limiting the Effectiveness of the Antismog Resolutions

This study also aimed to reconstruct the perspectives of eco-advisors—their observations and opinions regarding the practical implementation of antismog resolutions. Beginning with their general insights, without exception, all eco-advisors pointed to positive changes in air quality across various municipalities. Some supported this view with relevant data—such as a decrease in the number of days with excessive pollution levels—while others based their assessments on personal observation and intuition. The advisors emphasized the positive role played by the antismog resolutions in raising public awareness and reducing pollution. Although the relationship between these resolutions and observed outcomes was nuanced in different ways, all EAs recognized their pivotal importance, especially in the case of the resolution concerning Kraków. All interviewees also acknowledged a significant change that occurred in Małopolska: the installation of air-quality monitoring tools and public information systems. These tools have become part of the visual landscape of municipalities in the region—especially around schools, town squares, and municipal offices. This process has even led to the emergence of a specific informational ecosystem related to the communication of air-quality status.

Alongside these developments, a major portion of the interviews was dedicated to discussing the factors that, in the eco-advisors' view, limit the effectiveness of antismog resolutions. It is worth recalling that although EAs have access to unique insights into local conditions, they do not necessarily possess a full understanding of all processes relevant to air-quality protection. Keeping that in mind, the most frequently cited barriers to the effectiveness of antismog resolutions (and the Małopolska Air Protection Improvement Programs) are listed below—besides those already discussed (e.g., residents perceiving the act of reporting violations as "snitching").

Mentality and Habits

Academic literature includes attempts to conceptualize the psychology of polluters—factors related to cognitive patterns and modes of information processing that foster behaviors aimed at circumventing or ignoring environmental regulations (e.g., Rowell et al., 2021). A broad stream of research seeks to explain why individuals fail to adopt proenvironmental practices (e.g., why they do not separate waste or why they burn prohibited materials). Drawing on this perspective, some eco-advisors pointed to entrenched, "traditional" ways of thinking about environmental and household matters as a key barrier to the implementation of antismog resolutions. These attitudes were most frequently associated with older residents. Some eco-advisors even noted a "significant" or "large" share of residents in their municipalities who hold such views. In some localities, this group comprises "about half" of the population. As EA 11 (similarly EA 14 and EA 17) put it, "50% do not want to hear about it at all … air pollution? Come on—pollution has been around for decades and people still lived through it; nothing ever happened to them." It is difficult to fully capture this mentality, but EA 6 outlined some of its features as follows:

> We have a group of residents who approach the topic of boiler replacement in a somewhat selective way—at least here, in the municipality where I work—because they firmly believe that in rural areas, people should heat their homes with "natural fuels," like wood, rather than being forced to switch to gas boilers or, say, heat pumps. So, it's more of a mental approach, really. Not a financial issue or a technical problem, but a mindset.

These beliefs and accompanying practices are closely tied to historically self-sufficient lifestyles. Wood, for instance, has served as the dominant heating fuel for centuries, while coal continues to occupy a prominent place in the cultural imagination of the Polish people (Kuchler & Bridge, 2018). As EA 3 recalled, when he first began engaging residents on this issue in 2016, "people wondered what the point was—why even talk about this—when coal has been the main heating fuel for decades, centuries even." EA 7 echoed this sentiment, noting that for many, the prevailing belief was that "burning coal has always been good, so there's nothing wrong with continuing as we have—things have always been this way, and we'll keep it that way." Although coal only became widespread in what is now Poland in the nineteenth century, it is frequently perceived as a traditional, safe, and dependable fuel—its historical use seemingly unproblematic. As EA 14 recounted residents saying, "We burned it for years and there was never a problem"; "[burning coal] was not harmful, it didn't harm anyone." These narratives highlight the need for public education not only about current environmental risks but also about the region's environmental history—where persistent misconceptions continue to shape attitudes and behavior.

For some individuals, burning coal is a vital part of their lifestyle. EA 2 described "ninety-year-old grandmothers for whom firing up the stove is the only remaining goal in life"—indicating a deep attachment to a familiar world. Behind such attitudes lies not only a lack of awareness of pollution effects (including indoor air pollution) but also an ingrained way of life tied to a particular relationship with the environment. Notably, several eco-advisors, especially in rural or semi-rural municipalities, pointed out that many residents own forests, which for some is equal to "free fuel" (e.g., ED 3, ED 14, and ED 16). Since these beliefs form a coherent system of thought, embedded in daily routines, they are difficult to challenge—especially when they coexist with habits of frugality and resourcefulness. EA 12 captured this well:

> It's hardest to reach older people who are very rooted in tradition—"we've always burned coal, we've always burned wood"—and they simply cannot imagine using other types of fuel for their heating systems. For them, even the most basic upgrade like an eco-pea coal boiler is unacceptable. They ask, "What am I supposed to do with all the wood in my garden?" or "When I go to the forest, I bring back firewood, as I always have." These are the cheapest sources of fuel, in many cases. So, the rural mentality of the older generation is hard to overcome, and their worldview is difficult to change. They are, frankly, unreformable.

EA 11 elaborated on how some people approach the issue of boiler replacement in terms worth quoting at length:

> I think that for some of the older residents—those over 60 or 70 years old—it's a problem that can't be solved. We've inspected a few such households. You go into a home with an old stove that also functions as a kitchen range, and the man is cooking meals on it. And when you talk to him about possibly receiving 100% funding to replace it—with a gas boiler, full thermal insulation of the building, and so on—he'll say, "Where would I cook, then? What am I supposed to do? There's no way." These people just don't see the need for change. They've been rooted in that place for years and have a daily routine—they don't see the need for easing their burdens. I honestly don't think they'd agree to change anything, even if the municipality covered all the costs.

One could hypothesize that such attitudes are correlated with certain (conservative) political preferences and climate skepticism, although this would require empirical validation. Politicians, including local officials, sometimes "wink" at these skeptical segments of society, which often constitute more than just a fringe minority in many municipalities.

This resistance is not solely rooted in financial hardship but is also deeply embedded in habitual lifestyles and daily routines—particularly when combined with cognitive closure, limited administrative capacity, and, in some cases, a strong sense of self-sufficiency. Notably, EA 2 observed that many low-income residents do not apply for support available through programs such as *Stop Smog*, which covers up to 90% of retrofit costs. As he remarked, "Many of these people don't approach us. It's a bit of a mystery. It's strange. These poor individuals—some of them feel ashamed, I suppose. They won't come to us, because they're afraid they'll be seen as poor." In his view, the real paradox is that "those in need feel ashamed, while those who cheat do not." He was referring to "a whole group of people who are officially poor—on paper they earn 300 złoty a month—but when you see their house, you'd want to live there yourself. But that's a nationwide issue." These reflections underscore the structural injustices that arise when legal obligations are imposed without adequate attention to inequality in access to assistance. While some residents who genuinely need support refrain from applying due to stigma or institutional barriers, others—more resourceful or opportunistic—successfully obtain financial aid despite being able to cover the costs themselves.

Eco-advisors also pointed to additional attitudes that diminish residents' willingness to replace outdated boilers. EA 2 noted that while the majority of residents in his municipality comply with the antismog resolutions "and accept them without much resistance," there remains a subset who actively contest them. As EA 15 recounted, such individuals often say: "Whatever. In two or three years this might all change. It's just a law" or "Maybe the rule won't even come into force. I don't care ... this is my business." These arguments attempt to undermine the credibility and durability of public policy, casting doubt on both the legitimacy and political resolve behind the regulations. Similarly, EA 14 described residents who, even when confronted with legal mandates and scientific evidence, simply replied: "No, just no." EA 1 echoed this sentiment, observing: "We're dealing with a group of residents who just say, 'No, just no.' And that's the end of it. They refuse to accept any argument." Although this group appears to be small, their presence is significant. Perhaps most troubling, however, is the account provided by EA 12, who recalled hearing local officials themselves declare they would not replace their boilers because it was not cost-effective. When such views are voiced by those in authority, they risk legitimizing noncompliance and reinforcing resistance among the broader public.

Financial Issues

Among the factors limiting compliance with the antismog resolutions, financial issues featured prominently in the narratives of eco-advisors. As a reminder, the regulatory model adopted in Małopolska was based on a ban on the use of certain fuels (in the case of Kraków) and an obligation to replace heating sources (in the rest of the region). This legal framework was accompanied by various forms of financial support for individuals tasked with meeting these obligations. In Kraków, the system included almost full subsidies for the most disadvantaged residents. In the rest of Małopolska, residents have relied—and continue to rely—on grants from various sources. Over time, these grants have evolved and typically include support for thermal insulation, connections to heating networks, and the replacement and management of heating systems.

Many eco-advisors pointed out a key weakness in the adopted solutions: while replacing an old boiler with one compatible with more environmentally friendly fuels (e.g., pellets, gas, or oil) addresses environmental concerns, it also introduces new financial uncertainties. Chief among these is the future cost of such fuels. This unpredictability is a source of concern for residents, particularly because applying for subsidies requires scrapping the old "smoke-belching" furnace, making the transition effectively irreversible. As EA 7 observed, "People are afraid of prices, of rising [gas] prices. They're afraid that the supply of the fuel might be interrupted due to various political developments." This uncertainty—especially regarding the availability and affordability of gas in the context of the Russian invasion of Ukraine and the resulting sanctions on Russia—has discouraged some groups from making the switch. Although other alternatives, such as heat pumps, are available, they tend to involve significantly higher upfront costs. Following this line of thought, many eco-advisors emphasized the problem of lacking price guarantees for new fuels or the absence of public subsidies or protective mechanisms to keep those prices within a certain limit (EA 16, EA 8, EA 7, and EA 1). Residents also think in terms of flexibility. As EA 13 explained when reconstructing this line of reasoning, "If I have a boiler that can burn coal, I'll burn coal; if I have wood, I'll burn wood—this multi-fuel boiler gives me options." Switching to gas, by contrast, entails both uncertainty and a loss of flexibility. EA 3 offered an even broader perspective:

> There should be a national strategy with guaranteed prices. For example, if a person signs a contract for a utility like gas, they should be assured that the gas price won't change for 5–10 years. That would help residents understand their financial outlook and plan accordingly. They would know the price won't go up, and as a result, many would start switching to these cleaner heating sources.

This is a highly important perspective, as it highlights the need for a coherent, long-term national energy strategy that can serve as a foundation for related policy areas. Reducing uncertainty would enable residents to make informed, future-oriented decisions. It is difficult to disagree that the direction of antismog efforts in Małopolska should be closely integrated with broader, state-level energy and climate policies.

Several eco-advisors also mentioned insufficient funding. In areas where the pace of boiler replacement is high, there have been reports of a lack of sufficient resources to meet the demand from all residents seeking subsidies at a given moment (EA 1). Some provided more concrete details. EA 9, for instance, stated: "There's a lack of funds for replacing certain heating sources—especially those requiring major interventions in the building itself, such as traditional kitchen ranges or tiled stoves. Replacing these systems involves significant labor, and in such cases, the subsidies stop being attractive."

Although there are dedicated grants, the scale of building intervention needed often leaves residents with a significant out-of-pocket cost. Other concerns raised by eco-advisors related to how subsidies were distributed. For instance, under the *Clean Air* program (see Chap. 2), residents initially had to pay costs upfront and only later received partial reimbursement (e.g., EA 8 and EA 3). According to EA 1:

> For those in difficult financial situations, this mechanism is unacceptable. No bank will issue them a loan, no company will take on the burden of financing such a venture. So how can we expect a person earning minimum wage or living on a pension—who already spends half their income on medication—to undertake an investment worth tens of thousands of złoty?

Later, the program shifted away from the reimbursement model, though this change introduced new problems—such as fraudulent contractors persuading homeowners to make irrational and costly decisions (e.g., installing a heat pump in an uninsulated wooden cottage).

Eco-advisors also debated the idea of differentiating subsidy rules based on income (e.g., EA 1) and pointed out that the multiplicity of financing options created confusion and hindered decision-making. EA 1 emphasized that variation in subsidy levels between programs led some residents to delay action in hopes of better offers: "There was the PONE program funded by the Voivodeship Environmental Protection Fund, with subsidies around 13,000 PLN. Then new regional programs appeared that offered 1,000 more—and people waited, switched programs, and so on." Given such conditions, it is not surprising that some chose to wait.

The Role of Local Conditions and Factors

In their interviews, eco-advisors also pointed to local-level factors that limit the effectiveness of antismog resolutions—particularly the socio-demographic profile of the municipality, the nature of the housing stock, and certain legal legacies.

EA 7 (similarly EA 3 and ED 17) highlighted the generally poor technical condition of single-family homes and other buildings in their municipalities, many of which are old. In such cases, simply replacing the boiler or changing the heating system is not a sufficient solution. These buildings require either demolition or costly renovation, and installing a new boiler in them often makes little sense. Sometimes, residents are dealing with the consequences of building decisions made decades earlier under a different model of family life and lower social mobility. EA 2 illustrated this issue vividly when explaining why some residents are slow to replace their heating systems or abandon the idea altogether:

> In the past, homes were built for the entire family. They're around 200 square meters or more. Now the kids—say, three of them—one's in England, one's in Sweden, and one's in Kraków. And the parents are left alone in this 200-plus-square-meter house, right? They don't really know what to do with it. They can't sell it, because it's family property with sentimental value, and it's hard to maintain. So, they only heat one floor. So, what then? Should they switch to a gas boiler and insulate the ceiling? That's the kind of dilemma we're talking about.

Several eco-advisors also drew attention to unresolved property issues, including inheritance matters. Without clear ownership status—such as a formal decision on inheritance—residents are excluded from receiving subsidies (EA 9, EA 7, and EA 14 regarding plots of land). This is a significant barrier that not only complicates the application process but also affects the decision-making timeline. As EA 2 explained, at the stage of completing documents before signing a contract, it sometimes turns out that "Someone owns 1/164th of the building, and there are 20 or even 30 co-owners. Or someone has only a notarized deed from the 1940s, or there's no land and mortgage register set up—people just never followed through with this paperwork." EA 3 described a similar case: "Not far from here, in our municipality, a grandfather and grandmother had a house. The grandfather passed away, the grandmother is still alive, but the inheritance proceedings were never completed, so the legal status of the property remains unresolved. And what happens? 'You won't be able to sign a funding agreement,' they're told." This eco-advisor added that they had notified central authorities and called for a nationwide campaign to regularize land and property records, which would enable more people to access subsidies under the *Clean Air* program. Thus, resolving ownership and inheritance issues is a crucial part of the broader context that affects the overall effectiveness of antismog regulations.

"Paperwork"
Another set of limitations identified by eco-advisors concerned bureaucratic factors. Some pointed to the complexity of the documentation and difficulties in understanding the procedures required to obtain subsidies—particularly the necessity of submitting everything online. EA 8 remarked: "People are afraid of what we call 'paperwork'. When they come to us and we explain what documents are needed to submit an application for funding or payment, some just throw up their hands and never come back because they're overwhelmed by it all." This challenge is especially pronounced among those lacking the cultural or communication skills needed to navigate administrative procedures—but not exclusively. EA 3 described situations in which "Accountants or people who had worked with documents for 20 years came in and said, 'I've been working in paperwork for two decades, and I've never seen anything like this. I don't even know where to start.'" Although the Clean Air program eventually simplified the application process—for instance, in 2020, technical specifications were no longer required, and most documentation was replaced with declarations—many problems remained unresolved. Notably, the program was suspended in 2025 and was reintroduced a few months later in a slightly modified form. EA 10 (as well as EA 1 and EA 15) stressed the urgent need to simplify the process: "There's a pressing need to redesign the subsidy system—to make it easier and faster for the average resident on the street." It is worth remembering that a significant portion of the eco-advisors' workload consists of assisting residents with completing applications—time that could otherwise be spent on more proactive and strategic activities.

Challenges Related to Inspections
Several eco-advisors pointed to the lack of sufficient resources, which hinders effective and thorough enforcement. Only a minority of municipalities have municipal guards functioning alongside the police (see MPIAQ 2020, p. 30). Where such entities exist, they enable more extensive enforcement capabilities. Significant disparities in municipal budgets—often correlated with municipality size—translate into varied capacity for enforcing the antismog resolutions. This was clearly articulated by multiple eco-advisors. For example, EA 10 observed: "There is no dedicated institution for this purpose. In large cities we have municipal guards, and in some larger municipalities as well—but the core function of these institutions is to carry out precisely such inspection activities."

This advisor advocated for the creation of municipal guard units in a greater number of municipalities to ensure the enforceability of antismog laws. Meanwhile, EA 3, emphasizing limited resources, pointed out that setting minimum control targets is helpful but warned: "We can't leave local governments without support. Who are they supposed to send? An accountant? Sure, an eco-advisor would be great. But they're better used providing information rather than conducting inspections." According to some, the shortage of resources results in too few inspections to meet actual needs. As EA 1 stated, "Only increased inspection efforts can lead to residents complying with the anti-smog resolution." However, more inspections do not necessarily mean a more punitive approach. The same eco-advisor suggested that increased monitoring should involve warnings and education for first-time violations and only resort to penalties in cases of repeat offenses: "Only in cases of recidivism should penalties be imposed strictly." This softer approach was echoed by EA 3, who noted that while burning plastic in a stove is a "crime" that should be punished, other cases require a more situational response.

Eco-advisors expressed differing views on what level of fine would be appropriate. At the time of the study, local enforcement authorities could issue fines ranging from PLN 50 (approx. €10) to PLN 500 (approx. €100). If the fine was not accepted, the matter would be referred to court, which could impose a fine of up to PLN 5000 (approx. €1000), slightly more than the monthly minimum wage in Poland in 2024. During interviews, advisors debated whether fines of PLN 50 or 100 were effective deterrents—or whether even such seemingly modest sums could pose a hardship for some residents.

Their responses revealed a clear tension between the view that even the maximum fines were insufficient and the recognition that such fines could constitute a substantial burden for certain individuals. Close relationships with residents influenced how eco-advisors viewed penalties. EA 7 explained: "I had an inspection yesterday—cases like these are really hard. I visited a resident who's had two cancer surgeries, has tumors, his wife isn't working, his daughter is still dependent ... and for someone like that, it's really difficult to impose a fine ... they barely have enough to live on, let alone afford a new boiler." Eco-advisors have some latitude in how inspections are conducted, which can yield different outcomes—from taking into account an individual's personal situation to inadvertently signaling that bans are not being strictly enforced. With regard to the former, EA 7 voiced a proposal, echoed by several others, to scale penalties based on income in order to protect the most vulnerable and avoid imposing demands beyond their means.

4.4 Eco-Advisors' Perspective: A Quantitative Approach

4.4.1 Eco-Advisors: Where They Work and What Motivates Them

Addressing several key issues related to the work, responsibilities, and role of eco-advisers in the practical implementation of anti-smog resolutions required a quantitative approach. These include, among other things, variation in working

Table 4.2 Municipality size

Municipality size	Counts	% of total
Less than 5000	13	10.3 %
5000–10,000	44	34.9 %
10,000–15,000	30	23.8 %
15,000–25,000	21	16.7 %
More than 25,000	18	14.3 %

conditions and the degree of support provided by local political leaders in municipalities for the implementation of their tasks. Comparable estimates from eco-advisors regarding residents' awareness of smog and their attitudes toward combating it were also necessary. Similarly, the challenges and difficulties in combating smog require a quantitative approach, enabling comparisons across municipalities and the identification of broader trends.

It is essential to begin by outlining the basic conditions and characteristics of the eco-advisors' work, as well as their motivations for carrying out the assigned tasks and their general approach to combating smog.

By the time these quantitative studies were conducted in 2023, every municipality in Małopolska (of which there are 182) had at least one eco-advisor. These municipalities vary in size, character, and resources, which may potentially influence the work of eco-advisors as well as their perspectives. Looking at the research sample, some eco-advisors work in large or small municipalities (in terms of population), although the majority—58%—work in medium-sized municipalities (with populations ranging from 5000 to 15,000) (see Table 4.2). Therefore, the fight against smog should not only be viewed from the perspective of large municipalities, as eco-advisors working in urban municipalities represented only 10% of the sample.

The creation of the eco-advisor position in Małopolska represented an innovative step—at least within the Polish context. As a newly established profession, this novelty is reflected in the length of time respondents reported having held the position. Unsurprisingly, a majority of the research sample (52%) had worked as eco-advisors for more than 1 but fewer than 3 years (see Table 4.3). This relatively short tenure should be taken into account when interpreting the findings. On the one hand, it is likely too early for issues such as burnout or job dissatisfaction to become fully apparent. On the other hand, the limited duration may not yet allow for more comprehensive or systemic reflections to emerge.

The research aimed to determine what motivated eco-advisors in Małopolska to take on this job. This question is important because the position requires dense interaction with people, and much depends on one's initiative, assertiveness, and determination—qualities that are more easily cultivated when supported by certain motivations for the work. This profession can be performed "formally" or with a "heart" and even with a sense of mission. In this context, it is interesting to explore whether eco-advisors view themselves as public servants who could work in any area (but, for various reasons, their work now focuses on air protection) or whether they perform the job because they genuinely want to fight for environmental

Table 4.3 Time of working as an eco-advisor

Time to be an eco-advisor (years)	Counts	% of total
1 or less	24	19.0%
More than 1, less than 2	26	20.6%
More than 2, less than 3	39	31.0%
3 or more	37	29.4%

Table 4.4 Identification of eco-advisors

Idea (0) vs money (10)	Counts	% of total
0	11	8.7%
1	5	4.0%
2	10	7.9%
3	15	11.9%
4	10	7.9%
5	54	42.9%
6	5	4.0%
7	6	4.8%
8	6	4.8%
9	1	0.8%
10	3	2.4%

Table 4.5 Descriptive statistics of policies recommended by eco-advisors

	Encouragement policy (0) vs prohibition policy (10)
Mean	1.944
Std. error mean	0.216
Median	1
Standard deviation	2.428

values. Regarding self-identification of the surveyed eco-advisors, on a scale ranging from "work mainly to realize an idea" to "work mainly for financial gain," the most common response was balanced—in the middle (42.9%)—indicating a cautious stance. However, responses indicating an ideological motivation (40.5%) were clearly more frequent than those pointing to financial motivation (16.7%) (see Table 4.4)

Eco-advisors, as individuals responsible for the daily implementation of air protection laws, were asked about their recommended policy for combating smog: whether they believe that the "command and control" policy or the "incentive-based" policy is more effective. This distinction refers to the typical division in the literature (e.g., Goulder & Parry, 2008). Interestingly, eco-advisors clearly preferred the incentive-based policy (see Table 4.5). An overwhelming majority of eco-advisors fully support the incentive-based approach, while only a small percentage, even to a limited extent, lean toward the command-and-control policy. Only one eco-advisor strongly favored prohibitions. How can this be explained? According to prevailing views, softer methods are better and more effective, likely because they are less coercive and more flexible and do not provoke resistance from the target audience. However, the literature is not entirely uniform on this issue, and there are critical voices against the incentive-based approach (e.g., Stavins, 2001). One might ask whether these preferences influence the way eco-advisors work, for instance, in terms of emphasizing situational and individualized enforcement, or if they lead to greater leniency toward "polluters."

Outlining the context of eco-advisors' work also requires reference to how they assess the local authorities' support for the issue of combating smog. From the interviews, we know that eco-advisors are integrated into different parts of the municipalities' organizational structure. Their supervisors are most often the heads of departments dealing with environmental matters, or, less frequently, they hold independent positions, reporting directly to the mayor or municipal president. Notably, eco-advisers work in municipal buildings and rely entirely on the infrastructure provided by the municipalities. Therefore, eco-advisors have a clear understanding of the municipality's approach to air protection issues and the role of law enforcement agencies involved in enforcement. With this in mind, respondents were asked to evaluate (1) the involvement and activity of the local police or municipal guards in the fight against smog (which is crucial for the long-term monitoring of the implementation of antismog resolutions and other air protection regulations) and (2) how significant the issue of air protection is to municipal authorities, as this determines the scale of resource allocation and actual actions in this area.

The involvement of the police or municipal guards is assessed as significantly lower than the importance of air protection to municipal authorities (see Table 4.6). Notably, 32% of respondents indicated that the involvement of the police or municipal guards is low or very low (see Table 4.7). In contrast, no eco-advisor considered air quality to be a marginal issue for municipal authorities. Approximately 24% of eco-advisors stated that local authorities treat the air pollution problem as a priority, while 58% regard it as an important but not the most critical issue, which can be interpreted as a general openness to fighting smog. With some caution, it can be said that in the vast majority of municipalities, the attitude and approach of the authorities, according to our respondents, are not factors limiting the fight against smog. However, data indicate what has emerged from the qualitative part of the research: the challenges in enforcement (inspections) stem from the fact that law enforcement agencies have numerous diverse tasks and limited resources (and sometimes there are no municipal guards, relying solely on the police). Thus, the weakness of

Table 4.6 Descriptive statistics of variables related to authorities' activity

	Involvement of municipal guards/police	Relevance to the municipal authorities
Mean	2.984	3.992
Std. error mean	0.112	0.07
Median	3	4
Standard deviation	1.251	0.785

Table 4.7 Combined table: frequency of municipal guards/police involvement and perceived relevance to municipal authorities

Involvement of municipal guards/police	Counts	% of total	Perceived relevance to municipal authorities	Counts	% of total
Very low	23	18.4%	Treat this issue as marginal, completely not important	0	0%
Low	17	13.6%	Treat this issue as less important than most issues	8	6.3%
Medium	36	28.8%	Treat the issue as moderately important	15	11.9%
High	37	29.6%	Treat this issue as important but not as a priority	73	57.9%
Very high	12	9.6%	Treat this issue as a priority	30	23.8%

enforcement in the field of air protection is, to some extent, due to broader institutional factors. It can be speculated that since local authorities do not pose an obstacle to the implementation of resolutions and other regulations and do not create a negative atmosphere for the tasks assigned to eco-advisors, the limiting factor lies with the residents, at least with some of them.

4.4.2 Assessment of Residents' Knowledge and Awareness

It is interesting to observe how eco-advisors, based on their daily interactions and insider perspective, perceive the state of knowledge and awareness regarding the air pollution issue among the residents of their municipalities. It turned out that, according to the eco-advisors, a significant portion of the residents is still unaware of the smog problem. This issue was much more pronounced here than in the qualitative part of the study. Specifically, 23% of eco-advisors assessed that the majority or a large majority of residents in their municipalities are unaware of the problem. This is a substantial proportion, considering the range of informational and educational activities being carried out. At the same time, there are few municipalities where the overwhelming majority of residents are aware of the air pollution issue. The most common response (approximately 37% of answers) was the second most positive—meaning that most residents in the municipality of the eco-advisor are aware of the problem (see Table 4.8). It is reasonable to conclude that there is a significant variation in residents' awareness of air pollution issues, reported by EAs, which should definitely translate into intensified educational activities in certain municipalities.

The research also indicates that eco-advisors generally assess the increase in residents' awareness since 2017 in a positive light. Approximately 72% of respondents believe that awareness of the issue has increased significantly or very much, while only one person reported no increase at all (see Table 4.9). This rise in awareness is likely supported by the relatively high level of access to information about smog and antismog initiatives: about 76% of eco-advisors rated this access as broad

Table 4.8 Distribution of smog awareness

Smog problem awareness	Counts	% of total
The vast majority are unaware of the problem	5	4.0%
The majority are unaware of the problem	24	19.0%
About half are aware of the problem	41	32.5%
The majority are aware of the problem	46	36.5%
The vast majority are aware of the problem	10	7.9%

Table 4.9 Frequency of increased awareness since 2017

Increased awareness since 2017	Counts	% of total
No, it hasn't changed at all	1	0.8%
Yes, but only slightly increased	34	27.0%
Yes, it has increased significantly	73	57.9%
Yes, it has increased a lot	18	14.3%

Table 4.10 Frequency of access to information variable

Access to information	Counts	% of total
Narrow—even residents who are interested in the topic have difficulty accessing information.	2	1.6%
Rather narrow—a significant proportion of residents do not have access to information.	3	2.4%
Neither narrow nor wide—interested parties will find this information, but it is not widely disseminated.	25	19.8%
Rather wide—the vast majority of residents are exposed to information about the resolution.	72	57.1%
Wide—all or almost all residents, even those less interested, are exposed to information about the resolution.	24	19.0%

or fairly broad, while only 4% considered it narrow or fairly narrow (see Table 4.10). While these findings suggest that information is widely available and that residents' attitudes are shifting, they do not imply that the entire population is fully aware of the smog problem. Despite several years of information campaigns, considerable work remains to be done to reach all segments of the public and to deepen understanding of the issue.

The responses regarding the availability of information align with answers to the question about the presence of air-quality monitoring conducted by municipalities themselves (as opposed to monitoring by a designated public agency) (see Table 4.11). It is significant not only that air-quality monitoring is now present in the vast majority of municipalities but also that approximately 69% of the positive responses indicate that monitoring was initiated in 2018 or later. This suggests that most municipalities currently engaged in air-quality monitoring began doing so within the past 4 to 5 years. This development appears to be closely linked to the broader antismog strategy promoted through the EU LIFE project.

Table 4.11 Frequency of air-quality monitoring variable

Air-quality monitoring	Counts	% of total
No—does not use any sensors and does not plan to buy them in the near future.	7	5.6%
No—does not currently use any sensors but plans to buy them in the near future.	8	6.3%
Yes—in the last 5 years (since 2018 or later), the municipality has started monitoring air quality.	77	61.1%
Yes—the municipality was already monitoring air quality before 2018.	34	27.0%

Table 4.12 Descriptive statistics of variables related to the interest of residents in particular actions, treated as numerical

Interest (1–5 scale)	Replacement of boilers and solid-fuel furnaces	Installation of renewable energy sources	Thermomodernization of a building or part of it
Mean	3.54	3.532	3.571
Median	4	4	4
Standard deviation	0.891	0.892	0.794

The next issue concerns how awareness translates into action. According to eco-advisors, residents demonstrate considerable interest in taking various proenvironmental actions that impact air quality (see Table 4.12). For each of the three actions mentioned in the question, over 50% of eco-advisors assessed the level of interest as high or very high. A deeper analysis revealed that, although municipalities generally showed medium-to-high or high levels of interest among residents in these three activities, there are municipalities where each of the actions was associated with very high estimated interest from the residents.

Eco-advisors were also asked to assess the priorities of residents (see Table 4.13). They estimated what they believed to be the priority for the average resident of the municipality: air quality or lower heating costs. Eco-advisors had the opportunity to assess this on a scale from 0 to 10, where "0" indicates a priority for air quality and "10" indicates a priority for lower heating costs. Interestingly, in the vast majority of cases, eco-advisors estimated that the priority for residents was almost entirely or entirely focused on heating costs (in contrast to air quality). The average value was above 8, with the median being as high as 9 (where 10 points represented a complete priority for heating costs). Despite relatively high awareness of the smog issue (especially in some of the municipalities), residents, at least in the eyes of eco-advisors, are generally unwilling to incur higher costs in exchange for better air quality. This raises an important point—if this is the case, it means that clean air is not a fundamental value for them, nor does it rank highly on their preference scales.

Table 4.13 Descriptive statistics of compliance with the nonecological fuel ban and residents' priority

	Priority: air quality (0) vs heating costs (10)
Mean	8.286
Std. error mean	0.157
Median	9
Standard deviation	1.766

Table 4.14 Descriptive statistics of problem assessment variables, treated as numerical

Problem (1–5 scale)	Difficulties in informing citizens about the provisions of the resolution	Habituation of residents to traditional heating methods, e.g., coal	Residents' fear of contacting authorities and of writing applications	Low relevance of environmental issues for residents	Low relevance of environmental issues for municipal authorities	Poverty among residents
Mean	2.206	4.048	2.69	3.246	1.683	3.714
Std. error mean	0.084	0.087	0.08	0.079	0.088	0.075
Median	2	4	3	3	1	4
Standard deviation	0.941	0.979	0.899	0.883	0.985	0.838

Table 4.15 Frequency of problem assessments

Problem	Informing difficulties		Traditional heating methods, habituation		Fear of contacting authorities		Low relevance for residents		Low relevance for authorities		Poverty	
1	33	26.2 %	2	1.6 %	10	7.9 %	3	2.4 %	72	57.1 %	0	0 %
2	45	35.7 %	8	6.3 %	43	34.1 %	18	14.3 %	33	26.2 %	5	4.0 %
3	38	30.2 %	21	16.7 %	52	41.3 %	60	47.6 %	14	11.1 %	52	41.3 %
4	9	7.1 %	46	36.5 %	18	14.3 %	35	27.8 %	3	2.4 %	43	34.1 %
5	1	0.8 %	49	38.9 %	3	2.4 %	10	7.9 %	4	3.2 %	26	20.6 %

1—this problem was not present; 5—this is one of the most important problems

4.4.3 Challenges in Fighting Air Pollution

Another issue examined was the eco-advisors' assessment of the significance of various factors in the fight against air pollution in their specific context and municipalities. According to the results, the most significant barriers to combating smog are residents' habitual reliance on traditional heating methods (e.g., coal) and poverty among residents (see Tables 4.14 and 4.15). A frequently mentioned problem of considerable importance is also the low priority given to environmental issues by residents, which may also be linked to these habits. This strongly resonates with the findings from the qualitative part of the study. Interestingly, eco-advisors most rarely identified local authorities' engagement as a problem, which aligns with the earlier assessment of eco-advisors regarding whether municipal leaders prioritize environmental issues.

These findings align with the results of the qualitative analyses. According to eco-advisors, deeply entrenched habits and prevailing attitudes toward environmental issues constitute significant barriers to the effectiveness of antismog resolutions in Małopolska. Financial constraints—particularly poverty—are also frequently cited as major obstacles, with nearly 55% of eco-advisors identifying this as a serious concern. Importantly, the problem does not seem to lie with municipal authorities. Most eco-advisors—who could express their views candidly in the questionnaire, thanks to confidentiality safeguards—indicated that local authorities generally recognize the importance of air-quality protection. This conclusion is consistent with responses to the related question discussed earlier.

4.5 Conclusion

The two-stage research provided valuable insights into the broader context of implementing the antismog resolutions—particularly by reconstructing various aspects of eco-advisors' work, including how they perceive public awareness of air pollution, how they motivate residents to comply with the regulations, and their own assessments of the resolutions' functioning, with special emphasis on existing challenges.

(1) This leads to a picture of eco-advisors as individuals working across municipalities of varying sizes (interestingly, the second stage of the research revealed that there were no statistically significant differences between the answers of eco-advisors from different types or sizes of municipalities)—mostly medium-sized—who carry out their duties largely out of a sense of mission, considering economic incentives to be a more effective method of regulating environmental issues. What is important is that they operate in settings typically marked by the support of local authorities, yet also report shortcomings, particularly the lack of enforcement bodies.

The tasks of eco-advisors primarily revolve around assisting residents in applying for subsidies related to heating system replacement or household thermal modernization, as well as carrying out various informational and educational activities. Much of their work depends on the resources and initiative of the municipality. This resident-focused orientation is clearly reflected in the very title of the role—eco-advisors. However, what is particularly telling is that, despite the breadth and demands of their responsibilities, eco-advisors are not typically involved in the comprehensive management of air quality or broader environmental issues. The position, as implemented in Małopolska, does not include coordinating the local implementation of policies related to air pollution, nor does it extend to areas such as urban planning, spatial development, or transportation management (which are closely related to air pollution). Nor are eco-advisors formally involved in shaping local strategies or policies. Their role is narrowly focused on assisting residents—an essential and highly valuable function—but their insights and observations rarely find a direct pathway into relevant decision-making processes.

Regardless of these findings, in order to shed more light on this profession, it is worth considering whether eco-advisors can be classified as street-level bureaucrats—bearing in mind the important caution that "we need to be careful not to assume that all frontline workers are street-level bureaucrats" (Maynard-Moody, Portillo 2010: 263). Briefly engaging with this conceptual thread, it is important to recall that in his seminal work *Street-Level Bureaucracy: Dilemmas of the Individual in Public Services*, Lipsky (1980) laid the foundation for the street-level bureaucracy framework. He defined street-level bureaucrats as "public service workers who interact directly with citizens in the course of their jobs" (1980: 3), a group that includes police officers, social workers, and teachers—professionals who work under conditions of chronic pressure, limited resources, and often ambiguous goals. According to Lipsky, these workers exercise significant discretion and autonomy in their daily practice, using this leeway to adapt policies to local realities.

As is evident, the category of street-level bureaucrats is a broad one. At its core, however, lies a defining criterion: direct interaction with citizens as part of one's official duties. By this standard, eco-advisors clearly qualify as members of this category. Yet a closer examination reveals important nuances. Unlike classic street-level bureaucrats, eco-advisors do not hold formal decision-making powers—a distinction underscored by their official title, "advisors." They do not issue administrative penalties or make binding determinations in individual cases. Although they may conduct inspections of heating systems or fuel types, ultimate authority in such matters rests with other bodies, such as the municipal police or environmental protection inspectors. Similarly, they do not make final decisions regarding the distribution of subsidies; those remain the responsibility of separate administrative institutions. In this respect, eco-advisors operate largely without "hard" competencies and do not exercise the kind of nondelegable discretion traditionally associated with street-level bureaucrats. This absence of formal authority does not, however, diminish their significance. On the contrary, eco-advisors play a crucial role in shaping residents' knowledge, decisions, and attitudes. Their influence is "soft," but it targets precisely those factors—such as intrinsic motivation and long-term behavioral change—that ultimately determine the success of environmental policy. All these findings should be interpreted in light of the broader significance of street-level bureaucracy theory, which calls for "opening the black box" of what actually happens in implementation contexts. In this sense, studying the daily work of eco-advisers offers a valuable empirical window into the dynamics of policy implementation at the local level, especially in fields such as environmental protection, where regulations aimed at curbing air pollution are enforced through diffuse mechanisms and depend heavily on persuasion, cooperation, and local knowledge.

(2) Eco-advisors observe a growing awareness among residents regarding air-quality issues, a trend they attribute to improved access to information and the development of a comprehensive public infosphere that communicates real-time air-quality data. Nonetheless, significant knowledge gaps persist. Awareness of anti-smog regulations, available funding mechanisms, and the role of eco-advisors does

not necessarily translate into a deeper understanding of air pollution and its consequences. According to the eco-advisors, residents form a highly diverse group with varying attitudes toward environmental values such as clean air. This diversity is particularly evident in the realm of motivation. Some residents—such as newcomers to rural areas, parents of young children, or older individuals maintaining self-sufficient lifestyles—approach air quality from different value-based or pragmatic standpoints. Qualitative analyses revealed that motivations for replacing heating systems are often non-autotelic—that is, not grounded in an intrinsic rejection of poor air quality or in ecological reasoning related to planetary or interspecies well-being. Particularly noteworthy are the motivations of those who oppose the resolutions, as well as the deeper reasons—identified by several eco-advisors—for the lack of intrinsic environmental concern among many residents. These motivations are frequently shaped by ingrained habits, financial constraints, lack of cultural or technological competencies, resentment toward top-down regulations, or strategic cost-benefit calculations. Ultimately, financial concerns remain the most frequently cited barrier to compliance with antismog regulations—a finding especially pronounced in the quantitative phase of the research (similar results: Król & Gomola, 2022). However, some eco-advisors interviewed in the qualitative phase disputed this view, instead emphasizing the importance of sociocultural and psychological factors in shaping residents' decisions. Interestingly, political factors—such as party identification and ideological polarization—did not emerge from the data. This absence is particularly striking in the national political context. Between 2015 and 2023, the ruling Law and Justice party (*Prawo i Sprawiedliwość* (PiS)) often downplayed the urgency of addressing air pollution, prioritizing the protection of the coal-mining sector and economic growth instead. A telling example is the widely cited parliamentary speech by Minister Jan Szyszko, in which he attributed poor air quality primarily to the inferior quality of imported coal rather than to systemic reliance on solid fuels. Notably, in September 2022, under the shadow of the Russian invasion of Ukraine and the potential problems with carbon, PiS leader Jaroslaw Kaczyński told residents of Nowy Targ (one of the most polluted towns in Poland) to burn pretty much everything ("We should be burning everything, other than tires, or similar things, because this is unfortunately what happens here") (Euractiv, 2022). More broadly, the party frequently framed EU climate and environmental policies in critical terms. One might reasonably expect that political identity and ideological leanings could influence whether residents support or resist the legal obligations imposed by antismog regulations. However, as noted in the methodological section, such political factors remained largely unaddressed in the data. This may be due to the eco-advisors' general reluctance to raise politically sensitive issues, instead directing attention toward more technical matters.

(3) Despite differences in local conditions and the specific contexts in which eco-advisors operate, they generally expressed a shared perspective. Across interviews, they identified similar challenges, made consistent observations, and drew converging conclusions—although some variation naturally emerged between individuals and municipalities. Several key factors were cited as limiting the effectiveness of the antismog resolutions. First and foremost were residents' attitudes and habits,

which—according to both the qualitative and quantitative findings—are strongly correlated with age. Second, eco-advisors emphasized the absence of a clear, stable, and long-term public policy in Poland on energy, which undermines residents' willingness to make decisive and lasting choices regarding fuels and heating technologies. Linking antismog policies with national and European energy strategies is essential for achieving long-term environmental goals in a coherent and stable manner (see, e.g., Pilogallo et al., 2024). Financial constraints were also frequently mentioned, including issues related to the accessibility, complexity, or adequacy of stove replacement funding programs. Additionally, enforcement mechanisms were widely perceived as insufficient—often due to the limited capacity of municipal police or local guard units (where such units exist at all). Finally, broader contextual factors further complicated implementation, including the characteristics of buildings (e.g., age, infrastructure) and unresolved property ownership issues, which frequently hinder the ability to undertake necessary modernization efforts. They mentioned problems with the design and accessibility of subsidy programs and bureaucratic burdens. They also pinpointed the nuanced forms of social control directed toward polluters—or the lack of such efforts—as important determinants of antismog regulation effectiveness.

The advisors' insights lead to several recommendations for enhancing policy effectiveness—for example, the need to tailor information, incentives, support, and enforcement strategies to different categories of residents. Messaging and assistance should be differentiated: one approach for those whose use of wood or coal is deeply embedded in their lifestyle, another for those who have the means to switch but are waiting for more favorable financial conditions, and yet another for those who reject state authority in this domain altogether.

References

Bondarouk, E., & Mastenbroek, E. (2018). Reconsidering EU compliance: Implementation performance in the field of environmental policy. *Environmental Policy and Governance, 28*(1), 15–27. https://doi.org/10.1002/eet.1797

Bondarouk, E., Mastenbroek, E., & Scholten, P. (2017). Institutional capacity in the implementation of immigrant integration policies in Dutch municipalities: A fuzzy set qualitative comparative analysis. *Policy & Politics, 45*(2), 289–306. https://doi.org/10.1332/030557316X14552878016151

Bondarouk, E., Mastenbroek, E., & Scholten, P. (2020). Integrating immigrant integration governance: The role of coordination in Dutch municipalities. *Policy Sciences, 53*, 665–684. https://doi.org/10.1007/s11077-020-09388-0

Borghetto, E., & Franchino, F. (2010). The role of subnational authorities in the implementation of EU directives. *Journal of European Public Policy, 17*(6), 759–780. https://doi.org/10.1080/13501763.2010.486981

Braun, V., & Clarke, V. (2006). Using thematic analysis in psychology. *Qualitative Research in Psychology, 3*(2), 77–101. https://doi.org/10.1191/1478088706qp063oa

Buschmann, D., Koziol, K., Bausch, T., & Reinhard, S. (2022). Adaptation to climate change in small German municipalities: Sparse knowledge and weak adaptive capacities. *Natural Resources Forum, 46*(4), 377–392. https://doi.org/10.1111/1477-8947.12262

Deloitte Advisory. (2015). *Koncepcja funkcjonowania Eko-doradców oraz Centrum Kompetencji w województwie małopolskim*. Deloitte.

Euractiv. (2022, December 9). *"Burn everything": Poland chokes on the smog of war*. Euractiv. https://www.euractiv.com/section/eet/news/burn-everything-poland-chokes-on-the-smog-of-war/

Gollata, J., & Newig, J. (2017). Policy implementation through multi-level governance: Analysing practical implementation of EU air quality directives in Germany. *Journal of European Public Policy., 24*, 1–20. https://doi.org/10.1080/13501763.2017.1314539

Goulder, L. H., & Parry, I. W. H. (2008). Instrument choice in environmental policy. *Review of Environmental Economics and Policy, 2*(2), 152–174. https://doi.org/10.1093/reep/ren005

Guest, G., Bunce, A., & Johnson, L. (2006). How many interviews are enough? An experiment with data saturation and variability. *Field Methods, 18*(1), 59–82. https://doi.org/10.1177/1525822X05279903

Hennink, M., Kaiser, B. N., & Marconi, V. C. (2017). Code saturation versus meaning saturation: How many interviews are enough? *Qualitative Health Research, 27*(4), 591–608. https://doi.org/10.1177/1049732316665344

Hooghe, L., & Marks, G. (2001). *Multi-level governance and European integration*. Rowman & Littlefield.

Knill, C., & Liefferink, D. (2007). *Environmental politics in the European Union: Policy-making, implementation and patterns of multi-level governance*. Manchester University Press.

Kollmuss, A., & Agyeman, J. (2002). Mind the gap: Why do people act environmentally and what are the barriers to pro-environmental behavior? *Environmental Education Research, 8*(3), 239–260. https://doi.org/10.1080/13504620220145401

Król, M., & Gomola, A. (2022). How to reduce low-stack emissions? An assessment of the willingness of residents of single-family houses to replace Fossil Fuel heating systems. *Journal of Public Governance, 60*(2), Article 04. https://doi.org/10.15678/PG.2022.60.2.04

Kuchler, M., & Bridge, G. (2018). Down the black hole: Sustaining national socio-technical imaginaries of coal in Poland. *Energy Research & Social Science, 41*, 136–147. https://doi.org/10.1016/j.erss.2018.04.014

Lipsky, M. (1980). *Street-level bureaucracy: Dilemmas of the individual in public services*. Russell Sage Foundation.

Marks, G., & Hooghe, L. (2004). Contrasting visions of multi-level governance. In I. Bache & M. Flinders (Eds.), *Multi-level governance* (pp. 15–30). Oxford University Press.

Newig, J., & Fritsch, O. (2009). Environmental governance: Participatory, multi-level – and effective? *Environmental Policy and Governance, 19*(3), 197–214. https://doi.org/10.1002/eet.509

Newig, J., & Koontz, T. (2013). Multi-level governance, policy implementation and participation: The EU's mandated participatory planning approach to implementing environmental policy. *Journal of European Public Policy*. https://doi.org/10.1080/13501763.2013.834070

Pilogallo, A., Pietrapertosa, F., & Salvia, M. (2024). Are we going towards an effective integration of air quality and climate planning? A comparative analysis for Italian regions. *Journal of Environmental Management, 368*, 122138. https://doi.org/10.1016/j.jenvman.2024.122138

Polish Economic Institute (PEI). (2020). *Public attitudes toward climate policy in Poland*. Polski Instytut Ekonomiczny.

Rowell, A., Makuch, K., & Jackson, T. (2021). Regulatory avoidance and non-compliance in environmental law: Emerging trends. *Environmental Law Review, 23*(4), 293–308. https://doi.org/10.1177/14614529211054816

Stavins, R. N. (2001). Experience with market-based environmental policy instruments. In *Handbook of environmental economics* (Vol. 1, pp. 355–435). https://doi.org/10.1016/S1574-0099(05)01009-8

Steg, L., Bolderdijk, J. W., Keizer, K., & Perlaviciute, G. (2014). An integrated framework for encouraging pro-environmental behaviour: The role of values, situational factors and goals. *Journal of Environmental Psychology, 38*, 104–115. https://doi.org/10.1016/j.jenvp.2014.01.002

Steg, L., Perlaviciute, G., van der Werff, E., & Lurvink, J. (2015). The significance of hedonic values for environmentally relevant attitudes, preferences, and actions. *Environment and Behavior, 46*(2), 163–192. https://doi.org/10.1177/0013916512454730

Stępień, M. (2025). *Judges, decision making, and empathy: An empirical study of courtroom psychology*. Routledge.

Thomann, E. (2019). *Customized implementation of European Union food safety policy: United in diversity?* Palgrave Macmillan. https://doi.org/10.1007/978-3-319-92552-4

Thomann, E., & Sager, F. (2017). Toward a better understanding of implementation performance in the EU multilevel system. *Journal of European Public Policy, 24*(9), 1367–1384. https://doi.org/10.1080/13501763.2017.1314542

Thomann, E., & Zhelyazkova, A. (2017). Moving beyond (non-)compliance: The customization of European Union policies in 27 countries. *Journal of European Public Policy, 24*(9), 1269–1289. https://doi.org/10.1080/13501763.2017.1314536

Tortola, P. D. (2017). Clarifying multi-level governance. *European Journal of Political Research, 56*(2), 234–250. https://doi.org/10.1111/ejpr.12230

Treib, O. (2014). Implementing and complying with EU governance outputs. *Living Reviews in European Governance, 9*(1), 1–47. https://doi.org/10.12942/lreg-2014-1

Whitehead, J. C., & Cherry, T. L. (2007). Willingness to pay for a green energy program: A comparison of ex-ante and ex-post hypothetical bias mitigation approaches. *Resource and Energy Economics, 29*(4), 247–261. https://doi.org/10.1016/j.reseneeco.2006.12.001

Zeigermann, U., Buschmann, D., & Reinermann, J.-L. (2020). *Klimaschutz in Kommunen: Analyse von Aufgaben, Rollen und Qualifikationen kommunaler Klimaschutzmanagerinnen*. Umweltbundesamt. https://www.umweltbundesamt.de/publikationen/klimaschutz-in-kommunen-analyse-von-aufgaben

Zhelyazkova, A., Thomann, E., Ruffing, E., & Princen, S. (2024). Differentiated policy implementation in the European Union. *West European Politics, 47*(3), 439–465. https://doi.org/10.1080/01402382.2023.2257963

Chapter 5
The Usefulness of the Concept of Symbolic Law in Relation to Fighting Air Pollution in Poland and Małopolska

Mateusz Stępień

Abstract This chapter applies the theoretical framework of symbolic law and assesses its usefulness in understanding efforts to combat air pollution in the Małopolska (Lesser Poland) region of Poland. Drawing on the works of John P. Dwyer and Jens Newig, it seeks to deepen understanding of the Małopolska experience by employing the analytical lens of symbolic law and exploring what additional insights into the dynamics of air pollution policy can be gained from this perspective. At the same time, the chapter identifies the limitations of these conceptualizations of symbolic law and evaluates their explanatory value for understanding regulatory inertia, policy superficiality, and the complex interplay of political, administrative, and societal factors in environmental governance. Thus, using the Małopolska case as an empirical reference point, it assesses the putative explanatory potential of this conceptual framework and its usefulness for analyzing environmental policy implementation in practice.

Keywords Symbolic law · Air pollution · Małopolska's struggles against smog · Effectiveness of law

5.1 Introduction

Examining the case of Poland, a country that has experienced and continues to experience severe and long-standing air pollution (see, e.g., Zgłobicki & Baran-Zgłobicka, 2024), helps explain why meaningful improvements in air quality were so difficult to achieve over many years. Despite the extremely detrimental effects of air pollution on public health, the existing system of dedicated institutions and legal measures (see Chap. 2) failed for a long time to translate into tangible improvements in air quality.

M. Stępień (✉)
Department of Sociology of Law, Jagiellonian University, Kraków, Poland
e-mail: mateusz.stepien@uj.edu.pl

M. Stępień, M. Klinowski, *Fighting Air Pollution*, Law and Visual Jurisprudence 17, https://doi.org/10.1007/978-3-032-23909-9_5

Particularly important for the air pollution policy in Poland was the country's accession to the European Union (EU) in 2004 and, indeed, the preceding process of preparing for membership. EU integration marked a turning point in Poland's environmental governance. Membership brought long-term environmental objectives, binding legal obligations, and new accountability mechanisms, including the possibility of infringement proceedings before the Court of Justice of the European Union for failure to implement EU directives. It also provided access to substantial financial resources for environmental protection. In this sense, European integration introduced both new pressures and new policy instruments that could be employed to address air pollution.

However, even several years after accession, improvements in air quality, particularly in regions such as Małopolska, remained unsatisfactory (see Chap. 2). Importantly, although air pollution levels were objectively measurable and extensively documented through publicly available data generated by state-run monitoring systems, these data were, for many years, not presented in a form that was readily accessible or easily understandable to the public. As a result, the scale of the problem was not widely recognized by residents until around 2012–2013 (see Chap. 3). Likewise, for many years, air pollution failed to elicit a strong response from political actors, including those in the government. Indeed, politicians displayed remarkably little initiative in developing comprehensive and effective solutions.

This situation raises several important questions. Why did the existence of a relatively sophisticated system of air-quality protection fail to deliver meaningful outcomes? Why did regulatory solutions that appeared robust on paper prove so weak in practice? What explains the persistence of what might be described as symbolic or ineffective regulation, whereby legal frameworks formally work yet fail to generate substantive environmental improvements? More importantly, why, despite the evident urgency of the problem and its well-documented consequences, were rapid and effective implementation mechanisms not introduced?

The long-standing tradition of research on symbolic law, developed within both political science and legal studies, directly addresses these issues. This body of scholarship examines how law is often employed not to achieve substantive change but to signal intentions, respond to societal expectations, or create the appearance of action. In such cases, the communication of legal regulation may become more important than its practical effects. While this is not the place for a full overview of the diverse and multifaceted scholarship on symbolic law (see, e.g., van Klink et al., 2016), a brief reference to its intellectual roots is helpful. In legal studies, the tradition can be traced back to the somewhat forgotten American legal realist Thurman Arnold (e.g., Arnold, 1935), who emphasized the performative and rhetorical roles of law, suggesting that legislative acts often serve—referring to his words—as a form of public preaching rather than instruments aimed to be enforced. In political science, a foundational figure is Murray Edelman (e.g., Edelman, 1964), who argued that legal and policy measures frequently function to protect the interests of dominant groups by offering only a superficial appearance of addressing the needs of marginalized populations. What unites many approaches within this tradition is the rejection of a purely instrumental, means-ends view of legislation. Instead, laws are seen as vehicles of communication—performative acts that convey messages beyond their literal content. Such messages may shape public perception, legitimize political arrangements, or defuse social tension, even if the legal norms themselves are not effectively implemented or enforced.

Additionally, Gunnel Gustafsson—one of the early pioneers in the study of symbolic policies within the public policy field—observed as early as the 1980s that environmental issues often gave rise to a proliferation of symbolic and pseudo-policies (1983: 277). This observation remains relevant today. Supranational regulations, including those issued by the European Union, have frequently been characterized as symbolic policies due to their weak enforcement mechanisms (see, e.g., Matten, 2003; Blühdorn, 2007; Barry & Blühdorn, 2018). This raises a critical question: to what extent has EU law on air pollution functioned symbolically, and to what degree might this label apply to the transposing regulations adopted in Poland? Furthermore, how can the concept of symbolic law be operationalized within the framework of multilevel governance?

The literature highlights several characteristics of the environmental policy domain that make it particularly susceptible to the emergence of symbolic law (e.g., Dwyer, 1990; Gustafsson, 1983; Matten, 2003; Newig, 2007). Among these are the high social significance of environmental issues—in terms of both their economic implications and their connection to human health and well-being; the inherent complexity of ecological systems; the presence of conflicting interests and competing environmental values that require difficult trade-offs; ideological polarization surrounding environmental debates; pressure exerted by international organizations and obligations arising from international environmental law; intensive lobbying by both environmental nongovernmental organizations (NGOs) and powerful industry stakeholders; and the existence of abundant, yet fragmented and at times inconclusive, expert knowledge.

These factors collectively make decision-making especially difficult. On one hand, policymakers sometimes face pressure to demonstrate responsiveness and determination—often through legislative or regulatory action. On the other hand, meaningful environmental change frequently threatens entrenched economic interests and necessitates structural transformations that are politically costly or difficult to implement. As a result, symbolic measures can serve as politically expedient solutions: they allow governments to appear committed to environmental protection while avoiding the political and economic costs of deep and substantial reform. However, this represents only one—admittedly highly general—interpretation of symbolic law in environmental contexts.

This chapter focuses on studies on symbolic law that engage directly with the domain of environmental protection. Within this body of work, two contributions stand out as particularly insightful and well developed. The first is John P. Dwyer's (1990) concept of the "pathology of symbolic law." Although Dwyer's framework is not highly theorized—despite being presented in a text of over 80 pages—its strength lies in presenting an interesting case study. The author develops his argument through an in-depth analysis of a single case in American air pollution law, offering a compelling diagnosis of how environmental provisions can deliberately fail in practice despite ambitious official goals. The second, more theoretically sophisticated approach is Jens Newig's (2007) concept of "symbolic environmental legislation." Newig provides a broader conceptualization of symbolic law, grounded in both theoretical and empirical research. The contrast between the two scholars reflects their disciplinary orientations: Dwyer is an American legal scholar specializing in environmental law, whereas Newig—originally trained as a geoecologist—is a German political scientist and public policy scholar with a strong empirical focus, particularly on environmental legislation in Germany.

This chapter will reconstruct the perspectives of both authors—John P. Dwyer and Jens Newig—on the phenomenon of symbolic law in the context of environmental protection. It will examine how each conceptualizes the meaning, characteristics, underlying causes, and forms of symbolic legislation. These theoretical insights will then be applied to the legal and policy framework governing air pollution in Poland, with a particular focus on the Małopolska region. The central question guiding this analysis is whether these two approaches offer new explanatory tools for understanding the persistent difficulties in effectively addressing air pollution in Poland and Małopolska. If they do, what exactly do they contribute and in which dimensions of the problem—legal design, political strategy, administrative practice, or public communication? If they fall short, does this limitation reflect weaknesses in the theories themselves, or does it reveal something about the specific characteristics of air pollution governance in Poland and Małopolska? In either case, this theoretical exercise will serve a dual purpose: it will eventually deepen our understanding of the local struggle with smog in Małopolska and simultaneously provide an opportunity to evaluate the analytical usefulness of Dwyer's and Newig's propositions.

5.2 Dwyer's Critique of "Legislative Evasions"

5.2.1 The Clean Air Act Case

Dwyer provides a detailed analysis of a specific case from American federal air-quality law—namely, the legislative history and subsequent implementation challenges of a provision within the Clean Air Act (CCA) (42 U.S.C., § 7401 et seq., 1970). His focus is on Section 112 of the Act, which authorized the Environmental Protection Agency (EPA) to establish emission standards for so-called hazardous air pollutants—substances known to cause disease and endanger human health. Unlike in other provisions of the CAA (e.g., Section 111), Congress did not require the EPA to consider either the economic costs of compliance or the technological feasibility of emission reductions when setting these standards. Furthermore, Congress imposed highly ambitious deadlines: the EPA was given 90 days to compile a list of hazardous pollutants, 180 days to propose emission standards, and another 180 days to issue final regulations. According to Dwyer, both agency officials and external experts viewed these time frames as unrealistic. The absence of explicit cost or feasibility considerations, combined with the compressed schedule, contributed to an extended period of regulatory paralysis. For nearly two decades, no binding standards for hazardous air pollutants were adopted, owing to a complex interplay between the EPA, the federal courts, and shifting political priorities within the executive branch. Dwyer's entire analysis is centered on this single case.

5.2.2 *The Rationality Behind Creating Flawed Legislative Solutions*

Dwyer pondered whether legislators were aware of the flaws in the legislative process. He emphasized that although these issues were not publicly addressed during the legislative stage, this omission stemmed not from ignorance but from deliberate avoidance (1990: 249–250). According to Dwyer, legislators understood that setting emission standards without considering implementation costs or feasibility would make the EPA's task extremely difficult—if not impossible. This immediately raises the question: if lawmakers knew that the CAA provisions would be ineffective in this area, why were such provisions included at all?

Dwyer observes that legislators often make decisions strategically—a dynamic he refers to as a "deep pathology of lawmaking in representative democracy" (1990: 246). This pathology emerges from adherence to the internal "logic" of the political process: a logic shaped less by substantive problem-solving and more by the pursuit of political advantage. While Dwyer does not fully elaborate this insight, it opens the door to a broader reflection on how the structural conditions of democratic governance may generate "pathological" legal solutions through calculated political maneuvering.

Rather than offering a general theory of democratic politics, Dwyer zeroes in on the specific situation legislators faced. On one hand, there were "political benefits associated with supporting legislation issued for health protection regardless of the costs"; on the other, there were "enormous political costs in a situation where it would emerge that health benefits were sacrificed to lower regulatory costs." Caught "between a rock and a hard place," Congress sent a clear message to voters: "We are protecting your health at any cost"—while in practice avoiding swift and decisive regulatory measures that might antagonize powerful, organized interests. As Dwyer underscores, the symbolic benefits of the Clean Air Act—especially the political capital it generated—became paramount.

Dwyer argues that the rationality of symbolic legislation lies in its ability to reconcile conflicting pressures. Symbolic legal solutions may appear to pursue a specific objective (e.g., environmental protection) while in reality serving other functions: postponing difficult decisions, diffusing accountability, or avoiding political fallout. These strategies deliver tangible political gains. In the case of Section 112, Dwyer contends that the provision was enacted primarily as a symbolic expression of "commitment to solving this particular social problem" (1990: 283)—a performative gesture affirming the importance of public health and environmental values (1990: 249).

The "symbolic" character of such legal acts lies in the use of law not primarily to regulate behavior but to communicate political (or axiological) intent. Symbolic legislation projects resolve, affirms shared ideals, and cultivates public trust—often without producing real-world change. In this way, it functions as a form of axiological reassurance: a mechanism for expressing collective values, even when effective implementation tools are lacking. As Dwyer puts it, such laws serve as an expression of the legislature's aspirations and a reassurance to different voters and agencies (1990: 300). Legislators, he notes, gained political credit for voting in favor of "health and the environment" through the CAA—sending a bold public message against organized interest groups. Yet, at the same time, they postponed difficult decisions: "Congress was able to claim credit for protecting health and the environment while avoiding difficult policy questions and shifting the political problems to EPA" (1990: 282–283).

Importantly, Dwyer challenges a rigid distinction between "symbolic" and "instrumental" legislation. Symbolic law is not necessarily devoid of consequences. It expresses preferences, and the failure to achieve declared goals is itself a political outcome. Moreover, symbolic law fulfills political functions: it reinforces and legitimizes certain values and narratives. As Dwyer puts it, such laws "symbolize the government's commitment to certain public values." In this sense, they operate through communication and value affirmation rather than practical implementation. Echoing Arnold, Dwyer observes that "a law that is unenforceable or not administrable when read literally may be important symbolically because it establishes the proper ideals" (1990: 249). Symbolic legislation is valued not for its regulatory efficacy but for the ideals it embodies. The "symbolic weight" of a legal act is distinct from its behavioral effects. Often, symbolic law is created because it offers an efficient means of affirming widely held values—linking them to specific policies, political actors, or institutional narratives, even in the absence of enforceable mechanisms.

5.2.3 Motivations for Legislators to Create Flawed Legal Solutions

Dwyer draws attention to the variety of motivations among legislators for creating flawed legal solutions. Some of them, anticipating future elections (a prime example of strategic decision-making), propose or support "symbolic laws" because "it minimizes political costs and maximizes political recognition (credit)." Dwyer accurately speculates that legislators who truly regard the goals of symbolic actions as important, even if the legal act aiming to achieve them is merely an empty declaration, are more likely to accept symbolic solutions. When they know it is symbolic law, they do not oppose it because the cost of opposition is high (e.g., due to their own image). Furthermore, opposing it is also difficult for another reason. Developing Dwyer's argument, one could say that it is not easy to show how a given law will work in practice—this analysis requires time and a huge amount of work (including empirical work). In this sense, the cost of resistance is high. Moreover, in the analyzed case, some legislators knew the goal would not be achieved but wanted such an idealistic legislative response to promote certain values, even if it was a form of "deception"; "some legislators may support health-based environmental controls because they establish government priorities and public values promoting protection of public health" (1990: 249). Conversely, "other legislators may have been less interested in the dynamics of rulemaking and more committed to the symbol itself—that protection of human health has no price. Even though they privately acknowledged that the symbolic goal is unattainable, these legislators wanted the government to pronounce an idealistic social policy to preserve underlying values (...)" (1990: 248). Dwyer notes, referencing numerous examples, that in the legislative process, proposals that focus attention on the social "evil" personified by corporations and industry or on the social victim have significant advantages related to their popularity. For many legislators, it is more convenient to make a safe choice and vote for them due to voter support. After all, "agencies and courts will struggle with unresolved legal, ethical, and political questions" (1990: 245).

This leads to the conclusion that the decisions of individual legislators—driven by diverse motivations and levels of knowledge—are guided by reasoning that may be internally rational yet collectively produce what Dwyer terms a "pathological" outcome. In this sense, the legal act labeled as "pathological" is not the result of irrationality or oversight but rather the outcome of intentional and strategically rational actions taken by political actors operating within a specific institutional context and under particular constraints.

5.2.4 Consequences of Symbolic Law and Dwyer's Evaluations

The enactment of such legal acts—namely, symbolic legislation—has specific and far-reaching consequences. Relevant entities (in this case the EPA and, later, the courts) are compelled to respond to what Dwyer terms a case of faulty delegation. In some situations, the flawed legislative act may be "supplemented" or "repaired" during the implementation phase—e.g., through functional or creative interpretation. In the case analyzed by Dwyer, this involved transforming symbolic guarantees into enforceable legal standards. Although this dynamic is critical, Dwyer does not explicitly consider that such corrective measures at the implementation stage may be (1) anticipated and intended by the lawmakers themselves or (2) unforeseen and unintended or even undesirable. If the implementation challenges were truly unknown to the legislators, then what we are dealing with may be something other than symbolic legislation. Nevertheless, in the case Dwyer examines, the symbolic provision gave the agency discretionary options: to postpone fulfilling the legal requirement, to independently undertake a cost-benefit analysis, or to wait until court litigation forced a resolution. These options were shaped by—and responsive to—the broader political context.

The possibility of "correcting" symbolic law during implementation is noteworthy, as it sheds light on important institutional dynamics. Even when such corrections were not foreseen, the original lawmakers can retroactively claim that this was exactly the intention—and later credit themselves with any positive outcomes. In this way, the authors of symbolic laws retain a strategic advantage: they can frame and reinterpret the outcomes to suit political narratives and assign favorable meanings to subsequent developments. Symbolic legislation thus creates space for ambiguity, maneuverability, and selective attribution of responsibility—benefits that accrue to its creators.

Dwyer's assessment of this legislative practice is unequivocally critical: "The enactment of symbolic legislation reflects a breakdown of the policymaking machinery, a system that all too frequently addresses real social problems in an unrealistic fashion. It also creates a dilemma for regulators and judges" (1990: 234). Crucially, Dwyer identifies the most damaging consequence of symbolic law, not in its symbolic content *per se* but in the disruption of the regulatory process that follows. He points out that symbolic legislation distorts public discourse in agency proceedings and legislative hearings. It creates inflated expectations among advocacy groups (such as environmentalists) while simultaneously triggering opposition from powerful interests, who often work to sabotage the process. By making unrealistic promises that cannot be fulfilled, symbolic law undermines the possibility of political compromise—effectively paralyzing constructive policymaking. In this light, symbolic law is not merely rhetorical. It is a distinct political strategy for coping with intractable problems—one that shifts the problem temporally and institutionally but does not solve it. As Dwyer concludes, since symbolic laws attempt to solve real conflicts in an unrealistic way, "the underlying problems, such as widespread exposure to hazardous air pollutants, remain unresolved" (1990: 283).

5.2.5 Polemic Remarks and Summary

Dwyer emphasizes—crucially—that the legislative practice of enacting symbolic solutions is neither rare nor anomalous. Rather, it is a typical and systematic feature of democratic lawmaking, one that should be analyzed and explained as a normal part of legislative behavior. Against the backdrop of prevailing normative expectations about the rationality and functionality of legislation, he provocatively asserts: "Legislating in this way [i.e., as symbolic action] may not be responsible, but neither it is unusual nor surprising" (1990: 246). Symbolic legislation, therefore, is not an exception or marginal deviation—it is a recognizable and patterned strategy.

But what exactly is symbolic legislation? For Dwyer, symbolic law arises when "the legislature does not want the law to be implemented in the form materialized in the text." Elsewhere, he observes that a law that is unenforceable or unimplementable has significance because it reestablishes and refreshes the proper ideals or values (1990: 249). In his view, symbolic legislation is passed with the awareness—on the part of its authors—that it will not be effectively implemented, typically due to insurmountable practical, administrative, or political barriers. This insight leads to an important limitation of Dwyer's approach: he does not address the methodological and conceptual challenges of establishing lawmakers' intentionality, especially within the framework of collective decision-making. How can we reliably identify the subjective awareness or strategic motives of individual legislators, much less of legislatures as collectives?

The case study that Dwyer analyzes—Section 112 of the Clean Air Act—is a specific instance of what might be termed "symbolic law by delegation." This form of symbolic legislation allows political actors to avoid making potentially unpopular decisions while appearing to affirm important normative commitments (e.g., protecting public health or the environment). By delegating implementation to administrative agencies under unrealistic constraints, lawmakers communicate responsiveness to public concerns while effectively insulating themselves from the political costs of action or inaction. Dwyer's study thus exemplifies one particular form of symbolic law: a law that is "symbolic" not only in the sense of being ineffective but also in the sense of communicating values that are not meant to be realized in practice.

A key component of Dwyer's argument is that this strategy—despite undermining the goals nominally endorsed by law—was nevertheless rational for the legislators involved. In fact, Dwyer's reasoning closely aligns with public choice theory and other rational actor models in political science. Under certain institutional and political conditions, creating effective regulatory programs may not be the optimal strategy for political actors seeking to maximize electoral support or maintain influence. Sometimes, sending a reassuring signal to concerned constituencies—suggesting that a problem has been addressed—can yield greater political benefits than implementing a meaningful but controversial solution.

Recalling earlier points, Dwyer identifies several motivations behind support for symbolic legislation: genuine endorsement of the values the law is intended to promote, the desire to avoid difficult or unpopular decisions, and strategic cost-benefit calculations. From these diverse yet individually rational motivations, a collectively irrational outcome can emerge: a dysfunctional law that fails to address the social problem it ostensibly seeks to resolve. This leads Dwyer to a fundamental insight about democratic institutions: individual rationality—filtered through legislative procedures and shaped by institutional incentives—can, and often does, produce pathological policy outcomes.

Although Dwyer's analysis is fragmented at times, he touches on a broader set of constitutional, institutional, and organizational dynamics that shape lawmaking. He reduces the creation of flawed legislation to a constellation of measurable factors—especially individual motivations—but situates them within broader structural constraints.

As was mentioned, Dwyer begins his analysis with a classic distinction between instrumental and symbolic law, only to complicate and partially undermine it.

Symbolic laws often contain instrumental elements beneath the surface. He writes: "symbolic legislation is a political gesture. While it serves both instrumental and symbolic goals, the instrumental goals are beneath the surface." This perspective resonates with Murray Edelman's theory of symbolic politics: legal acts often publicly affirm goals (such as protecting public health or the environment) that threaten powerful interests, but in practice, they are designed to preserve the status quo by avoiding real conflict with those same interests. Dwyer thus draws attention to the communicative function of symbolic law: it signals political intent and performs value affirmation. The legislation does not directly challenge entrenched interests but reassures voters that something is being done. In this light, Section 112 of the CAA was addressed less to the EPA, which was formally tasked with implementation, and more to the public and interest groups, as a symbolic performance of political will. In this way, Dwyer's account weaves together microlevel motivations with broader institutional and structural forces, providing a multifaceted picture of how symbolic legislation operates in practice.

5.3 Symbolic Law as an Expression of Rationality: Jens Newig's Concept of Symbolic Environmental Legislation

5.3.1 Starting Point

Jens Newig, in his interdisciplinary research, also takes up the issue of symbolic legislation—likely because it resides at the intersection of legal effectiveness, its limitations, and the political dimension of law. Newig critically evaluates earlier studies, noting that research on this topic remains quite limited, and many of the key questions have not yet been answered (2007, p. 277). Even years after this observation, Newig's assessment remains accurate, despite his own important contributions to advancing the field.

According to Newig, the underdevelopment of research on symbolic law stems from several sources. First, the well-established tradition of rationalist legal theory—especially prominent in continental jurisprudence—tends to overlook the phenomenon of the intentional creation of flawed or ineffective laws. Moreover, Newig rightly points out that "the relationship between symbolic legislation and the issue of effectiveness still awaits explanation." The conceptual link between symbolic law and legal effectiveness remains undertheorized, particularly in terms of clarifying what kind of effectiveness is being questioned: legal, behavioral, political, or symbolic. Discussions that label symbolic law as "ineffective" often fail to specify which dimension of effectiveness is at stake.

Newig also highlights the lack of systematic understanding of the conditions that foster the production of symbolic legislation. This gap is compounded by a tendency (established by Murray Edelman) to reduce symbolic law to mere deception of citizens by political elites or interest groups. Such an approach overlooks earlier, more nuanced treatments of the topic—particularly those of Thurman Arnold and later by Gunnel Gustafsson—who offered alternative interpretations. Newig calls for a broader and more sociologically informed perspective, suggesting that symbolic law can also be understood as a form of social self-deception. This line of inquiry, explored by some Dutch scholars (see van Klink et al., 2016), encourages scholars to adopt a macrolevel analytical perspective—what Newig refers to as a "bird's eye view" (2007, p. 278).

Importantly, Newig's approach moves beyond the traditions established by Arnold and Edelman. As highlighted in the introductory remarks to this chapter, Arnold regarded law as inherently permeated by ineffective norms that persist due to their deep embeddedness in social structures, often fulfilling important functions despite their instrumental shortcomings. Edelman, by contrast, stressed the intentionality of elites, framing symbolic law as a strategic instrument designed to pacify demands for justice without materially threatening the interests of powerful groups. Newig, however, introduces a third possibility: that symbolic legislation may not always result from top-down manipulation but from collectively produced narratives and beliefs that obscure the ineffectiveness of law even to those who create or support it. In this view, symbolic law—or to be more precise, one of its types—is not merely imposed on society by cynical elites but can emerge from systemic patterns of social cognition, institutional inertia, or diffuse political pressures—reflecting broader dynamics of self-deception in liberal democracies.

5.3.2 Newig's Perspective on Symbolic Legislation in Environmental Policy

Newig's thinking on symbolic legislation in the environmental domain consistently relies on one research perspective—the theory of public choice, which is based on methodological individualism and the rational actor paradigm and also expresses a realistic view of politics (2007, p. 292). Newig's way of thinking about processes in modern democracies is guided by a simple assumption in the spirit of public choice theory, which says that politicians are interested in "maximizing electoral gains and popularity rankings." Politicians are rational actors focused on their own benefits. Similarly, the public—although citizens are concerned about the environment (the area that Newig's analyses focus on)—shows a strong tendency to minimize personal costs associated with fighting for a "better" environment (including air). A typical voter is, as Anthony Downs put it, a "rational ignorant." Furthermore, the entire principal-agent structure in democracy creates incentives for the ruling parties to "exploit their information and potentially deceive voters to some extent." For Newig, public choice theory "assumes that law makers tend to deliberately deceive citizens" (2007, p. 283). This assumption can be regarded as partially accurate, although this way of thinking overlooks other important motivational elements (some may focus on electoral success due to the opportunity to implement a specific ideology or axiology, while others may do so for financial or prestige reasons).

Building on this, Newig analyzed the conditions that favor the enactment of symbolic laws, "the way various external factors decide to what extent a law is symbolic" (2007, p. 289, 291). He placed mechanisms and factors that foster the creation of symbolic law at the center. Additionally, he presented two case studies on environmental protection issues, in which he applied the previously introduced divisions. These relate to two German legal acts: the Ozone Law (*Ozongesetz*) from 1995 and the Regulation on Large Combustion Installations (*Großfeuerungsanlagen-Verordnung*) from 1983. As Newig writes, these "two cases serve to illustrate the effectiveness and ineffectiveness of (symbolic) legislation, the law makers' clear intentions, the relevant mechanisms involved [in their functioning], and the issue of deception and self-deception" (2007, p. 278). The choice of these cases was already based on a preliminary assessment aimed at conducting a "contrastive" case study within symbolic legislation. Although these cases themselves are interesting, they will not be discussed in detail because, for the purposes of this chapter, Newig's theoretical framework is much more important. It is worth noting, however, that Newig did not develop these case studies thoroughly. While the text includes a brief historical background and statements from politicians involved in their creation, they are more general analyses than classic case studies. Newig relied on media materials, statements from interest groups, and literature and conducted in-depth interviews with politicians closely connected to the legislative processes (he conducted 16 interviews with parliamentarians and officials from the relevant environmental agency).

5.3.3 Characteristics of Symbolic Law

Newig begins his deliberations with a strong assumption that law is an instrument of social ordering. It serves "to guide, regulate, and control society in a desired fashion" (2007, p. 278), which excludes the more subtle roles of law as meaning making and identity creation. For Newig, law directly affects order as a top-down tool, which shows his presupposition about its role and place. Nevertheless, even sticking to this way of understanding the law, one could add that the general control of the lawmaking process by political powerholders is a valuable tool in their hands—it provides them with a wide field, among other things, to engage in "symbolic" actions.

On this backdrop, the specificity of symbolic law becomes evident, as it "deliberately fails to meet its declared objectives" (2007: 278); it is law "that was never intended to fully realize the goals it seemed to aim for" (2007: 277), "passed by the legislature against the better knowledge of its creators" (2007: 279). The subjective component must be emphasized—the creators of symbolic law *ex ante* know about its flaws, which are even assumed and intentional. Even further, Newig argues that they make decisions "against" their best knowledge, suggesting that they possess the knowledge necessary to achieve the intended goals but, for some reason, do not use it in the legislative process. In another paper, coauthored by Newig, it is stated that in the case of "symbolic policies or legislation ... policy makers formulate dishonest aims while pursuing a hidden agenda, e.g., to depoliticize hot public issue" (Newig et al., 2019, pp. 3–4). This formulation highlights the "hidden goals" of such legislative efforts. According to Newig, the essence of symbolic law is "deception" (2007, p. 291), creating a sort of cover. In a similar vein, Newig described symbolic environmental legislation—despite often ambitious and officially declared goals, some actions are designed to remain ineffective in ecological terms (2007, p. 277). Symbolic law is based on the manipulation of goals—there are official goals, but they are not the ones the creators actually want to achieve.

The question arises whether such a situation (namely the manipulatron of goals) is a hallmark of symbolic legislation or just one of its subtypes. More specifically, does every instance of pursuing a "hidden" goal, while assuming and expecting that the officially declared goal will not be achieved, fall within the category of symbolic law? It seems that not every form of goal manipulation (more precisely axiological manipulation) constitutes a case of symbolic law—otherwise, the element of "symbolism" would be lost.

Symbolic legislative acts are "created" to be ineffective with respect to their official goals. These are, therefore, planned, intentional activities of the law creators. Although Newig rightly emphasizes this, there is a lack of a more precise elaboration of this element, which is a broad category (which is why the definition stating that symbolic legislation involves making decisions "against" one's best knowledge is useful).

The last of Newig's definitions of symbolic legislation refers to "ambitious, officially declared goals." These are cases where the official axiological basis is clear and simultaneously "ambitious." What this means is not explained. Nevertheless, the direction of the deliberations is important—this is precisely the nature of goals that is significant for how legislators are perceived, but it also suggests difficulties in achieving them. While Newig does not expand on this thread, it seems that the category of "ambitious goals" is important when determining the presence of symbolic law (including explaining the failures associated with its implementation by creators of such solutions). The core of symbolic lawmaking lies in communicating these "ambitious goals."

What does "ecologically ineffective" mean? Unfortunately, Newig does not clarify this. One might assume that it refers to achieving the declared, official goals. However, such a symbolic act will be effective in some sense if these hidden goals are achieved. Newig, in fact, points this out. He even goes further by asserting that "all legislation is symbolic (to a certain extent), and almost all symbolic laws are also effective (at least in a political sense)" (2007, p. 278). Some degree of "symbolism," i.e., creating elements of law without assuming that it will achieve its intended goals, is common. It is unfortunate that Newig does not elaborate on this issue. It seems that such an approach leads to some inherent properties of law as an ordering tool.

5.3.4 *The Legislative Activity Matrix*

The core of Newig's considerations revolves around modeling legislative activities. He differentiates between two dimensions of legislative action.

The first dimension is described as "political-strategic." This involves political goals (e.g., increasing popularity, addressing a particular issue). These are "intentions aimed at purely political outcomes." Newig emphasizes that lawmakers, when creating laws, may be under pressure to show that a problem has been addressed, to meet the emotional needs of people (and to achieve other goals), but without producing any real effects, without a genuine improvement in the social conditions indicated by the specific legal act (2007, p. 276). These "political-strategic" motivations can vary widely. The second dimension is "issue-related substantive." This aspect involves achieving "substantive" goals (which requires, as Newig writes, "legal effectiveness")—"manifested, explicit goals for which the legislative act serves as a means." In this case, the law is used to actually achieve certain social goals. Based on this distinction, Newig creates a matrix (Table 5.1), which results in four types of legislative acts (2007, p. 280). Every legal act fits somewhere within this matrix.

Symbolic law, unlike the other three types, involves a situation in which the creators do not care about the substantive effectiveness of the proposed intervention (e.g., they do not select the right tools to achieve declared goals) but only focus on its political effectiveness (2007: 280). This requires actively communicating the mere fact of enacting or specifying the content of the given act, without concern for the substantive side of the law. In this view, symbolic law "includes those legal acts that are not intended, nor expected, to be effective legally and substantively, but which are enacted with certain political-strategic intentions" (2007: 280). Such legislative intervention is intentionally and deliberately designed to be defective—that is, not an effective tool for achieving the declared goals. Its shortcomings are not accidental but reflect a conscious decision shaped by the broader horizon of objectives and the expectations of its drafters.

One should immediately note that the gradation of "substantive" and "political" characteristics of a legal act requires better description (see Lembcke, 2016, p. 90). In a liberal democracy, it is precisely the combination of these aspects, their integration in the institutional framework, that should be the starting point. Moreover, the division itself is not as clear as it might seem. For example, there are situations where the correct tools are chosen but there is no political will to actually apply the given legal solution. The question arises as to how substantively "effective" (in a substantial sense) such a regulation is. In this case, ineffectiveness results from something other than a flaw in the knowledge used to create the intervention.

Table 5.1 Types of legislative acts according to Newig (based on Newig, 2007)

	Nonpolitical-strategic	Political-strategic
Issue-related substantive	"Do the job"	Integrational potential
Non-issue-related substantive	"For the files"	Symbolic

5.3.5 Locating Symbolic Law

How can symbolic law be identified in practice? This question is particularly important given that lawmakers are unlikely to openly admit that a legal act is ineffective—or even symbolic in nature. Jens Newig addresses this challenge by distinguishing between "objective" and "subjective" criteria, the latter referring to the intentions and mental states of legislators. Although he notes that "alongside these 'objectively measurable' criteria, the 'subjective' criterion of legislative intent plays a key role in understanding the symbolic nature of statutes" (2007: 281), he does not explain how such intent can be identified in practice. Instead, his analysis focuses almost exclusively on the "objective" criteria.

Newig first identifies a set of "objective" indicators meant to assess the issue-related effectiveness of a legal act. These include (1) substantive suitability—the degree to which the content of the law corresponds to its stated goals (the lower the fit, the more likely the law is symbolic); (2) enforceability—the presence of provisions specifying the institutional actors responsible for monitoring compliance and imposing sanctions (if absent, this may suggest symbolic intent); and (3) implementation context—including available resources, administrative capacity, and the willingness of the target group to comply (the more limited these factors, the more probable the symbolic nature of the law).

While these criteria offer a starting point, they remain general and not particularly precise. For example, enforceability, especially in the form of sanctioning mechanisms, is a problematic metric. A law may deliberately lack sanctions not out of disregard for effectiveness but because it seeks to encourage certain behaviors or values without coercion—such as moral appeals or soft regulatory guidance. Newig does not adequately address the diversity of legislative types or their normative rationales. Furthermore, conflating resource limitations (affecting lawmakers) with willingness to comply (affecting recipients) raises analytical concerns. A technically sophisticated law, supported by expert input and strong institutional backing, might still fail in practice due to political resistance or public distrust. Conversely, a law adopted with minimal resources may succeed because it resonates with a community's identity, values, or aspirations.

Newig also introduces "objective" indicators of political-strategic effectiveness, including (1) whether the law provides specific legal consequences for nonimplementation (suggesting genuine commitment to execution); (2) the law's position in the legal hierarchy (with higher-level acts presumed to be more strategically significant); and (3) the timing of the act (e.g., if passed before elections or during the holiday season, potentially indicating symbolic aims such as media visibility or political appeasement).

These criteria, however, are not particularly persuasive. For example, legislation passed before elections could serve a genuinely substantive function—such as addressing urgent public demands—rather than merely symbolic goals. Similarly, passing controversial laws during holidays may reflect strategic obfuscation rather than symbolic posturing. Moreover, legal hierarchy is not a reliable indicator: an executive decree in a crisis may be more politically strategic than a constitutional amendment passed through routine procedure. As with enforceability, the presence or absence of sanctions does not neatly differentiate between symbolic and nonsymbolic legislation. Newig again appears to overlook the diversity of legal forms and functions. Ultimately, while Newig's effort to define objective markers of symbolic law is valuable, the criteria he proposes are conceptually ambiguous, inconsistently justified, and insufficiently attentive to the complexity of lawmaking as a political and institutional process. The question remains whether these indicators are truly "objective" and whether they meaningfully capture the inherently political, contextual, and contested character of symbolic legal acts.

5.3.6 Factors Promoting Symbolic Law and Hypotheses Proposed by Newig

Newig relied on public choice theory, including the assumption that politicians are motivated by electoral success. This generally leads him in the right direction—allowing the decision to apply symbolic law to be placed within a broader context and structural conditions that affect motivations. He assumes that (1) media, interest groups, and the opposition influence the priorities of the ruling party, which leads to (2) pressure to create a solution (to some problem), and there are associated costs of doing nothing, but at the same time, there are (3) costs of implementing a solid, good, well-thought-out solution. According to Newig, when the costs of passivity (e.g., the costs of doing nothing) or creating a reliable solution are high and there is significant pressure, there is a tendency to create symbolic law. As a result, symbolic law minimizes the risk of losing popularity for lawmakers and "mutes" the entities demanding action from the ruling party. In this view, creating symbolic law is a way out of a specific situation involving the accumulation of several factors. For Newig, these three variables (pressures, the costs of creating a real solution, the costs of doing nothing) determine the creation of symbolic laws, which are a "cheap" and quick way of acting, bringing a "double benefit" to the creators (they take action presented as solving the problem and minimizing costs).

Newig's considerations about the information asymmetry between lawmakers and citizens, resulting from the different roles of both groups in politics, are very important. This asymmetry opens the way for the use of tactical means by which politicians can aim to satisfy the greatest number of voters while minimizing the number of those who might feel offended or unhappy by the planned policy (2007: 283). From this perspective, it is rational for a legislator to create symbolic law when the anticipated ineffectiveness in key areas will go unnoticed. Citizens might not perceive it, and organized players, the media, and the opposition might not raise it (for various reasons) (2007: 283). Newig rightly points out that lawmakers have the opportunity to explain themselves when someone points out the symbolic nature of a given law—"the politicians who have to take responsibility can still refer to the complexity of the issue, to unclear causal relations and similar factors which help them to deflect the blame" (2007: 284).

Newig operates with a distinction between solving and managing a social problem. Symbolic legislation represents "measures aimed at managing, not solving environmental problems" (2007, p. 291); it is part of managing the situation related to defining social problems and adopting a certain governance strategy. Creating symbolic law is a way of managing the "agenda"—certain topics are relatively easily highlighted (and later forgotten), while others are marginalized. This is also important because it shows that symbolic law can be a tool in internal struggles among political powerholders.

Based on this vision of factors influencing the creation of symbolic laws, Newig derived several detailed hypotheses. According to him, the greater the political pressure, the greater the chance that political-strategic dimensions will be highlighted in the creation of law. Next, a significant social problem—which either lacks an appropriate solution (it is unknown) or has only one that entails short-term costs exceeding short-term benefits—will likely be addressed through symbolic laws. Newig also hypothesized that the greater the social conflict of interests between competing groups, the higher the likelihood of creating symbolic legislation and that in the case of conflicting interests, the legislator seeks to satisfy the "more important" interest groups in a "substantive" way, while "less important" groups are satisfied only symbolically. And the last hypothesis goes that the more complex and opaque the political issue, the greater the likelihood that it will be addressed by symbolic legislation.

5.3.7 Summary and Commentary

Without a doubt, Newig's approach to symbolic law is original, even though it builds on ideas previously developed by other scholars, including Gustafsson and, to some extent, Dwyer. The analysis of "mechanisms and conditions conducive to the creation of symbolic laws," undertaken within the adopted research perspective (public choice theory), directs studies on symbolic law in the right direction. Based on simple assumptions inherent in this perspective, Newig established, supported by case studies, that the following factors condition the creation of symbolic laws: "high level of public attention, high regulatory costs relative to low regulatory benefits, sharp conflicts marked by values, asymmetric distribution of information, and high complexity of the issue" (2007: 291; in this way, he expanded his three-element proposal). Despite Newig's undeniable contribution to the study of symbolic law, some issues require polemical commentary.

A crucial distinction—one that Newig does not elaborate on but which is undoubtedly necessary—concerns the knowledge available to lawmakers. The first scenario involves lawmakers who possess the knowledge needed to make sound decisions but fail to utilize it or who, for various reasons, do not activate the available mechanisms for acquiring it. The second scenario involves the deliberate enactment of laws that are believed to be ineffective, without the lawmakers having—or potentially having access to—knowledge of effective alternatives. The absence of this distinction reflects a broader underdevelopment of the subjective dimension of the legislators. Moreover, the concept of "knowledge" alone does not adequately capture the full range of motivations or subjective factors involved in the lawmaking process. Overall, Newig's argument lacks clear definitional boundaries and fails to analytically distinguish between the different modalities that may lead to the deliberate creation of flawed laws. This critique extends to much of the literature on symbolic legislation.

While the attempt to identify factors conditioning the emergence of symbolic laws is both timely and valuable, it is important to note that Newig frames their creation as largely driven by external pressures on political powerholders. In this sense, Newig presents a reactive account of symbolic legislation. However, there are also situations in which political actors proactively resort to symbolic law—for example, when time constraints preclude a thorough legislative process, leading them to deliberately enact flawed laws. In some cases, political powerholders may even construct or exaggerate a social problem in order to be seen as addressing it. Restricting the analysis to external pressures appears overly limiting. Moreover, Newig's reference to "political pressure" later in the text is underdeveloped. It is said to consist of (1) public attention and (2) the certainty of involved actors—both of which are broad, loosely defined categories that do not lend themselves to precise operationalization or measurement. In sum, while Newig offers a coherent account of one subtype of flawed legislation, his framework lacks analytical refinement and fails to capture many important distinctions and specificities of legislative practice.

5.4 Applying Dwyer's and Newig's Concepts to the Context of Air Pollution Fight in Poland and Małopolska

5.4.1 Initial Thoughts

The situation in Poland and in the Małopolska region, both before and after EU accession in 2004, was dramatic in terms of air quality, as confirmed by monitoring data (see Chaps. 2 and 3). Although a comprehensive system of air-quality standards, monitoring, reporting, and public information formally existed, it failed to deliver the expected and officially declared outcomes. Fully uncovering the reasons for this ineffectiveness would require a broader, cross-sectoral analysis encompassing state capacities, the application of legal instruments (and their inherent limitations), and the overall functioning of administrative systems. The present analysis, however, adopts a narrower focus. Its primary aim is to assess whether two reconstructed concepts of symbolic law, both concerned with similar dimensions yet emphasizing different aspects, can provide meaningful insights into the shortcomings of Poland's air pollution regulation and policy. In doing so, the analysis seeks not only to clarify the dynamics of the case examined in this book but also to demonstrate the strengths, limitations, and distinctive features of these theoretical frameworks.

At the outset, it is important to sum up the core elements that both authors (Dwyer and Newig) share in their understanding of symbolic law. First, they agree that the creation of symbolic law is neither rare nor inexplicable—on the contrary, it is a frequent and systemically embedded feature of the legislative process. Second, both concepts focus on the political entanglement of lawmaking and the social roles that law plays, which makes law a convenient tool for advancing various goals, at least formally, with political objectives often taking precedence. Third, symbolic law can be broadly defined as law whose drafters are aware, or at least accept, that it is unlikely to achieve its declared objectives yet choose to enact it because it serves other political, communicative, or social purposes. Fourth, both approaches emphasize the subjective dimension of lawmakers, including their knowledge, intentions, and motivations. As a result, assessing whether a legal act qualifies as symbolic law requires some reconstruction of the beliefs and intentions of its drafters, since the symbolic nature of such acts is often not openly acknowledged. A careful examination of the subjective dimension of key legislators, particularly those who initiate, promote, and ultimately support a proposal, therefore becomes essential for identifying symbolic legislation. Fifth, both authors highlight the conditions that incentivize such legislative practices, including the structure of democratic political processes, public pressure, interest group influence, and the role of the media. Sixth, while both approaches emphasize the negative consequences of symbolic legislation, Newig leaves somewhat more room for interpreting these practices as self-deceptive rather than deliberately misleading, thus offering a slightly more neutral perspective.

It is also worth noting that, in Dwyer's approach—strongly influenced by the work of Murray Edelman—symbolic law, although ineffective in material terms, is embedded in a broader game of competing interests. Legal provisions may appear to protect the interests of group X, a perception often accepted and welcomed by members of that group, while in reality serving the interests of group Y, whose goals are in conflict with those of group X. Symbolic law may therefore create the impression that it improves the situation of a particular social group, while in practice, owing to its lack of real effectiveness, it reinforces the position of those who benefit from existing arrangements. Drawing on classical social theory, symbolic law can thus be seen as creating a form of false consciousness: it functions as a mechanism of political eyewash, fostering the appearance of change without producing substantive results.

In line with the initial observation, the theoretical approaches developed under the umbrella of symbolic law can, and indeed should, be applied to real-world processes of lawmaking and policy implementation aimed at protecting air quality. This includes, of course, the case of efforts to combat smog in Poland and, more specifically, in the Małopolska region. These frameworks undoubtedly direct our attention to important questions and areas of inquiry, such as the possibility of deliberately creating ineffective or "lame" legislation, the need to focus on the actual motivations of lawmakers, the existence of various rational reasons for adopting ineffective legal measures, and the use of legislation as a signaling device. In this sense, they offer a conceptual lens that generally appears both useful and appropriate. However, as the analysis progresses, it becomes clear that although these frameworks draw attention to several crucial dimensions of the legislative process, their limitations and relative superficiality become increasingly apparent. Ultimately, they prove unable to fully describe and explain the dynamics of this particular case.

To anticipate the conclusion somewhat, rather than asking why symbolic law emerged in this area, it may be more appropriate to ask why solutions resembling symbolic law were not adopted in the first place, given the near-total inaction of the central government (see Chap. 2). Nevertheless, thinking in terms of symbolic law and applying this perspective to the Małopolska case provides valuable resources for understanding its specific features and distinctive characteristics. It helps illuminate aspects of the political, legal, and social dynamics of air pollution governance that might otherwise remain overlooked, even if the concept itself ultimately proves insufficient as a comprehensive explanation of the case. Additionally, examining the struggle against smog in Poland and the Małopolska region through the lenses of the two conceptualizations of symbolic law provides insights into how thinking about symbolic law can be further refined and nuanced.

5.4.2 Multilevel Governance Context

The case discussed in this book suggests that questions concerning legal effectiveness, decision-making dynamics, and policy strategies within systems of multilevel governance (MLG), which characterize EU air-quality policy (see Chap. 4; see also Weale et al., 2002), require far more nuanced analyses than those offered by the concepts of symbolic law presented above. In other words, existing theories of symbolic law appear to be tailored to a comparatively simple model of lawmaking and policy implementation. They are less well equipped to account for decision-making processes involving multiple actors, overlapping competencies, diverse motivations, and interconnected arenas of governance operating at different institutional levels. MLG introduces new dynamics among multiple actors, as well as novel institutional pressures and opportunities. For example, in the context of air pollution policies, Paolo Giardullo et al. (2016: 5, 6) emphasize that MLG creates legislative gaps that "may provide room for lobbying activities by international groups (car manufacturers, fuel companies) or by other groups at national and regional level" and makes room for "frictions between different institutional levels." MLG generates both new spaces and new constraints for the creation of symbolic law—or, more precisely, for the emergence of only certain forms of it. While Dwyer's example and analysis refer to provisions of legislation in a federal state, it was the Environmental Protection Agency that was the addressee of a flawed authorization to set emission standards—the "game," therefore, unfolded on only two levels (and in the relationship between them). By contrast, the situation within the EU's MLG framework is considerably more complex.

In the case of MLG, EU directives and regulations concerning air-quality protection (increasingly, and fortunately, embedded in broader EU climate policy) often represent compromises that conceal the diverse motivations and strategies pursued by member states and their representatives in EU institutions, including the European Parliament. Even among representatives of a single country, some may support particular measures with the genuine intention of implementing them, while others may do so primarily for political reasons, without any real commitment to implementation, especially when political actors aligned with them hold, or expect to hold, power. Others may simply postpone action while waiting for future political developments. In other words, a multiplicity of actors is involved, each pursuing different strategies for coping with the complexity of the system (see Kobus et al., 2016). This means that, for at least some actors, laws and policies are not symbolic in nature, as they are intended to be complied with and effectively implemented. For others, however, the same legal acts may serve primarily symbolic purposes, for example, signaling a cooperative stance toward other member states and EU institutions or providing a strategic façade that facilitates subsequent political maneuvering at the domestic level. More broadly, both at the EU level and across other levels of governance, the MLG context makes it considerably more difficult to reconstruct the subjective dimension of decision-making. The multiplicity of actors, overlapping strategies, opportunities to shift or conceal responsibility behind the decisions of others, and the coexistence of competing or only partially compatible objectives significantly complicate the picture. This complexity poses a genuine challenge for identifying what should count as a symbolic legal act. Moreover, within a system of MLG, legal acts themselves become increasingly fluid. The relationship between goals and means is often loosened, as actors operating at different levels may pursue different objectives while relying on the same legal instruments. As a result, the traditional linkage between a legal act, its intended purpose, and its implementation becomes less clear-cut. This creates additional difficulties for identifying symbolic legislation, as the very logic of multilevel governance tends to "de-ontologize" legal acts, separating them from any single, stable purpose and embedding them in a complex web of actors, interpretations, and implementation practices.

At the level of the member states, approaches to EU policies and legal acts can differ significantly—especially in the field of air-quality protection, where compliance deadlines are frequently postponed and where multiple buffers exist in the form of exceptions, derogations, and other flexibilities. For some actors, the capacity to bend EU law—whether by failing to fully implement it, relying on exemptions and extensions, exploiting its intended flexibility, leveraging the threat or reality of political blackmail, or simply counting on the slow pace of enforcement proceedings—constitutes not a constraint but a political resource. Moreover, narratives about protecting key values or implementing specific environmental projects can be tailored to one group of voters while simultaneously presenting a more conservative stance—emphasizing local interests or alternative ideological perspectives—to another audience. In this context, member states can, and at times do, strategically "play" with regulations emanating from Brussels, adopting approaches that range from (1) open resistance and contestation, through (2) instrumentalization and selective compliance, to (3) diligent transposition and implementation.

This does not exclude the possibility of symbolic law being created through, for example, the transposition of a fragment of EU law that is formally required but not backed by actual implementation. However, for a legal act to be symbolic in this sense, it would require public communication presenting the act as something important and necessary—and often the opposite occurs. The narrative frequently emphasizes that "we do not want this, but we are forced to do it," which disqualifies the act from being symbolic in the classic sense. It is worth noting that the amendments to EU air-quality law adopted in 2024 (Directive 2024/2881 of the European Parliament and of the Council of 23 October 2024 on ambient air quality and cleaner air for Europe) (see Chap. 2) aim to limit the ability of member states to manipulate the system—for example, through measurement practices, modeling methodologies, or zone designation—practices that were previously common. These changes are intended to increase the internal coherence of the system and to reduce opportunities for strategic manipulation. In this sense, the functioning model of MLG remains in a state of flux—the boundary conditions for decision-making at various levels are being actively reshaped.

Moreover, the very logic of MLG presupposes a certain degree of differentiation, varied emphases, and flexibility regarding what takes place at different levels of governance. This stems not only from the structure of the MLG model itself but also from the need to reach compromises in adopting key decisions—including compromises involving a degree of "turning a blind eye" to implementation failures in order to achieve broader, often existential, goals for the survival of the EU. In a certain sense, this creates a new source of potential symbolic lawmaking at the national level. When undertaking transposition, governments can adopt different approaches—since there is a deadline, the task can be approached with full determination and ensured enforceability or merely "on paper," where the required solution exists only formally (a practice repeatedly criticized by the Court of Justice of the European Union). At times, given the large scale of legislative activity, purely performative acts may be produced that presuppose the absence of real action—a result of haste and the inability to focus attention on all fronts. Once again, much depends on a range of factors: time, resources, political objectives, external pressures, and so on. What matters for our analysis is that MLG creates space for many forms of legislative activity at the national level that may closely resemble symbolic law.

At this stage, symbolic law may emerge through the mechanism of delegation, as described by Dwyer. A national legislator may position themselves as a defender of certain values, draw public attention to a particular issue, and then delegate the details downward, effectively shifting responsibility while maintaining an image of advocacy and commitment—despite lacking resources or financial capacity to support meaningful implementation. This would constitute a form of symbolic signaling. MLG facilitates such shifting of responsibility—delegation aimed at avoiding accountability—and creates room for symbolic effects precisely because it becomes more difficult to monitor the functioning of the whole system. As noted earlier, the

MLG model itself presumes a degree of flexibility, which further enables such practices.

Another important point is that symbolic law, as conceptualized by Newig and Dwyer, always includes a communicative component (which was mentioned below)—that is, it involves signaling that a problem is being solved and that certain values are being protected. Both concepts, however, fail to account for temporal complexity (see Suska, 2025), which is a crucial element of MLG. In other words, a law may be passed in good faith, with a genuine determination to implement it effectively; the implementation may also be carried out sincerely, aimed at producing long-term effects. But later, new political actors may come to power at the national level who do not continue along this path, who do not prioritize the fulfillment of these commitments, or who do not pursue necessary adjustments. More generally, they may do nothing beyond maintaining the bare minimum of the machinery that was once introduced and still operates to some degree. In such a scenario, the regulation becomes increasingly hollow—more of a formality on paper—not through any new act that is publicly promoted but through a lack of political will and failure to sustain a context conducive to effective implementation. It must be emphasized that symbolic law without this aspect of public signaling loses its analytical value—the quiet creation of flawed legal solutions behind closed doors does not serve a political function and therefore cannot be considered "symbolic" in this strict sense.

5.4.3 Air Protection Inaction and Symbolic Signaling

In Poland, the process of transposing European air-quality legislation began even before the country's accession to the European Union (e.g., the Environmental Protection Act of 27 April 2001, Journal of Laws 2001 No. 62, item 627). At the time, however, this was largely a technical and administrative exercise that attracted little public attention and generated little political controversy. In subsequent years, by contrast, the central government displayed a notable lack of initiative in tackling air pollution (e.g., Citkowska-Kimla, 2019; see also Sect. 3.5). Of course, the elements formally required by EU law were introduced. These included strategic policy documents, selected legislative instruments (for instance, those relating to public access to environmental information, including information on air pollution), and, at a later stage, financial programs supporting the thermal modernization of buildings. However, these measures did not amount to a coherent, ambitious, and centrally coordinated policy and law framework. In particular, the central government failed to introduce a comprehensive set of nationwide bans, standards, and enforcement mechanisms, supported by adequate funding, that could have produced a rapid and effective improvement in air quality across the country.

As previously discussed, inaction cannot itself be classified as symbolic law—although this does not exclude the possibility that inaction sent signals to particular interest groups. The strategy adopted by national authorities allowed them to avoid introducing unpopular measures (such as general bans) that could have provoked strong opposition and would have required comprehensive implementation and enforcement mechanisms. At the same time, by refraining from systemic measures against low-stack emissions, the government could sustain the narrative that an air protection system was in place and functioning. This approach also safeguarded the interests of powerful stakeholders, including the coal lobby, coal wholesalers and retailers, and furnace manufacturers.

Moreover, in the absence of sufficient funding and given the lack of a strong top-down policy, space emerged for decentralized and diversified forms of financing (e.g., heating system replacements), as well as for local initiatives. What followed was a decentralization of antismog efforts, accompanied by uncoordinated, fragmented, and often unsynchronized attempts to introduce partial measures at the central level (see Chap. 2). A pivotal moment came in 2008, when responsibility for preparing Air Improvement Plans (*Programy Ochrony Powietrza*) was delegated to regional assemblies (*Sejmiki Wojewódzkie*). These plans are regional legal instruments adopted whenever air-quality standards are exceeded, as has regularly been the case in many parts of Poland, and they introduce binding measures aimed at reducing pollution within a given region. From that point onward, the principal policies and legal instruments designed to address air pollution, including antismog resolutions (see Chap. 1), began to emerge at the regional level and continue to evolve there, differing considerably in both scope and content. This shift proved fruitful and led to several important innovations in the Małopolska region. At the same time, however, it underscored the absence of decisive action by the central government, which failed to introduce a coherent set of nationwide bans, standards, and incentive schemes capable of addressing the problem across the entire country. As a result, responsibility for many of the most ambitious air-quality measures gradually shifted to the regional level.

Until around 2012–2013, however, there was relatively little social pressure demanding action against smog (see Chap. 3). Despite the serious consequences of governmental inaction, this lack of public pressure meant that national politicians had little incentive either to construct a broader political narrative around air pollution or to adopt legislation serving primarily symbolic functions. Indeed, one of the structural conditions conducive to the emergence of symbolic legislation identified by Newig is strong media and public pressure to address a particular problem. In the case of air pollution in Poland, however, such pressure did not emerge until approximately 2012–2013. Prior to that period, air pollution, although objectively severe and well documented, remained largely absent from public debate and was not perceived as an urgent political issue. As a result, the political incentives for adopting even symbolic forms of environmental regulation were relatively weak.

It should also be noted that air pollution policy directly affects millions of households and their finances, making it politically far less attractive than, for example, "penal populism"—rapid and highly visible legislative responses to criminal justice concerns that symbolically project decisiveness and control. In contrast, addressing low-stack emissions from domestic heating and hot water systems at the national level carried a high political risk. In this light, the decision to decentralize was a politically safe solution, but it did not amount to issuing symbolic legislation in the classic sense. Rather, it illustrates a situation in which symbolic law was deliberately not created at the central level. Had the national government assumed ownership of the issue, the effectiveness of its policies would have been relatively easy to measure (e.g., by counting the number of stoves replaced) and, thus, equally easy to assign blame—likely triggering widespread public dissatisfaction among hundreds of thousands of citizens. Recall that, according to Newig, difficulties in assessing the effectiveness of a legal act may create incentives for adopting legislation in a symbolic form. Conversely, when the effectiveness of a measure can be evaluated relatively easily, the incentives to enact symbolic legislation are reduced. In the Polish case, however, the core problem was not the existence of a distinctive legal act presented as a successful solution despite its ineffectiveness. Rather, it was the inertia and prolonged inaction of the central government. The main challenge was therefore the absence of ambitious and effective nationwide measures.

Indeed, the model pursued by successive governments in Poland has largely involved shifting responsibility for governance and problem-solving not only to regional authorities but also to individual citizens. The mushrooming energy crisis was addressed not through the construction of nuclear power plants or the development of a stable, centrally managed energy supply but rather through subsidy schemes for renewable energy sources. As a result, Poland became a country dominated by solar panels, heat pumps, and other decentralized solutions, rather than relying primarily on centrally supplied affordable energy generated through large-scale infrastructure projects, including nuclear power plants. With the help of subsidies and grants, citizens themselves financed a significant portion of the country's energy production infrastructure—one that remains unreliable and lacks sufficient energy storage capacity. A similar dynamic played out in the fight against smog. After years of experimentation with the legal instrument provided under Article 96 of the Environmental Protection Act, numerous court rulings, and several legislative amendments, regional authorities finally began using this tool (see Chap. 2)—enabling them to impose bans on certain fuels or types of heating appliances. This represented a significant breakthrough. However, it still did not lead to the creation of a coherent, coordinated national legal framework addressing air pollution and smog. In sum, rather than enacting comprehensive measures or symbolically charged legal acts at the national level, the approach has been marked by fragmentation and delegation. While regional governments—depending on their political will—have taken on the burden of implementing bans and restrictions on fuel types and furnace standards, all in the absence of a unified national vision of the whole energy sector, citizens have been left to navigate complex subsidy schemes (as the antismog resolutions impose direct obligations on users of heating systems). Although this model may allow for some degree of local innovation or experimentation (as in the case of Kraków), it falls short of constituting a centrally coordinated commitment to tackling air pollution in Poland.

This Polish model of air pollution management cannot be described as symbolic in the classical sense, although particular elements may be read as signals—primarily to EU authorities and national NGOs—that measures against smog were being introduced (albeit too late, after lengthy drafting processes, often slowed by internal cross-ministerial consultations). Each measure therefore requires careful scrutiny to assess whether it carries characteristics of symbolic law. The core feature of the Polish state's (neoliberal in many instances) approach, however, has been the absence of uniform national measures that could have ensured a faster and more coordinated replacement of old furnaces or imposed a ban on certain solid fuels. Instead, authorities publicly emphasized the introduction of partial measures—such as coal-quality standards, registries of heating sources, or funds for thermomodernization (dependent on individual initiative). These measures served a dual signaling function. On the one hand, they demonstrated to the European Union that the problem of air pollution was being addressed and that Poland was taking steps to comply with its obligations. On the other hand, they signaled to domestic constituencies, particularly those aligned with conservative and right-wing political forces, that the state would not introduce drastic air-quality policies or far-reaching environmental regulations imposing substantial obligations on citizens. In the case of the government led by the Law and Justice party (Prawo i Sprawiedliwość (PiS)), between 2015 and 2023, a political narrative often prevailed that downplayed the urgency of combating smog while prioritizing the interests of the mining sector, defending traditions associated with solid-fuel heating, and avoiding the imposition of environmentally motivated requirements on households. The outcome was a form of policy inconsistency, rooted in part in the multilevel governance structure of EU air-quality policy. On the one hand, a series of partial measures signaled commitment and responsiveness to EU institutions and legal requirements. On the other hand, their limited scope, strong decentralization, and political framing communicated to domestic constituencies and interest groups that combating smog was not a central political priority and that substantial room for flexibility remained. As a result, the same policies could simultaneously serve as evidence of compliance in the European arena and as reassurance at the domestic level that no radical transformation of existing energy and heating practices would be imposed.

5.4.4 Applying the Concept of Symbolic Law to the Case of the Antismog Resolutions

The considerations presented above concerned mainly the treatment of air pollution policy at the central level and the largely decentralized model that emerged in the second decade of the twenty-first century. Although a lack of action cannot itself be regarded as a form of symbolic legislation, it is worth asking whether the legal acts adopted at the regional level, including those introduced in the Małopolska region, can be interpreted in such terms or whether viewing them through the lens of symbolic law helps us better understand both their origins and their functions.

As noted in Sect. 2.3.2, during the second decade of the twenty-first century, two separate antismog regulations were adopted: one for Kraków, the capital of the region (in 2016), and another for the remainder of Małopolska (in 2017). While the resolution applying to Kraków introduced a complete ban on the use of coal and wood for heating purposes, the regulation covering the rest of the region established a gradual, three-stage phase-out of specific categories of heating installations. The objective was to first eliminate the most polluting furnaces, then progressively replace more advanced but still environmentally suboptimal devices, and ultimately ensure that only low-emission heating systems remained in operation. The first regulation therefore represented a clear and unconditional ban on the fuels being used, whereas the second constituted a long-term process of replacing the devices in which combustion took place.

It is noteworthy that the same legislative body, the Małopolska Regional Assembly, adopted two different regulatory approaches to address the same social problem, even though it was foreseeable that these measures would vary in their effectiveness. At first glance, the regulation applicable to the rest of Małopolska might be considered an example of symbolic law: a legal act adopted with the expectation that it would not achieve its stated objectives and would serve merely to signal that the problem was being addressed. However, a closer examination of both the legislative process (see Sect. 2.3.2) and the political and social conditions under which the antismog resolutions emerged suggests that the resolution for Małopolska outside Kraków does not fit this interpretation. There are several reasons for this conclusion.

The decision to adopt a less ambitious regulatory strategy was not without justification. Kraków constitutes a relatively compact urban area with a well-developed district-heating network, making it comparatively easy for residents to connect to centralized heating and hot-water systems. In most parts of the remaining region, however, such infrastructure was either limited or entirely absent. Furthermore, public pressure for far-reaching measures was considerably stronger in Kraków. Indeed, many residents of the rest of Małopolska viewed even the adopted regional solution as highly demanding and controversial. In this context, selecting a less radical regulatory path was understandable, particularly when contrasted with the much stricter regime introduced in Kraków. The phased and long-term character of the regulation also had practical advantages. It provided households with additional time to adapt and created opportunities for educational campaigns and public outreach. A more immediate and stringent ban might have generated widespread resistance and proved politically impossible to implement. Admittedly, from the perspective of combating smog, the adopted solution was too gradual and insufficiently ambitious, but at the same time, it enjoyed a higher degree of social and political legitimacy.

The legislative process itself demonstrates that the abovementioned issues were actively considered by policymakers. The first reason was *expressis verbis*, mentioned in the explanatory memorandum accompanying the resolution for the rest of

Małopolska.[1] Moreover, the political majority ultimately opted for a solution that was not optimal in environmental terms but was considered implementable, reasonably effective, and unlikely to provoke such strong opposition as to lead to its repeal. It would therefore be incorrect to argue that the regulation was adopted on the assumption that it would fail. Rather, regional lawmakers selected a policy instrument that could achieve meaningful results over the long term precisely because it was sufficiently acceptable to the public and politically feasible. In this respect, the adopted solution represented a form of political compromise within the then ruling coalition in the Regional Assembly. Moreover, some political actors may have supported the regulation or not opposed it furiously in the expectation that it would later be weakened or even abandoned, and attempts to reverse or soften the adopted measures were indeed made. This also suggests that different motivations underlay support for the regulation. While some actors may have viewed it as a temporary or politically expedient compromise, others supported it as a realistic and implementable strategy for improving air quality under existing social, economic, and political constraints.

Moreover, the legislative effort was accompanied by attempts to secure financial resources to support implementation. In particular, the LIFE Program (see Chap. 4) provided crucial funding for the creation of a network of eco-advisors, clearly demonstrating an intention to facilitate implementation rather than merely create the appearance of action. Of course, these efforts were not entirely successful, and important shortcomings remained, including those associated with the central-government funding program discussed in Chap. 2 and weak enforcement (see Chap. 4). Nevertheless, the existence of implementation-oriented measures and supporting institutions significantly weakens the argument that the antismog resolution for the rest of Małopolska should be regarded as an instance of symbolic law.

Consequently, the chosen solution, although imperfect and still not fully implemented due to enforcement deficiencies, low penalties, and other obstacles (see Chap. 4), cannot be described as purely symbolic. Viewed in the broader context of the legislative process, the long-term struggle for cleaner air, driven by social movements (Chap. 3), supported by opportunities and pressures arising from EU membership, and accompanied by efforts to secure financial and institutional resources for implementation, was far more than a law "on paper." While the adopted measures did not eliminate all implementation problems, they reflected a genuine attempt to address air pollution through instruments that were intended to be as effective as possible, politically feasible, and socially acceptable over the long term.

[1] See: https://bip.malopolska.pl/umwm,a,1283900,uchwala-nr-xxxii45217-sejmiku-wojewodztwa-malopolskiego-z-dnia-23-styczna-2017-r-w-sprawie-wprowadze.html.

5.5 Conclusion

There is a need to explore different types of weak or even fake legislation (on placebo legislation, see Stępień & Zomerski, 2025). The concept of symbolic law is particularly promising, as it allows us to move beyond the assumption that legislation is always rational in an instrumental sense and draws attention to its communicative and signaling functions. At first glance, symbolic law seems to be an attractive analytical tool for describing and explaining antismog policies and legislation in Poland—particularly in Małopolska—which for years remained largely ineffective despite the existence of a broad set of legal and institutional instruments. However, the conceptualizations of symbolic law developed by Dwyer and Newig reveal important limitations when applied to the Polish and Małopolska cases.

They presuppose a simple and linear model of lawmaking, in which a regulation is drafted primarily to achieve political rather than substantive goals. In this framework, "symbolicness" is attributed at the very moment of drafting. Such an understanding is ill-suited to the context of MLG, where the effectiveness of law is far more complex, involving strategic maneuvering, uncertainty, and a wider spectrum of possible outcomes. The MLG framework also changes the direction of symbolic signaling: in the Polish case, signaling often targeted EU institutions rather than domestic citizens, further complicating the picture. This leads to a broader argument: while Dwyer's and Newig's concepts are useful for identifying the "symbolic" character of individual legal acts, they offer limited analytical tools for assessing broader legal and institutional systems. In particular, they struggle to capture the systemic effects of legal and administrative machinery that persistently fail to achieve officially declared goals.

These concepts also neglect the possibility that a regulation may acquire symbolic characteristics later—after drafting and enactment. This is not merely hypothetical: legislation may be adopted in good faith, with genuine intent to be effective, but later remain only "on paper" due to political shifts or a lack of implementation support. Yet such laws may still be publicly communicated by those in power as if they effectively solve the problem. In other words, symbolic law can take different forms and temporalities that are not fully grasped by Dwyer's and Newig's conceptualizations.

Moreover, the conceptualizations of symbolic law developed by Dwyer and Newig lack the capacity to capture situations in which governmental action is not entirely absent but instead consists of marginal, fragmented, and poorly coordinated measures that may themselves be interpreted as symbolic. In the Polish case of combating smog, such measures often functioned primarily as communicative gestures directed both at EU institutions and at particular domestic constituencies, signaling that the problem was being addressed. Following Dwyer's interpretation, which draws heavily on Murray Edelman's theory of symbolic politics, this situation can be understood as an instance in which a set of policies was officially presented as a response to air pollution while, in practice, avoiding any serious challenge to the interests of coal producers, coal distributors and importers, as well as important segments of the electorate, particularly during the period of government led by the right-wing *Prawo i Sprawiedliwość* (Law and Justice party) (2015–2023). From this perspective, the adopted measures could be viewed as signaling concern and responsiveness without substantially altering the underlying political and economic arrangements associated with the problem.

All this points to an important limitation of existing conceptualizations of symbolic law. They are insufficiently equipped to describe and explain situations more complex than the enactment of a legal act whose ineffectiveness is knowingly accepted by its drafters. The Polish experience of combating air pollution demonstrates the need for more refined analytical tools capable of capturing different forms and constellations of symbolic action while simultaneously situating them within broader processes of institutional inertia, path dependency, and multilevel governance. Indeed, it is relatively easy to label a regulation as "symbolic," often using the term in a vague and imprecise manner. Although the conceptualizations proposed by Dwyer and Newig make the notion of symbolic law more concrete and analytically useful, the concept remains overly broad and lacks the theoretical instruments necessary to distinguish between more specific subtypes of symbolic legislation and symbolic policy instruments. As a result, its explanatory value is limited when confronted with complex empirical cases such as the governance of air pollution in Poland and the Małopolska region.

References

Arnold, T. (1935). *The symbols of government*. Harvard University Press.

Barry, J., & Blühdorn, I. (2018). *Politics of unsustainability: Eco-politics in the post-ecologist era*. Routledge.

Blühdorn, I. (2007). Symbolic politics and the politics of simulation. *Environmental Politics, 16*(2), 251–275. https://doi.org/10.1080/09644010701211874

Citkowska-Kimla, A. (2019). Poland and the problem of smog – Political action versus social expectations. *Krytyka Prawa. Niezależne studia nad prawem, 26*(2), 127–137. https://doi.org/10.17951/k.2019.26.2.127-137

Dwyer, J. P. (1990). The pathology of symbolic legislation. *Ecology Law Quarterly, 17*(2), 233–316. https://doi.org/10.15779/Z38D81P

Edelman, M. (1964). *The symbolic uses of politics*. University of Illinois Press.

Gustafsson, G. (1983). Symbolic and pseudo-policies as responses to environmental problems. In J. Forester (Ed.), *Critical theory and public life* (pp. 268–290). MIT Press.

Kobus, D., Maione, M., Skotak, K., Fuzzi, S., & Pollini, F. (2016). Air quality from a social perspective in four European metropolitan areas: Research hypothesis and evidence from the SEFIRA project. *Environmental Science & Policy, 65*, 58–64. https://doi.org/10.1016/j.envsci.2016.05.002

Lembcke, O. W. (2016). Symbolic legislation and authority. In B. van Klink, B. van Beers, & L. Poort (Eds.), *Symbolic legislation: Theory and developments in Biolaw (Legisprudence Library)* (Vol. 4, pp. 87–104). Springer. https://doi.org/10.1007/978-3-319-33365-6_6

Matten, D. (2003). Symbolic politics in environmental regulation: Corporate strategic responses. *Business Strategy and the Environment, 12*(4), 215–226. https://doi.org/10.1002/bse.362

Newig, J. (2007). Symbolic environmental legislation and societal self-deception. *Environmental Politics, 16*(2), 276 296. https://doi.org/10.1080/09644010701211783

Newig, J., Lenschow, A., Challies, E., Cotta, B., & Schilling-Vacaflor, A. (2019). What is governance in global telecoupling? *Ecology and Society, 24*(3), 5. https://doi.org/10.5751/ES-11046-240305

Stępień, M., & Zomerski, W. (2025). Exploring legislative placebo: A new framework for understanding deliberate ineffective legislation. *The Theory and Practice of Legislation, 13*(2), 181–212. https://doi.org/10.1080/20508840.2025.2507465

Suska, M. Ł. (2025). Becoming symbolic: Some remarks on the judicial rewriting of the offence of animal abuse in Poland. *International Journal for the Semiotics of Law, 38*, 1271–1289. https://doi.org/10.1007/s11196-024-10084-5

van Klink, B., van Beers, B., & Poort, L. (Eds.). (2016). *Symbolic legislation: Theory and developments in Biolaw (Legisprudence Library)* (Vol. 4, pp. 87–104). Springer. https://doi.org/10.1007/978-3-319-33365-6_6

Weale, A., Pridham, G., Cini, M., Konstadakopulos, D., Porter, M., & Flynn, B. (2002). Air pollution control and multi-level governance. In A. Jordan (Ed.), *Environmental policy in the European Union* (pp. 384–409). Oxford University Press. https://doi.org/10.1093/acprof:oso/9780199257478.003.0015

Zgłobicki, W., & Baran-Zgłobicka, B. (2024). Air pollution in major Polish cities in the period 2005–2021: Intensity, effects and attempts to reduce it. *Environmental Research, 240*(Part 2), 117497. https://doi.org/10.1016/j.envres.2023.117497

Chapter 6
The Utility of the Concept of Wicked Problems in the Context of Air Pollution in Małopolska

Mateusz Klinowski

Abstract The case of combating smog in Małopolska (Lesser Poland) offers an opportunity to test the descriptive and explanatory potential of the concepts used in the scholarly literature to account for the difficulties in improving air quality, particularly the notion of wicked problems, introduced by Horst W. J. Rittel and Melvin M. Webber in the 1970s. This concept has frequently been applied to issues of air pollution, emphasizing the intrinsic complexity of a certain class of problems that, in a sense, resist definitive solutions. The case of Małopolska allows for an application of this framework to assess the insights it may provide for understanding the region's ongoing struggle with smog. The aim, therefore, is to examine whether the concept of wicked problems helps illuminate the processes through which relevant actors attempt to address intractable challenges—specifically the persistent issue of air pollution in Małopolska. In doing so, the analysis contributes both to a deeper understanding of the Małopolska case and to a critical evaluation of the broader utility of this conceptual approach.

Keywords Wicked problems · Air pollution · Lesser Poland · Social problems

6.1 Introduction: The Puzzle of Małopolska

The preceding chapters have reconstructed a prolonged attempt to improve air quality in Kraków and the Małopolska region. However, this history presents a puzzle. The principal sources of air pollution have long been identified, and the health consequences of exposure to it are well documented. Despite public awareness of the problem, expert knowledge, and decision-maker experience, air pollution remains a serious problem in much of Małopolska. The regional antismog resolution adopted in 2017 has been implemented slowly and unevenly. Deadlines have been

M. Klinowski (✉)
Department of Law and Administration, Jagiellonian University, Kraków, Poland
e-mail: mateusz.klinowski@uj.edu.pl

M. Stępień, M. Klinowski, *Fighting Air Pollution*, Law and Visual Jurisprudence 17, https://doi.org/10.1007/978-3-032-23909-9_6

postponed, large numbers of noncompliant heating installations have remained in use, and the pace of their replacement has slowed down.

The persistence of pollution appears surprising. It provokes the question of why such a well-understood problem as air pollution in a particular region of Poland—with identifiable sources, technically available remedies, and measurable outcomes—remains so difficult to resolve. In the area of policy science, an influential way to answer such a question is to look at the intrinsic properties of the problem and to classify it as "wicked"; hence, one should not expect it to be easy to resolve.

It was Horst Rittel and Melvin Webber who, for the first time, articulated in their famous paper (1973) the claim that policy dilemmas relating to social problems cannot be analyzed in the same way as the choices scientists or engineers face when dealing with "ordinary" scientific or engineering problems. According to the authors, policy problems are of a distinct, "wicked" nature because unlike typical problems that (natural) science and engineering deal with, they lack a definitive description.

Problems in science and engineering are well defined—they are "bounded" by descriptions expressed in scientific terms, so a theorist or engineer can develop a clear idea of how to solve them. They can locate a specific problem against the background of the causal network provided by the broader context in which the problem appears, and both the definition and location of the problem are fixed by the objective nature of the terms used in scientific or engineering discourse. Since there are accessible criteria for evaluating whether particular actions taken in response to the problem are appropriate, ordinary scientific problems seem to have definitive solutions. For this reason, the authors called them "tamed"—as opposed to "wicked"—social problems.

On the other hand, social problems are defined in hindsight—through the actions planners (i.e., decision-makers) assume to be their solutions. Planners do not follow the typical procedure of defining and locating the problem and then looking for solutions. Rather, they define the problem in terms of the actions they have at their disposal. Instead of matching means to the end, social planners match ends to the means. When those means change, the social problem is redefined and resolved, and that process is never finished. In other words, the definition and location of a social problem depend on the context provided by the set of measures presented at a given moment as the potential solutions accessible to a planner. That set is subject to change over time, leading to redefinition of the problem. Hence, no particular action can be considered by a social planner as a definitive solution to a social dilemma. On the contrary, what is considered an appropriate reaction to the problem in a particular moment could turn out to be a wrong move later as the problem acquires a new description and comes to be understood in a different way than before. It is the very nature of social problems that they lack a final description.

Rittel and Webber summarized their intuitions in ten points, which were intended to serve as a useful characterization, helping planners understand the nature of wicked problems (Rittel & Webber, 1973, pp. 161–167).[1] Over time, their characterization became a subject of various interpretations and discussions, contributing to the inception of the theory of wicked problems.

Rittel and Webber believed that "social problems" and "wicked problems" are terms with the same extension. For them, as far as their original paper is concerned, all social problems are wicked, at least from the perspective of natural sciences and engineering. One of the fundamental properties of wicked problems is the phenomenon of their "transformation." However, such transformation can occur at various levels and mean something different. For instance, social problems are prone to evolving social perceptions, so the meaning of the problem (i.e., the answer to the question *what* is wrong) and the possible solutions change. As technology and scientific knowledge progress, the number and types of solutions available to planners evolve, so the social problem can be reformulated in terms of a new set of solutions—and so on.

Still, another sense of dynamics specific to a wicked problem can be derived from the list provided by Rittel and Webber (see point 5). According to it, a solution often contributes to worsening a problem. In other words, any attempt to solve a truly wicked problem leads to its transformation, and the new form is even more damaging and more difficult to address than the previous one. Hence, wicked problems are sometimes characterized by the existence of a specific feedback loop, making them especially difficult to solve or even impossible to tackle.

For Rittel and Webber, such a contribution of a proposed solution to an original problem was a reason to believe that policy decisions are irreversible. But the significance of that feedback loop seems to be much greater, and over time, some authors started to differentiate between standard social problems, which are relatively easy to address, and problems that are especially difficult and, thus, considered wicked. We will come back to this differentiation shortly.

The idea of distinguishing between tame and wicked problems especially gained popularity in policy sciences recently. Nonetheless, even just after its inception, the concept was utilized to characterize environmental problems, including air pollution (Goldsmith, 1969). Interestingly, even in these early uses of the wicked-problems concept, the category was applied to a specific subclass of social problems rather than treated as equivalent to social problems as such.

[1] Some of those points seem to be more important than others. The first one expresses the idea that if social problems are defined through their solutions, there are no definitive formulations of those problems. The second is that social problems "have no stopping rule," as new solutions may always emerge; conversely, planners may halt their efforts to solve a problem because the idea of a solution is a matter of political agreement. There are no independent, objective criteria for telling when a solution has been found, so the conventional character of the problem manifests also in the conventional character of its solutions, as well as a conventional character of the idea of its final solution. To put it more simply, the problem is solved when parties (stakeholders) agree that it is solved. Such an agreement is subject to change, though. The third and fourth points refer to the fact that any changes to social systems generate a cascade of consequences that are impossible to track, so no solution could be pointed out as the most sound or true at the moment of its application. It is a matter not only of convention or stipulation but also of indispensable ignorance.

Currently, the theoretical framework of wicked problems is utilized to analyze many important topics, such as climate change (FitzGibbon & Mensah, 2012) and the COVID-19 pandemic (Lilleker & Stoeckle, 2021). In the context of climate change, the original concept of wicked problems was further advanced with the introduction of the notion of "super wicked problems" by Levin et al. (2012).

For that reason, the goal of this chapter is to test whether the concept of wicked problems could help explain the persistence of air pollution in Małopolska, despite knowledge of its sources and the relevant efforts undertaken by regulators—in other words, whether describing air pollution in Małopolska as an example of a wicked problem improves our understanding of why the regional policy response has remained ineffective and whether it helps identify more appropriate forms of intervention.

But it is also interesting to test the concept against the body of factual evidence collected during our study. We expect that our case study will contribute to the theory of wicked problems also in this respect, helping to assess the adequacy of the concept itself.

The chapter combines conceptual analysis with a case-based assessment of the explanatory and practical value of the wicked problem framework. Its primary purpose is to improve understanding of why antismog policy in Małopolska has produced divergent and frequently insufficient results. The analysis therefore does not treat the Małopolska case as a neutral sample selected for the purpose of testing a general theory. Nor does it claim that one regional case can determine the value of the wicked problem concept across all areas of public policy. We do not establish how frequently political actors in Małopolska explicitly used the concept of wicked problems or whether they consciously adopted the framework. Instead, the concept is used as one possible interpretive framework for the case, whose principal institutional, political, and regulatory characteristics have already been established in the preceding parts of the book. The relevant question is whether this framework identifies the mechanisms responsible for the persistence of air pollution more accurately than alternative descriptions based, for example, on complexity, institutional fragmentation, regulatory design, political incentives, or symbolic legislation.

6.2 The Question of Adequacy of the Concept of Wicked Problems

In modern philosophical literature, concepts are considered representational devices, whose task is to provide a successful analysis (e.g., Cappelen, 2018). New concepts are introduced (or engineered) to acquire new knowledge or understanding of a certain phenomenon—to achieve a new *analysis*. Hence, the implementation of a new concept within the language of our theories should be subject to evaluation, during which one could—and even should—test the meaning (its intension as well as extension) of a particular lexical item (word) in order to estimate its utility. In the end, this utility of course derives from the entire *analytical project*, that is, the idea of employing a certain concept to acquire new understanding.

In the context of our study, thus, the question of the validity of the concept of wicked problems can be understood as a question of the proper formulation and usefulness of this analytical category. We can divide that question into a number of subquestions.

First, we can ask whether the concept of wicked problems is *explicable*. This means it is well defined and capable of capturing what a wicked problem is. It is also a question of whether the phenomenon has the proper characteristics and is useful for distinguishing wicked problems within the more general group of problems. In other words, it is a question of whether Rittel and Webber provided an appropriate description of the concept that suffices to differentiate it from other similar notions and whether it contributes to any helpful typology or classification of phenomena that planners encounter in the area of governance.

Second, we can ask whether the category of wicked problems is *adequate*. This means that the category is a good representational device. Hence, we will consider air pollution as an instance of a wicked problem only if air pollution bears the characteristics of a wicked problem, i.e., it fits well into this specific analytical category. If air pollution is a phenomenon that can only sometimes or only partially be categorized as a wicked problem, such a category may be qualified as inadequate for planners or researchers dealing with the issue.

Additionally, the adequacy of an analytic category could even be understood in a stronger sense here. The motivation for the adoption of the concept of wicked problems in the theory of (public policy) planning seems to be the enrichment of the theory with a conceptual tool helpful for governance. In other words, the category of wicked problems should provide planners (decision-makers) with some hints on how to manipulate the reality in order to achieve progress on air pollution (i.e., better air quality). Ultimately, considering air pollution as a wicked problem should help us not only to describe the issue more precisely or understand it more deeply but also to deal with it in a more adequate manner (more effectively or efficiently). This will be our third subquestion.

Therefore, in this chapter, we will consider three separate problems:

1. Is the concept of wicked problems *valid*?
2. Is the problem of air pollution *wicked*?
3. Do positive answers to 1 and 2 help us address the problem more effectively?

6.3 Problem 1: The Validity of the Concept

Let us start with the question of whether the concept of wicked problems has been properly explicated in the literature and is, thus, free of any deficiencies.

Although the distinction between tamed (solvable) and wicked (intractable, hard) problems has gained a significant amount of attention, the concept of wicked problems has been questioned nonetheless. Various authors pointed out that the concept is murky and has a low analytical value, as it adds nothing to our understanding of the specificity of the problem under consideration (see, e.g., Peters, 2017; Alford & Head, 2017; Turnbull & Hoppe, 2018). For this reason, alternative concepts have been proposed relatively quickly. For example, Herbert Simon argued for the category of ill-structured problems as a more useful analytical tool for public policy science (Simon, 1973). This category arguably makes more sense because it is more descriptive and therefore simpler to implement by social planners in their day-by-day practice. In contrast to well-structured problems in the natural sciences or engineering, ill-structured problems lack a clear and definitive description and, hence, some of the necessary information required for effective policy decisions. Actually, such a definition does seem to provide us with a better grasp of the nature of difficulty in the case of social problems. By adopting the concept of ill-structured problems, planners should pay more attention to the structure of information they have at their disposal, for example, by implementing measures addressing knowledge gaps in the process of policymaking.

More recently, Rob Hoppe (2010) explicitly argued against the concept of wicked problems, on the grounds that it misleadingly suggests that the intractability of some difficult social problems is an inherent property of the problems themselves. Instead, he proposed the category of "unstructured" social problems to describe situations in which relevant knowledge is uncertain and stakeholders disagree over the values and norms that should guide action. For Hoppe, dealing with those hard problems consists in making them more structured and thus manageable by producing more relevant knowledge of those problems and aligning the values and interests of all parties involved. This can be achieved through iterative democratic debate and policy processes, leading to incremental, temporary, and partial solutions.

Whether Simon considers his concept of ill-structured problems as equivalent to wicked problems remains a matter of discussion. Definitely for Hoppe, the category of ill-structured or unstructured problems and wicked problems are mutually exclusive. However, we can also imagine that someone might assume that wicked problems are a subcategory of ill-structured problems because the meaning of the former term is not exhausted by the characteristics of the latter term, as provided by Rittel and Webber. Specifically, the wicked problem category suggests that the difficult nature of social problems lies in their inner structure (their *essence* or *nature*), while Simon's and Hope's proposals focus on rather external circumstances and are limited to factors such as available information and shared values.

The problem is that this additional quality of wickedness that we attribute to difficult social problems needs to be explained (defined) somehow. A proponent of this approach should explain why wickedness is something more than, for example, the ill structure of the problem that Simon describes. The trouble is that when he tries to provide such an explanation, it seems to go no further than what had already been said about the difficulties associated with governance long before Rittel and Webber formulated their ideas. Namely, the concept of wicked problems seems to add nothing to the explanation of the exceptional nature of societal problems proposed by

Robert K. Merton (1936), who pointed out the unintended consequences of any social action, which are in principle difficult or even impossible to foresee.

Merton, among others, argued that social systems are stochastic in the sense that there are various and complex circumstances that influence the final results, so social action is always a game of chance, so to speak. Moreover, the practice of governance requires acting with confidence even when necessary information is lacking; thus, policymaking is often based on guesses, opinions, and estimates. This invites ignorance of the political process, inevitably followed by unexpected results, thereby contributing to the initial problem. Finally, public planners are often concerned with the immediate consequences of their actions, especially when they are driven by political interests, ignoring potential long-term consequences.

The proponents of the concept of wicked problems, therefore, appear obliged to demonstrate that the phenomenon they consider as an important part of the nature of every social problem is something different from the phenomenon of unintended consequences pointed out by Merton. That task is even more difficult as Merton also took into account the phenomenon of a feedback loop "peculiar to human conduct," describing how mere predictions of the consequences of actions distort the very process of predicting, thereby leading to unforeseen consequences. Meanwhile, such feedback loops are often described as an immanent property of social problems and linked to their alleged wickedness. For that reason, one could reasonably claim that the concept of wicked problems lacks any analytical value and brings nothing new to the table, as the characteristics proposed by Rittel and Webber point instead to some well-known and already explained properties of social problems.

More recently, there are authors who identify the increasing difficulty in solving social problems with their increasing complexity, instead of unintended consequences (see, e.g., Room, 2011). At first glance, such an explanation seems to fit better with the perceived dynamics of policymaking dilemmas in the modern world, where societal problems are demonstrably becoming more and more difficult. In this case, perhaps the term "complex problem" might be the desired label for a category that refers to a certain class of difficult-to-solve societal problems. However, the fundamental issue remains: how to define the term in a way that adds something significant to the science of public policy, for example, by serving as a useful tool for systematizing social problems. Those who advocate replacing the notion of wicked problems with the notion of complexity underscore that complex problems are something more than just complicated societal problems, as the former type of issues all share a certain inner structure characterized—through various feedback—by nonlinear functional connections between different variables within the policy area and are thus largely unpredictable. Problems that are not complex may still be complicated and difficult to solve, but they remain predictable and thus controllable.

Although some authors directly suggest that the term "wicked problems" could merely refer to complex cases where there is no linear relation (proportionality) between supposed goals and undertaken interventions (see Duit & Galaz, 2008), the original characteristics proposed by Rittel and Webber do not relate to an internal structure of a problem categorized as wicked, nor do they mention any nonlinear dynamics within such a problem.[2] According to this original approach, to be wicked in the first place means being difficult to define or to single out possible solutions, not to manifest nonlinear dependencies. In that case, the two terms denote different concepts and refer to different cases.

On the other hand, if nonlinearity and uncontrollability are not derivatives of a particular structure of a societal problem, what is the source of those phenomena? One possible answer is that difficult policy problems are intractable not primarily because of their cultural, political, historical, or economic context, but because of their essense. For example, poverty or crime are presumably not wicked problems in one period and non-wicked in another simply because, for instance, the economy is booming or prevailing social norms have changed. Rather, these problems are wicked or complex because of what they actually are, not because of their cultural or political context. In fact, most authors seem to speak about wicked problems, having the internal structure, logic or nature of these difficult societal issues in mind, regardless of any external circumstances. Authors who reject this line of argument therefore face the task of explaining how genuine difficulties in defining a policy problem and identifying an adequate solution can arise if they do not stem from the problem's inherent nonlinearity.[3]

The explanation proposed in response to this problem is the concept of "intractable policy controversies," which emphasizes the role of alternative interpretative frames—that is, structures of often tacit beliefs and perceptions underlying policy positions—in shaping disputes over important societal issues (see Schön & Rein, 1994). Different interest groups apply different frames to the same policy problem, often emphasizing different facts and values as most relevant. This makes it difficult to describe the problem in a uniform way or to agree on how it should be addressed. According to this approach, it is the discourse and competing interpretative frames surrounding a societal issue that make it difficult to resolve. Therefore, the concept of wicked problems could be regarded as superfluous and replaced by an analysis of the political and social context in which a difficult societal problem is framed and contested.

Another interpretation of the notion originates in the observation that wicked problems are considered the opposite of tamed problems. This suggests that wickedness has something to do with being beyond or out of control. For example, it could mean that planners have no means to limit the unintended consequences of their actions. Sometimes this lack of control over the problem may arise from its internal dynamics (nonlinearity of the problem), but it may also be due to the lack

[2] However, there are authors who believe that wicked problems are indeed nonlinear in nature, although for rather different reasons. They define the linear model of solving societal problems as "based on determinate problems which have definite conditions," where the role of the planner is merely "to identify those conditions and then calculate a solution." Wicked problems fit into this scheme, as their specificity, according to this view, pertains to the lack of definitive conditions upon which a solution could be calculated (see Buchanan, 1992).

[3] Additionally, in the literature, it is sometimes called "the technical nature of the issue"; see Peters and Tarpey (2019), p. 221.

of a proper description of the problem or a description of its solutions. Hence, such a view of wicked problems fits both aforementioned perspectives (external or internal) on what presumed wickedness in fact is.

It is also worth mentioning that some authors have proposed reinterpreting the original concept of wicked problems as referring primarily to solutions rather than to the problems themselves (Peters, 2017). Problems in policymaking are often the consequences of the personal skills and capacities of planners rather than solely the internal structure of the issues they deal with. According to this view, it is the reactions to problems that may be wicked, not the problems themselves. We will return to this idea in a moment.

Finally, a serious—and maybe even the most decisive—argument against the concept comes from the empirical study by Guy Peters and Matthew Tarpey (2019). Policy experts interviewed by the authors only rarely identified, in the problems they examined, the characteristics originally proposed by Rittel and Webber. What is worse, the interviews proved that these characteristics do not provide necessary or sufficient criteria for qualifying a difficult policy problem as wicked. Moreover, the problems typically described as wicked in the literature do not have the attributes assumed by Rittel and Webber, and conversely, many problems described as tame possess some of those attributes. The study demonstrates, first, that "wicked problems" is only a subclass of the broad category of societal problems and, second and more importantly, that the concept of wicked problems has in fact very limited practical usefulness.

On the other hand, the belief that most of the policy problems exhibit at least some of the traits included in the characteristics provided by Rittel and Webber is also shared by Newman and Head (2017). That, however, seems to undermine the original effort of Rittel and Webber, since they claimed, in turn, that all societal problems are wicked and fit their ten-point characterization entirely. Interestingly, despite this original assumption, even in the earliest attempts to apply the concept of wicked problems to policy dilemmas, the category was used to refer to a particular subclass of social problems rather than to social problems in general (see, e.g., Goldsmith, 1969).

All of this creates a rather confusing picture. There is a lack of agreement among scholars regarding the meaning of the term "wicked problems," as well as its reference. According to the cited authors, the term could be replaced by "ill-structured" or "complex." Wicked problems might also be understood as the subjects of intractable policy disputes. It is not clear whether wicked problems are just a subclass of societal problems—referring, especially, to difficult ones—or a fancier name for societal problems in general. Moreover, it is debatable whether the specificity of problems one prefers to call *wicked* stems from the internal structure of those problems or from external circumstances that provide the context.

In that case, the question of the analytical utility of the concept remains open. Supposedly, the concept should have *an analytic dimension* (to use the term introduced in Peters, 2017), as well as *a taxonomic (typological) relevance*, bringing us closer to understanding difficult social problems and helping us locate them within the complex background of our social or political life. For now, it is plausible to assume that the concept has neither of these traits; however, we cannot exclude the possibility that in the future, these deficiencies may be removed through clever concept engineering.

Meanwhile, having this in mind, let us now go back to the original formulation of wicked problems theory developed by Rittel and Webber in order to find out whether the situation in Małoposka fits their characteristics.

6.4 Problem 2: The Adequacy of the Concept

The brief overview of the debate presented above shows that, for a variety of reasons, the concept of "wicked problems" remains contested. We believe that our case study can contribute to this debate in two ways. First, if air pollution in Kraków and Małopolska exhibits the characteristics identified by Rittel and Webber, this would provide additional support for the theoretical adequacy of the concept as a way of describing complex societal problems. Second, if the persistence of air pollution in Małopolska, or the limited effectiveness of the 2017 antismog resolution (and, by extension, similar resolutions adopted elsewhere in Poland), can be plausibly explained in terms of wicked-problems theory, this would demonstrate the concept's explanatory and practical utility.

Before we go any further, one additional distinction must be introduced. The problem of air pollution can be interpreted as (a) an environmental hazard, (b) a policy problem, or (c) a governance problem. In such cases, the problem consists each time of finding an appropriate answer to the relevant question, depending on the interpretation we use: (a) how to reduce the volume of emissions, (b) which instruments to choose, and (c) how to implement them within the current legal and institutional context.

At face value, air pollution—understood as an environmental hazard—seems to be a much less difficult issue than an exemplary wicked problem described in the original paper of Rittel and Webber. It is true that air pollution is, in a sense, a unique phenomenon, and air pollution in Poland has different characteristics than in Germany. Yet it does not seem difficult to understand what that phenomenon is and what the general solutions to it are. Atmospheric processes and chemistry may be scientifically complex, but the reduction of pollutant emissions is not something that is too difficult to comprehend. When we interpret air pollution primarily as a physical phenomenon, the problem consists of the presence of harmful substances in the atmosphere, their emission from identifiable sources, their dispersion under particular geographical and meteorological conditions, and their effects on human health and the environment. At this level, one can state a problem (for instance, how to reduce these particular emissions over a particular area), but the problem is definitely well defined and not so complex. Actually, it is rather technical than societal—tamed rather than wicked.

What about the second meaning? The problem of air pollution—understood as involving the challenge of selecting politically or socially acceptable instruments for reducing emissions—also does not seem to be very complicated. Across the world, many policy instruments have been tested so far, and there seems to be a consensus about which of them work. These solutions, worth noting, are testable, since air pollution is a measurable physical phenomenon. Any particular selection of a set of solutions would, in the sense indicated by Rittel and Webber (1973), regressively define the problem. But this is a property of every policy problem, not a characteristic of the most difficult ones.

Finally, the problem of air pollution may be defined as a question of effective governance. In this case, the problem domain is reduced to issues of implementation of previously selected instruments. The implementation of air-quality policies has its own problems, and many obstacles have been identified so far. Effective implementation may require a multilevel approach and complex analysis. But does it create unique issues, unprecedented in their complexity and not replicable elsewhere? In fact, many implementation challenges are common across policy areas, and there is little reason to assume that air-pollution policies are fundamentally different in this respect.

Of course, the adoption of certain policies (passing a law) and their implementation (enforcing a law) may become difficult, but it is not because the underlying issue (a phenomenon that manifests itself physically) is inherently insoluble but rather because political and institutional arrangements prevent known measures from being applied consistently. However, the factors that prevent, in a particular case, the adoption and then the effective implementation of certain policies are usually well identified, and planners take them into account when dealing with the problem. Therefore, the issue of how to deal with the problem is not insolvable by necessity; on the contrary, it is usually successfully approached step by step.

In that case, it is certainly not true that planners dealing with air pollution have no right to be wrong or have no opportunity to learn through trial and error. As far as the history of air pollution is concerned, incrementalism seems to work, and decision-makers are not held liable if their initial efforts did not turn out as planned. On the contrary, in the case of Małopolska, we observed consecutive attempts to solve the problem of emissions, and those attempts did not lead to the worsening of the initial situation, although sometimes they transformed understanding of the problem. For example, successful measures to curb industrial emissions (i.e., the adoption of emission standards and their enforcement) increased the significance of residential emissions. This, in turn, required additional efforts in the form of adopting new public policies and implementing them. It is disputable, however, whether such transformations also changed the nature of the problem. One could claim, for example, that residential emissions were always there, and the decrease in industrial pollution only made them visible and thus significant in the public debate. In that account, the nature of the environmental problem did not change. Air pollution is simply a multifaceted phenomenon, and the evolution of policies addressing it can be understood as a gradual shift in attention from one dimension of the problem to another.

Finally, there are conventional criteria for determining when the problem of air pollution can be regarded as "solved," such as the air-quality standards established by national and international law. These criteria appear to address both dimensions of the problem: the physical phenomenon itself and the adoption and implementation of policy responses. Of course, such criteria may change over time, particularly as scientific knowledge about air pollution and its health effects develops. Nonetheless, at any given point in time, policymakers can determine whether pollution levels are under control and identify what further measures are required to achieve that state.

As we see, at least according to our admittedly simplified understanding of the situation, air pollution, however understood, does not fully fit the original description of a wicked problem. Yet it does exhibit some of the characteristics identified by Rittel and Webber. Certain dimensions of the air pollution problem—the physical phenomenon itself, the adoption of a particular policy, and the implementation of that policy—appear to conform to some of the characteristics of wicked problems. For example, air pollution—understood as an environmental phenomenon—appears to have no definitive formulation (point 1), partly because of its physical complexity: it arises from multiple processes, has both natural and anthropogenic sources, and involves a variety of substances and forms, including particulate matter and gaseous pollutants, whose classification as "pollutants" may depend on the context. For example, carbon dioxide (CO_2) from natural or anthropogenic sources can be considered a pollutant in some contexts, while in others it is not classified as an air pollutant. Alternative formulations of the problem may, of course, influence the way it is understood but may also help determine possible solutions. Because air pollution has multiple physical manifestations, it can also be addressed through different policy instruments, each of which, in turn, gives rise to distinct problems of policy adoption and implementation.

The problem itself has also undergone substantial transformations over time. For centuries, our comprehension of air pollution focused on point emissions, usually associated with industrial activities. For this reason, the subject of the first antismog regulations was mainly industrial processes. As time passed and those initial regulations started to bear fruit, understanding of the problem evolved toward areal and line emissions, reflecting our changing focus on pollutants produced in residential zones and by car traffic. Interestingly, the Małopolska case examined here reflects these broader historical shifts in how the air pollution problem has been understood. At the outset, air pollution in Kraków was considered a product of heavy industry, and sulfur dioxide (SO_2) was a major concern, but later, as the implemented regulations brought intended effects, air pollution came to be seen as a consequence of domestic heating. As the solid-fuel ban in Kraków took effect, planners' attention shifted again—this time toward pollutants transported from neighboring communities and traffic emissions. We have already discussed whether such reformulations of the initial understanding of what the problem is should be considered changes in the nature of the problem. Whatever the answer is, according to empirical evidence provided by our case study, it is plausible that the solutions implemented in response to air pollution are consequential in ways that fit point 5 of Rittel and Webber's original characteristics of wicked problems. These solutions are responsible for transforming the initial problem into another, often unexpected, version, which indeed is usually even more difficult to tackle from the perspective of governance. In the case of Kraków and Małopolska, industrial emissions were easier to control because they were the consequences of economic activity, and their sources were easy to pinpoint. Residential emissions are much more problematic since they are unintended consequences of housing, and their sources are difficult to find. This is precisely why residential emissions are described as areal.

But even if certain interpretations of the problem of air pollution are transformed as a consequence of initial responses, does that mean every attempt to solve air pollution makes the issue more problematic? This kind of feedback, in which attempts to solve a problem alter its structure and potentially make it more difficult to address, is sometimes regarded as a distinctive feature of wickedness.[4]

Let us start with the fact that some authors have indeed mentioned the connection between attempts to introduce air pollution regulations and the exacerbation of this phenomenon in unexpected ways and places. This is evident, for example, in the case of ultrafine particulate matter (PM0.1 or UFP) fractions, whose emissions increase in response to stricter standards for PM10 and PM2.5 (see Oberdörster & Utell, 2002). Ultrafine particles are more toxic and penetrate the bloodstream more easily and, therefore, are more harmful to health (see, e.g., Nel, 2005). However, as their emissions are not yet regulated or measured during inspections, companies responsible for PM emissions (e.g., car manufacturers) remain unconcerned. They select operating parameters for the equipment they produce to minimize regulated emissions, which usually increases unregulated emissions they still have no need to worry about. In this way, regulatory attempts to curb emissions bring about consequences that make the problem worse.

Our study also revealed some traces of this specific phenomenon, which is characteristic of wicked problems. We already mentioned twice in this chapter that the effectiveness of regulations aimed at industrial emissions contributed to the increased public visibility of residential emissions. But in Chap. 3, we also described how those regulations caused a real increase in residential emissions, meaning their causal force operated also at the level of physical phenomena.

Another effect of regulations on coal and its combustion was the increased social awareness of the negative effects of its extraction and combustion, which results, in turn, in increased interest in the use of wood-burning room heaters (i.e., wood-stack fireplaces). According to data from the Central Register of Building Emissions (CEEB) database,[5] at the end of 2023, there were 1,571,838 wood fireplaces and stoves in use in Poland. Each year, Poles install between 80,000 and 100,000 new stoves and fireplaces. If we combine this with the information that in 2024 the Polish construction sector recorded a year-on-year decline of approximately 9%, the persistently high number of new fireplace installations during the slowdown in

[4] This is rather in conflict with the original idea of Rittel and Webber. According to them, solutions to social problems are consequential in the sense that they cannot be simply undone; there is no replicability of their initial conditions, and planners are unavoidably responsible for them.

[5] Central Building Emissions Register, https://zone.gunb.gov.pl/pl.

the construction sector suggests that demand is driven by the antismog resolutions, which made the use of coal appliances illegal.[6]

The problem is that experiments involving different biomass products and combustion regimes designed to reproduce actual patterns of biomass use in Poland showed that emission factors (the mass of pollutants emitted per unit of fuel burned) for carbon monoxide (CO), nitrogen oxides (NOx), and organic carbon—including highly carcinogenic polycyclic aromatic hydrocarbons (PAHs) and other organic micropollutants—were not only high enough to pose health risks but, surprisingly, were often higher than those associated with hard coal. The only clear environmental benefit of biomass combustion was a reduction in sulfur dioxide emissions (Wielgosiński et al., 2017). Hence, regulations intended to reduce health risks by limiting coal combustion may, under certain conditions, have the unintended effect of increasing some health risks if coal is replaced with biomass burned in highly emitting installations.

Therefore, in the case of smog in Kraków and Małopolska, we do observe nonlinear dynamics in which successive reformulations of the problem make some of its dimensions more difficult to address. However, contrary to what a strong reading of wicked-problems theory might suggest, these reformulations do not render policy intervention futile. On the contrary, in the long run, gradual reformulations of the initial problem seem to favor planners looking for solutions to difficult societal issues. Complex problems cannot be solved in a single step. Their solutions consist of many incremental steps, and it is plausible that the adoption of one step leads to a reformulation of the initial plan of action. We have already mentioned that incrementalism works, and the revaluation of the initial design is an essential part of any reasonable strategy for dealing with complicated issues.

In particular, the regulations implemented in Kraków and Małopolska proved only partially effective in achieving the intended improvements in air quality; however, the process of adopting and implementing them, and of identifying the respects in which they fell short, generated practical knowledge about the nature of the problem and its complexity. Decision-makers are already planning corrective actions, thanks to the unique knowledge of the smog phenomenon they have gained through the implementation of earlier solutions, even though those solutions themselves have not proven sufficient, as was too hastily assumed. Wickedness of the problem, as we understand the original idea, shall prevent planners from moving forward and achieving genuine progress on the problem. In the case of smog in Lesser Poland and Kraków, however, there is certainly progress in understanding the problem, which should ultimately lead to further improvements in air quality.

Finally, it also seems true that air pollution can be considered a symptom of another problem from another domain (point 8 of the characteristics), and there are indeed multiple possible explanations for air pollution (point 9).

---

[6] This phenomenon is, of course, not limited to Poland, as the number of solid-fuel appliances in Europe alone is estimated to be well above 70 million (Vicente & Alves, 2018).

There is, of course, a wide range of interpretations of air pollution and its causes. Depending on the political narratives prevailing in public discourse, air pollution may be framed as a consequence of uncontrolled capitalism (particularly in relation to industrial smog or acid rain), poverty (in the case of residential pollution), the political influence of mining unions and the economy's dependence on coal (in relation to particulate-matter pollution), or corporate misconduct (as in the Dieselgate scandal). Yet the existence of these competing interpretations does not necessarily prevent the adoption and implementation of effective solutions, as some accounts of wicked problems might suggest. Air pollution may legitimately be understood as arising from a variety of socioeconomic causes, but addressing it does not require policymakers to eliminate all of them. On the contrary, competing interpretations may help reveal the full complexity of the problem, and a better understanding of its multiple causal pathways may facilitate the design of more effective policy responses. For example, once policymakers recognize that air pollution results from a range of different conditions, they may favor instruments that operate across several causal domains over measures whose effects are much narrower. Prohibitions may sometimes function in this way, because their application does not depend directly on the income or attitudes of those subject to them, whereas economic incentives may be less effective when the financial response they seek to induce is weakened by either very high or very low incomes, or by entrenched cultural preferences.

Table 6.1 summarizes our considerations so far. On the left, we list the original characteristics of wicked problems; on the right, we indicate whether, in our view,

Table 6.1 The problem of air pollution in Małopolska vs wicked-problem characteristics

Features of wicked problems proposed by Rittel and Webber	The problem of air pollution in Małopolska
1. There is no definitive formulation of a wicked problem.	+
2. Wicked problems have no stopping rule.	–
3. Solutions to wicked problems are not true or false but good or bad.	+
4. There is no immediate and no ultimate test of a solution to a wicked problem.	–
5. Every solution to a wicked problem is a "one-shot operation"; because there is no opportunity to learn by trial and error, every attempt counts significantly.	+
6. Wicked problems do not have an enumerable (or exhaustively describable) set of potential solutions, nor is there a well-described set of permissible operations that may be incorporated into the plan.	–
7. Every wicked problem is essentially unique.	–
8. Every wicked problem can be considered to be a symptom of another problem.	+
9. The existence of a discrepancy representing a wicked problem can be explained in numerous ways. The choice of explanation determines the nature of the problem's resolution.	+
10. A planner has no right to be wrong.	–

the smog problem in Małopolska (in any of its layers) meets these characteristics, even to a limited extent. The symbol "+" should be interpreted as "at least partially present," while "–" should be interpreted as "weakly present or absent."

It seems that air pollution, as a multifaceted, cross-domain, and complex problem that can be described from several complementary rather than mutually exclusive perspectives, exhibits some characteristics of a wicked problem. The apparent wickedness of air pollution may stem from the multiplicity of its physical sources and sociocultural drivers; the diversity of pollutants involved; differences in cultural perceptions, customs, and habits; the complex and evolving causal structure of the phenomenon; and persistent gaps in knowledge. The specific character of air pollution is also reflected in the fact that both the choice and effectiveness of possible policy responses depend on contextual factors such as climate and weather (Kinney, 2008). Recent satellite observations have shown that even lightning discharges can be a significant source of air pollution in the form of nitrogen oxides and ozone (Allen et al., 2021). Atmospheric processes are inherently variable, while weather dynamics are nonlinear and partly chaotic. As a result, interventions aimed at controlling air quality cannot be expected to produce outcomes with the same degree of predictability as interventions addressing problems that are not embedded in chaotic systems. But should we really interpret this fact as evidence of some property of the phenomenon other than its complexity—namely, its wickedness? There is no good reason to do so, at least as long as wickedness is defined by a specific set of characteristics that air pollution does not fully satisfy.

Why does anyone, therefore, want to describe air pollution as a wicked problem? The propensity to qualify air pollution as wicked may be a consequence of the behavior of certain political or market actors that deliberately try to dismantle public policies and regulations designed to tackle air pollution. It so happens that public policies regarding polluting emissions interfere with important interests of several powerful actors, including international and state corporations, unions, and, of course, the electorate. It is thus reasonable to expect that those who profit from the current state of affairs—however deleterious it is for public health—will likely do everything to preserve it, effectively undermining or softening regulatory efforts.

The phenomenon of regulatory capture is well known in the policy literature (see, e.g., Hempling, 2014), and various companies have previously employed such strategies to prevent certain regulations from being adopted or even discussed.[7] In the context of Poland, attention is usually drawn to the role of the mining industry and miners' unions in resisting governmental attempts to reduce the country's dependence on coal for heat and energy production. However, producers and distributors of solid-fuel boilers and room heaters, often relatively small local enterprises, have constituted another important group influencing national-level regulation and, for many years, resisting more stringent regulatory measures.

[7] It is not a coincidence that, so far, the ban on cigarettes has not been proposed in any of the Western countries, nor has any limit on gas combusted by privately owned cars. Tobacco companies, oil companies, and car manufacturers still have an enormous amount of power, and they use it to set the boundaries of public discourse in accordance with their corporate interests.

The case of Polish air pollution policies demonstrates that various actors, including those involved in household heat and energy provision, were able to promote competing narratives—for example, portraying coal as an indispensable element of national energy independence, wood as a natural, clean, and sustainable resource, and air pollution as a form of moral panic allegedly orchestrated by foreign economic interests seeking to promote renewable-energy technologies at the expense of domestic industry. Existing cultural beliefs, identities, and perceptions could be mobilized in support of such narratives.

The distortion of public discourse and the ability of organized interest groups to influence policymaking may be particularly pronounced in relation to causally complex issues such as air pollution or climate change, where understanding sources and consequences requires specialized knowledge. The complexity of the underlying phenomenon, its multicausal nature, and its multiple possible framings may therefore create opportunities for strategic actors to shape public perceptions of the problem and influence the adoption and implementation of policy responses. According to this interpretation, the "wickedness" of the problem may lie partly in the difficulty of addressing it effectively when organized interests intervene in the political process in ways that obstruct or weaken anti-smog policies.

Even the language used in public discourse may play a significant role and contribute to the wickedness of the problem in this sense. The terminology used to describe air pollution can itself make both public understanding and policy implementation more difficult. For instance, the term "low-stack emissions," used to describe a major source of air pollution in Poland, is translated into Polish as "niska emisja", which literally means "low emissions." Because of this, claims such as "low emissions are problematic" or "low emissions are the major contributor to the high levels of pollution measured in Poland" may sound paradoxical to a lay audience, potentially contributing to confusion about the nature of the problem and, in turn, to its perceived intractability.

Summarizing this section, it should be noted that air pollution only partially meets the characteristics proposed by Rittel and Webber. While studying the problem of air pollution and the responses proposed over time, it is easy to get the idea that the source of the alleged wickedness of the problem is, in fact, its complexity. In the case of Małopolska, the said complexity consists of the elaborate socioeconomic context in which air pollution policies are designed and operated. The Małopolska case thus provides a useful example of how such complex circumstances, including the influence of organized interest groups, can make a problem difficult to understand and address—not because of its intrinsic nature, but because of the surrounding configuration of competing views, interests, and values. It also illustrates how the unintended consequences of earlier interventions can shape subsequent developments and become reference points for later assessments and actions, thereby creating an additional appearance of wickedness.

Therefore, it seems that we do not have a sufficient reason to believe that air pollution is a genuine wicked problem. In particular, we are not convinced that the concept of wicked problems adds anything valuable to our understanding of complex societal problems. Moreover, we suspect that such a description, although fashionable and thus attractive as a narrative tool, could even stop planners from searching for effective solutions. We will elaborate on these points in the next section.

6.5 Problem 3: Practical Significance of Considering Air Pollution as a Wicked Problem

From the point of view of governance praxeology, the most interesting question is not whether the concept of wicked problems is properly constructed or explicated nor whether air pollution is a proper instance of such a problem. Rather, what counts the most is the question of whether the use of the concept contributes to more effective (or more efficient) solutions to air pollution, providing us, for example, with valuable insights into the problem or a useful classification—both leading to better public policies. In particular, from the perspective of our case study, the fundamental question is whether the concept of wicked problems can help explain the persistence of air pollution in Małopolska and the limited effectiveness of the antismog resolutions adopted to address it.

In trying to test the usefulness of the concept of wicked problems in governance practice, however, one immediately encounters a rather fundamental problem. Presumably, the concept is intended to denote problems that are untamed and intractable. At first glance, therefore, asking whether classifying air pollution as a wicked problem helps policymakers address it may seem almost paradoxical: such a classification appears to rule out the possibility of any definitive solution. Nonetheless, allegedly wicked problems remain the object of deliberate policy efforts. According to the original formulation by Rittel and Webber, as we have seen, the class of wicked problems was effectively coextensive with the class of societal problems, and hence governance is largely concerned with searching for ways of addressing wicked problems. Such a search may be open-ended, yet surely it was not the authors' intention to claim that attempts to address societal problems are futile. It therefore remains reasonable to ask whether the analytical category proposed by Rittel and Webber actually assists policymakers in these efforts. Moreover, identifying a problem as wicked should, in principle, provide some practical advantage by helping planners anticipate the kinds of difficulties they are likely to encounter.

This conclusion makes sense, however, only in the absence of competing explanations. The value of the wicked-problems framework should therefore be assessed against alternative analytical categories that may offer competing explanations of air pollution, the adoption of policy responses to it, and their subsequent implementation. In the case of Małopolska, there are several alternative explanations for the persistence of air pollution in the region, as indicated in our study. For example, we claim that the 2017 antismog resolution is ineffective due to institutional arrangements that disperse responsibility for its implementation—and this explanation seems to offer a better understanding of the underlying issue than the broader category of wickedness. The latter merely restates the difficulty of the problem, obscuring any specific mechanisms that could be investigated to propose more practical solutions to the problem. In that case, one may even hypothesize that qualifying air pollution as a wicked problem could impair governance.

This is particularly important because the preceding analysis suggests that the continued difficulty of improving air quality in Małopolska cannot be adequately explained by any inherent wickedness of the air pollution problem itself. We know that the principal emission sources are identifiable, the main categories of intervention are established, and environmental outcomes can be measured. Importantly, the experience of Kraków demonstrates that sufficiently clear and consistently implemented restrictions can produce substantial change. In fact, our case study of regulations in Kraków and Małopolska leads us to conclude that considering air pollution as a wicked problem could in fact help justify ineffective public policies. More specifically, it renders the adoption and implementation of effective policies and regulations less plausible.

Politicians often refer to the allegedly complex nature of air pollution to explain why they are not successful in dealing with the problem, despite millions of euros spent on subsidies, education, and enforcement. However, there is evidence proving that planners intentionally overlooked important data and created a nexus of interdependencies and mutually conditioned decisions to render public policies ineffective while deflecting responsibility to act. In our view, these choices were at least partly driven by an effort to avoid electoral backlash from voters culturally attached to solid-fuel heating and resistance from organized interests representing the solid-fuel production and heating industries.

The persistence of pollution therefore requires an explanation focused not only on the environmental problem but also on the institutional system constructed to address it. Analysis of the official documents leading to the 2017 resolution revealed disturbing facts. Its adoption was preceded by the preparation of a scientific study on the actual distribution of air pollution in the province, as well as the mathematical modeling of the predicted future distribution of pollutants after the hypothetical implementation of various regulations differing in their stiffness. That initial assessment of the effectiveness of different potential regulations stated that no form of regulation other than a ban on all solid fuels (identical to the one in Kraków) would improve air quality in Małopolska to the levels required by international and domestic law (see Lochno, 2017). Yet that evidence was ignored, and the measures implemented in Kraków by the 2016 resolution were not replicated in the 2017 regulation. Apparently, the representatives assembled in the regional parliament had something in mind other than the effectiveness of the regulation they voted for. Moreover, at the time the 2017 resolution was passed, no sufficient financial resources were secured for its implementation—namely, partial subsidies directed to the residents of Małopolska to support the replacement of high-emission appliances. As it later turned out, even the scale of the challenge—i.e., the number of those appliances—was not known to the planners. A central register of heating installations (CEEB) was established much later. Therefore, antismog regulations were adopted in Małopolska, and then elsewhere, without proper assessment of the task.

But the real challenge turned out to be multilevel governance. This is where an interesting phenomenon emerges—at the intersection of different institutions at the local, regional, and national levels, which are responsible for the implementation of public policies concerning air quality. Decisions taken at various levels of governance (i.e., national parliament, ministry, regional parliament, municipal councils) and administration (the National Fund for Environmental Protection with its regional branches, the Regional Inspectorates for Environmental Protection, the state's Trade Inspection)—all aimed at tackling air pollution—have created a patchwork of regulations and mutual relations, where the effectiveness of the actions of one institution depends entirely on the decisions and actions of another, often operating at a different level of politics or administration.

For example, the regulation banning certain types of high-emission boilers could not be effective if such appliances continued to be offered on the market. But the power to exclude certain installations from the market was assigned to the ministry and trade inspectorate, while the power to regulate their use lay with local parliaments. Similarly, the technical requirements for heating installations, determined by local parliaments, were meaningless if the quality of coal was not regulated, which fell under the competence of another ministry. Such complicated relations of cross-competence and powers were the result of subsequent changes in the law by the national parliament, and at least some of them seemed to be a deliberate tactic aimed at dissolving responsibility between different players, and thus also dissolving agency, leaving the field open to various lobbies seeking to dismantle any decisive attempts to tackle pollution.

Additionally, the effectiveness of various antismog regulations depended on enforcement, and when they were adopted, nobody really cared if such enforcement would ever be possible. For example, the effectiveness of the 2017 resolution is strongly dependent on the efforts of municipal guards. Yet such guards, necessary for enforcing the resolution, exist in only about 15% of all communities in Małopolska. Authorities of some communities, as we directly observed on many occasions, openly question the need to establish such guards, since they oppose the very idea of environmental law enforcement.

In this context, our study suggests that existing approaches to difficult societal problems should be supplemented by greater attention to the institutional conditions shaping air pollution and the policies designed to address it. We refer to this set of conditions as the *institutional dimension* of a societal problem. The theory of wicked problems does not originally take into consideration the dynamics of the state, regional, and local institutions involved in solving various societal problems. Our hypothesis is that such institutional dynamics may actually be responsible for the difficulties observed in the case of many societal problems qualified as *wicked*. We could even coin another term—*institutional inertia*—to describe situations in which institutions responsible for taking action—thanks to complex or ambiguous divisions of tasks and competencies—enter into a kind of drift, refraining from action while pretending to deal with the problem. This *institutional inertia* often seems designed, as it fits the actual needs of political leaders. However, it may instead arise from a sequence of deliberate institutional and political choices, each of which is intelligible from the perspective of the actor making it. Legislators may distribute competences in a manner that avoids concentrating political responsibility, and regional authorities may adopt less-demanding instruments to reduce electoral resistance. Municipalities, in turn, may avoid costly enforcement. Ministries may postpone technical standards that threaten national industries. The cumulative effect of these choices may be a governance system whose inertia is foreseeable and politically convenient even if it was not designed by a single actor. Rather, particular choices contributing to it are intentional, and their combined consequences may be welcomed and preserved because they protect planners from political costs.

Institutional inertia in this sense does not mean also complete inactivity. On the contrary, authorities adopt regional strategies, programs, implementation reports, subsidy schemes, and public awareness campaigns. Yet such accumulation of activity does not necessarily produce the intended policy outcomes. In fact, in Małopolska, public institutions demonstrate that they combat air pollution, despite the number of noncompliant appliances remaining high and air quality decreasing.

The phenomenon of institutional inertia also explains why the language of wickedness may become politically useful. Where responsibility is already fragmented, describing the problem as intrinsically complex and resistant to definitive solutions provides a general narrative suitable for legitimizing failures. Planners involved in the implementation of policies can always justify their inability to curb the problem by invoking its wickedness. The persistence of pollution then appears to confirm the wicked diagnosis.

The Małopolska case therefore suggests that what appears as wickedness may often be a property not of the underlying societal problem but of the failed governance structure developed to address it. Therefore, the wicked problem theory, as we argued before, does not explain the persistence of air pollution in the region. Moreover, it is important to avoid this framework when seeking to comprehend the problem because it distracts us from examining circumstances that are plausibly more fundamental for finding effective solutions (e.g., the institutional context of the problem).

6.6 Conclusion

Good concepts constitute good analytical categories. Preferably, those categories fit our language practices and, in consequence, our perceptions of the reality. A useful analytical category should possess a sufficiently stable meaning and should make it possible to distinguish the phenomena to which it applies from those to which it does not. This chapter therefore asks whether the characteristics proposed by Rittel and Webber constitute reasonably clear criteria and whether they differentiate wicked problems from other subtypes of social problems proposed in the literature (e.g., ill-structured problems, complex problems, and intractable policy controversies). Our answer is that the concept of wicked problems possess limited taxonomic usefulness.

Good concepts are also practically useful and help us not only to describe our world in their terms but also to understand it or manipulate it efficiently in order to increase utility. The chapter elaborates then whether the characteristics associated with wicked problems correspond to the actual features of air pollution and antismog governance in Małopolska. Our conclusion is that there is only a partial fit, as the concept captures only some of the observable properties of the air pollution problem.

The last question is whether the concept of wicked problems constitutes a good explanation of the persistence of air pollution in Małopolska or whether the theory of wicked problems has anything to offer to those interested in understanding the inefficiency of antismog resolutions. If the answer is positive, it is a strong argument for the concept and its **practical, policy-guiding value**.

We argue that the concept not only fails to expand the set of reasonable policy responses, but there are reasons to believe that by classifying air pollution as a wicked problem, experts, planners, or journalists may even make antismog policies less effective.

It is worth noting that our analysis of the situation in Lesser Poland is consistent with the phenomenon of so-called *placebo governance* (see Stępień & Zomerski, 2025). Placebo governance produces symbolic legislation, whose aim is to deflect responsibility for the problem by creating an illusion of its solution. Notably, the appearance of placebo policies is described by scholars as an expected result of the attempts of the political class to deal with wicked problems. For example, Head considers it one of the general strategies of governance toward wicked problems (Head, 2022, p. 43). In contrast to this conception, however, we propose to look at the notion of wicked problems as an alleged example of newspeak—a pseudo-scientific jargon used not solely because it is fashionable but mostly because it is convenient. This jargon does not, in fact, add much to our understanding of air pollution and does not expand our inventory of policy actions to counter the problem. In fact, we believe that the proponents of the concept of wicked problems should be obliged to describe how its adoption expands the toolkit planners can utilize to address air pollution. Perhaps we should even consider such expansion as a counterpart to Popper's procedure of falsification in the area of governance. In that case, one could regard air pollution as a wicked problem only if describing it through wicked problem theory actually helps planners tackle the problem in ways that were inaccessible (or impossible) when framed in other terms.

In the previous sections of this chapter, we indicated that it is interesting to contemplate whether the concept of wicked problems adds anything valuable to governance beyond the claim that a certain problem is difficult or complex. Yet, here, we suggest something more profound. Namely, ascribing a wicked nature to a certain problem could work as an alibi to avoid involvement in more effective, albeit politically risky, policies. Therefore, it is reasonable to avoid it in political and expert discourse. In the end, the necessity of inventing "more analytic terms" that will enable better classification of problems and policies, and thereby allow policymakers to construct more effective policies, has already been declared in the literature (see Hoornbeek & Peters, 2017).

References

Alford, J., & Head, B. W. (2017). Wicked and less wicked problems: A typology and a contingency framework. *Policy and Society, 36*(3), 397–413. https://doi.org/10.1080/14494035.2017.1361634

Allen, D., Pickering, K. E., Bucsela, E., Van Geffen, J., Lapierre, J., Koshak, W., & Eskes, H. (2021). Observations of lightning NOx production from Tropospheric Monitoring Instrument case studies over the United States. *Journal of Geophysical Research: Atmospheres, 126*, e2020JD034174. https://doi.org/10.1029/2020JD034174

Buchanan, R. (1992). Wicked problems in design thinking. *Design Issues, 8*(2), 5–21.

Cappelen, H. (2018). *Fixing Language: An Essay on Conceptual Engineering*. Oxford University Press. https://doi.org/10.1093/oso/9780198814719.001.0001

Duit, A., & Galaz, V. (2008). Governance and complexity – New issues in governance theory. *Governance, 21*, 311–335.

FitzGibbon, J., & Mensah, K. O. (2012). Climate change as a wicked problem: An evaluation of the institutional context for rural water management in Ghana. *SAGE Open, 2*(2). https://doi.org/10.1177/2158244012448487

Goldsmith, J. R. (1969). Air pollution epidemiology. A wicked problem, an informational maze, and a professional responsibility. *Archives of Environmental Health, 18*(4), 516–522. https://doi.org/10.1080/00039896.1969.10665446

Grzegorz, W., Patrycja, Ł., Olga, N. (2017). Emission of some pollutants from biomass combustion in comparison to hard coal combustion. *Journal of the Energy Institute, 90*(5), 787–796. https://doi.org/10.1016/j.joei.2016.06.005.

Head, B. W. (2022). *Wicked problems in public policy: Understanding and responding to complex challenges*. Palgrave Macmillan.

Hempling, S. (2014). "Regulatory capture": Sources and solutions. *Emory Corporate Governance & Accountability Review, 1*, 23.

Hoornbeek, J. A., & Peters, B. G. (2017). Understanding policy problems: A refinement of past work. *Policy and Society, 36*(3), 365–384.

Hoppe, R. (2010). *The governance of problems: Puzzling, powering and participation*. Policy Press.

Kinney, P. L. (2008). Climate change, air quality, and human health. *American Journal of Preventive Medicine, 35*(5), 459–467. https://doi.org/10.1016/j.amepre.2008.08.025

Levin, K., Cashore, B., Bernstein, S., & Auld, G. (2012). Overcoming the tragedy of super wicked problems: Constraining our future selves to ameliorate global climate change. *Policy Sciences, 45*(2), 123–152.

Lilleker, D., & Stoeckle, T. (2021). The challenges of providing certainty in the face of wicked problems: Analysing the UK government's handling of the COVID-19 pandemic. *Journal of Public Affairs, 21*(4). https://doi.org/10.1002/pa.2733

Lochno, A. (Ed.). (2017). *Attachment No. 2 to the Resolution No. XXXII/451/17 of the parliament of the Lesser Poland Voivodeship of 23 January 2017: The Air Protection Programme for Lesser Poland Voivodship "Małopolska in a Healthy Atmosphere"*.

Merton, R. K. (1936). The unanticipated consequences of purposive social action. *American Sociological Review, 1*(6), 894–904.

Nel, A. (2005). Air pollution-related illness: Effects of particles. *Science, 308*(5723), 804–806. https://doi.org/10.1126/science.1108752

Newman, J., & Head, B. W. (2017). Wicked tendencies in policy problems: Rethinking the distinction between social and technical problems. *Policy and Society, 36*(3), 414–429.

Oberdörster, G., & Utell, M. J. (2002). Ultrafine particles in the urban air: To the respiratory tract--and beyond? *Environmental Health Perspectives, 110*(8), A440–A441. https://doi.org/10.1289/ehp.110-1240959

Peters, B. G. (2017). What is so wicked about wicked problems? A conceptual analysis and a research program. *Policy and Society, 36*(3), 385–396. https://doi.org/10.1080/14494035.2017.1361633

Peters, B. G., & Tarpey, M. (2019). Are wicked problems really so wicked? Perceptions of policy problems. *Policy and Society, 38*(2), 218–236. https://doi.org/10.1080/14494035.2019.1626595

Rittel, H. W. J., & Webber, M. M. (1973). Dilemmas in a general theory of planning. *Policy Sciences, 4*(2), 155–169.

Room, G. (2011). *Complexity, institutions and public policy: Agile decision-making in a turbulent world.* Edward Elgar.

Schön, D. A., & Rein, M. (1994). *Frame reflection: Solving intractable policy disputes.* Basic Books.

Simon, H. A. (1973). The structure of ill-structured problems. *Artificial Intelligence, 4*(3-4), 181–201.

Stępień, M., & Zomerski, W. (2025). Exploring legislative placebo: A new framework for understanding deliberate ineffective legislation. *The Theory and Practice of Legislation, 13*(2), 181–212. https://doi.org/10.1080/20508840.2025.2507465

Turnbull, N., & Hoppe, R. (2018). Problematizing "wickedness": A critique of the wicked problems concept, from philosophy to practice. *Policy and Society, 38*(3), 315–337. https://doi.org/10.1080/14494035.2018.1488796

Vicente, E., & Alves, C. (2018). An overview of particulate emissions from residential biomass combustion. *Atmospheric Research, 199*, 159–185. https://doi.org/10.1016/j.atmosres.2017.08.027

Chapter 7
Conclusion

Mateusz Stępień and Mateusz Klinowski

Abstract This final chapter summarizes the challenges and lessons arising from efforts to combat air pollution in the Małopolska (Lesser Poland) region of Poland. It highlights the role of geographic and climatic conditions in shaping pollution levels, as well as the influence of historical socioeconomic decisions concerning energy infrastructure, industrial development, and patterns of urbanization. Political and ideological factors, operating at both the regional and national levels, also play a significant role in shaping policy design and implementation. The chapter points out that the contrast between Kraków's strict ban on the use of solid fuels and the more flexible regulatory approach adopted in the rest of Małopolska illustrates the tensions inherent in a decentralized system of air pollution governance. At the same time, this contrast provides an opportunity to reflect on the relative effectiveness of command-and-control measures and incentive-based policy instruments. The chapter also summarizes the role played by eco-advisors in combating smog. Finally, it revisits and critically evaluates the theoretical frameworks of symbolic law and wicked problems, demonstrating how these concepts may, at times, obscure the role of deliberate political choices and institutional constraints in hindering effective interventions. The Małopolska case underscores the need for analytical tools capable of accounting for the sociopolitical, historical, legal, and geographical determinants of environmental governance when addressing complex environmental challenges.

Keywords Air pollution · Wicked problems · Symbolic law · Fighting smog · Lesser Poland

---

M. Stępień (✉)
Department of Sociology of Law, Jagiellonian University, Kraków, Poland
e-mail: mateusz.stepien@uj.edu.pl

M. Klinowski
Department of Law and Administration, Jagiellonian University, Kraków, Poland
e-mail: mateusz.klinowski@uj.edu.pl

M. Stępień, M. Klinowski, *Fighting Air Pollution*, Law and Visual Jurisprudence 17, https://doi.org/10.1007/978-3-032-23909-9_7

In this section, we would like to highlight some issues that the case of combating air pollution in Małopolska (Lesser Poland) brings to light.

(1) The case underscores the role of spatial, geographic, and climatic determinants, which significantly hinder efforts to improve air quality in Małopolska, though their importance may vary elsewhere. Kraków is situated in a particularly unfavorable location in this regard, and the same applies to other towns in Małopolska, often located in valleys and basins along rivers and streams, where topography amplifies pollution levels. The role of geographic determinants is often mentioned by other authors writing about the problem of air pollution in Poland.

The Małopolska case also highlights the significance of socioeconomic history. Past decisions—regarding sources of energy, the location of industry, the layout of transportation arteries, or even the way residential buildings were constructed (for instance, obstructing natural wind corridors)—continue to shape current air quality and the country's capability for changing it. The structural obstacles to the development of system heating illustrate how strongly historical infrastructural and regulatory choices influence present-day options, for example, for reducing low-stack emissions. Another noteworthy phenomenon is the suburban expansion around Kraków, driven by the search for cheaper housing and better quality of life. As the city population is moving from the districts of apartment buildings to suburban zones, this contributes to emissions because in the densely urbanized areas of Kraków, buildings are heated by district heating network, whereas in the suburbs, typically each building has its own heating installation.

Additionally, suburban expansion has produced a specific cut-off problem. While Kraków was made subject to a ban on solid fuels, the municipalities surrounding the city were not, as they became subject to the regulatory regime adopted for the rest of Małopolska, based on the gradual replacement of old and suboptimal heating installations with new ones. According to the so-called doughnut theory, itself the subject of disputes, a substantial share of Kraków's air pollution currently originates from this ring of neighboring communities surrounding the city. Hence, we argue that socioeconomic processes, such as spontaneous suburban growth, are key to understanding both the scale of pollution and the possibilities for effective intervention.

(2) The careful reconstruction of the long-term process of combating smog in Małopolska offers important insights into environmental governance and the factors that induce policy change. In the Małopolska case, this process unfolded in distinct stages, beginning with the political recognition of air pollution as a social problem, followed by the adoption of regional legal measures and, subsequently, their implementation. The detailed analysis of the role played by *Krakowski Alarm Smogowy* (Kraków Smog Alert), the grassroots organization that brought the issue of smog onto Kraków's public agenda, shows that it contributed significantly to the first stage and helped facilitate the second. The role of KAS presented in this book nuances our understanding of how civil society contributes to addressing serious social problems. Rather than directly producing policy change, social movements may play a crucial role in problem recognition, agenda setting, public mobilization, and the creation of political conditions conducive to policy intervention.

(3) The Małopolska case shows how important political and ideological factors are. Different political formations (parties), present even at the regional level in municipal councils, hold divergent views on environmental issues and prioritize them differently, influencing the direction, pace, and determination with which remedies are sought and implemented. Between 2009 and 2023, the region of Małopolska was governed by the centrist coalition, and this political configuration enabled innovative steps to be taken. However, from 2015 to 2023, at the national level, Poland was governed by a conservative majority that approached environmental and air-quality issues differently, aligning its stance with its critical orientation toward the EU (note that it was the Polish government formed by the PiS party that unsuccessfully challenged the National Emission Ceilings (NEC) Directive before the Court of Justice of the European Union, arguing that it imposed a disproportionate burden on Poland compared to other member states (*Case C-128/17*)). After all, environmental policies largely originate at the European level. This tension—between municipal authorities willing to take real steps to protect air quality, even at financial cost to residents, and (some) regional and central authorities who, for reasons of ideology, prejudice, or populism, motivated primarily by their party memberships, resisted such measures—to a large extent determined the pace and direction of antismog policies in Poland.

It must also be emphasized that in Poland, the parliament decided to move antismog public policies to the regional level. At this level, ideology and party membership is still important, and at the same time this level is still significantly far from the real situation and problems of any particular local community. Hence, by choosing the regional level as the main locus for antismog regulations, political leaders decided to deliberately lower the effectiveness of possible regulations while retaining political and ideological control over antismog policies. While the decentralization of antismog policy may, at first glance, appear beneficial due to its flexibility and capacity to accommodate local circumstances, in practice, it deserves a more critical evaluation. As a consequence of this decentralization, the level of protection of human health and life against air pollution varies across regions and even between individual cities in Poland, with neither uniform standards nor consistent enforcement. Political and ideological factors, alongside differences in the development of gas distribution networks, also help explain why the Małopolska Regional Assembly adopted two distinct antismog resolutions for the province: a strict and relatively rapid ban on the use of solid fuels in Kraków and a more flexible, phased timetable for the replacement of boilers and furnaces in the rest of the region.

(4) The Małopolska case illustrates the importance of multilevel governance in air-quality policy. Achieving clean air goals is a long-term process shaped by actions across multiple levels and influenced by countless factors that shape interactions among those levels. As noted, Poland's decentralized antismog model—deepened by the discretion granted to regions in adopting antismog resolutions and the lack of coordination—represents both a challenge and an opportunity. The Małopolska case not only reveals a small fragment of this multilevel governance system but also highlights the efforts required to create conditions for implementing EU-driven

policies locally. The LIFE project, for example, introduced eco-advisors in every municipality in Małopolska. Yet the Małopolska model of the eco-advisor assigned primarily educational and informational tasks, without providing them with significant powers to coordinate activities across relevant sectors. One could imagine a different model, with broader responsibilities. The Małopolska case therefore helps clarify these institutional choices and allows us to evaluate the rationale behind them.

(5) The Małopolska case also contributes to the discussion on the effectiveness of command-and-control instruments versus economic incentives. The introduction of two different regulatory regimes in Kraków and in the rest of Małopolska can be viewed (with some important reservations) as a kind of natural experiment, offering valuable insights into the broader debate on optimal policy instruments for addressing air pollution and, more generally, environmental problems. Which of the two resolutions proved more effective? The book provides a detailed analysis using different quantitative criteria for assessing the effectiveness of both regulatory approaches. These include measured air quality in the two areas (Kraków and the rest of Małopolska), as well as the number of inefficient solid-fuel heating installations remaining in operation. The findings primarily reveal the difficulties and ambiguities associated with using these criteria as indicators of policy effectiveness.

Nevertheless, the overall conclusions lean somewhat closer to a preference for command-and-control measures, namely, a clear ban. Such instruments were easier to communicate, more unambiguous in their requirements, and better suited to assessing the scope of their effectiveness. At the same time, the analyzed case highlights the conditions under which such measures can be successfully introduced and implemented, including the availability of alternative heating sources, social acceptance, political support, and sufficient implementation capacity.

Interestingly, empirical research on eco-advisors—as actors involved in the implementation of antismog laws and policies at the municipal level—identified several factors limiting the effectiveness of the antismog resolutions, the key legal instruments for improving air quality in Małopolska.

Among these factors, residents' attitudes, habits, and everyday practices that affect the environment, particularly air quality, also matter. The region's population includes groups whose lifestyles are rooted in traditions of self-sufficiency in household heating, including the continued use of wood-burning kitchen stoves. Changing such practices is often difficult due to age, cultural attachment, or financial constraints. At the same time, there are significant groups whose everyday practices can broadly be described as proenvironmental, including reduced reliance on private cars—another source of emissions that has become increasingly important. While this distinction inevitably simplifies a more complex reality, the relative proportions of these groups shape pressures on local and regional policymakers and, consequently, influence the effectiveness of efforts aimed at reducing air pollution or the lack thereof. Another, more structural, factor is the lack of a transparent, stable, and long-term energy policy in Poland, which translates into difficulties for residents when making decisions regarding household heating technologies. Financial constraints were also identified as an important factor limiting effectiveness, particularly in relation to the design and operation of stove-replacement and thermal modernization funding programs. As emphasized throughout this book, enforcement mechanisms remain insufficient, largely due to the limited capacities of municipal police and local guard units, where such units exist at all. Additional factors are related to the situational context, including the characteristics of buildings (e.g., their age and technical infrastructure), unresolved property ownership issues, as well as the design, accessibility, and administrative complexity of subsidy programs. Another important factor is the relatively high level of tolerance toward polluters and the limited extent of neighborhood-level social control directed at enforcing antismog norms.

As can be seen, the factors limiting the effectiveness of antismog resolutions in Małopolska are highly diverse in nature. Some are linked to broader structural issues, such as the absence of a coherent national energy strategy; others are institutional, while still others are rooted in broader cultural patterns, including lifestyles and the weak social pressure exerted on those contributing to air pollution.

(6) The juxtaposition of two analytical frameworks—symbolic law and wicked problems—with the Małopolska case reveals their limitations. The concept of symbolic law is suited to simple legislative situations but fails to capture the dynamics of multilevel governance. Meanwhile, the notion of wicked problems obscures rather than illuminates the array of factors shaping the difficulties in fighting smog. Worse still, it can serve to legitimize ineffective public policies: politicians often invoke the allegedly insurmountable complexity of air pollution to justify their own lack of success.

Our considerations demonstrate that the concept of wicked problems is not so much useless as misleading. While the problem of air pollution shares at least some of the characteristics described by Rittel and Webber, the difficulty in solving it appears not to stem from its internal properties, identified causal relationships, or external mechanisms of politics, economics, or other cultural conditions but rather from deliberate actions by politicians aimed at deflecting responsibility for the problem and eliminating the need to respond. Using the concept of wicked problems may, therefore, lead to the omission of important aspects of the politics surrounding difficult social problems and, de facto, hinder the search for a resolution of such problems.

Perhaps, based on our research, we should also explicitly demand an end to such a classification of social problems, which assumes the existence of a distinct class of problems that are essentially super-difficult to solve or are even insoluble. It is likely that social problems are difficult not because they are specific in nature but because, for various reasons, those responsible for dealing with them are unwilling or unable to solve them. Carefully chosen conceptual frameworks and esoteric terms can effectively conceal this from us. The wickedness of the problem can thus serve as an alibi for avoiding more effective, albeit politically risky, policies. This demonstrates the need for new conceptualizations capable of capturing the specific contexts and various determinants of the modern struggles over air quality throughout the world.

Kolibri 360 GmbH
Ferdinand-Jühlke-Straße 7
99095 Erfurt, Deutschland
produktsicherheit@kolibri360.de